Generation on Fire

Generation on Fire

Voices of Protest from the 1960s

An Oral History   Jeff Kisseloff

THE UNIVERSITY PRESS OF KENTUCKY

Publication of this volume was made possible in part by a grant from the National Endowment for the Humanities.

The University Press of Kentucky

Scholarly publisher for the Commonwealth, serving Bellarmine University, Berea College, Centre College of Kentucky, Eastern Kentucky University, The Filson Historical Society, Georgetown College, Kentucky Historical Society, Kentucky State University, Morehead State University, Murray State University, Northern Kentucky University, Transylvania University, University of Kentucky, University of Louisville, and Western Kentucky University.

Editorial and Sales Offices:
The University Press of Kentucky
663 South Limestone Street, Lexington, Kentucky 40508-4008
www.kentuckypress.com

10 09 08 07 06   5 4 3 2 1

Library of Congress Cataloging-in-Publication Data

Kisseloff, Jeff.

Generation on fire : voices of protest from the 1960s : an oral history / Jeff Kisseloff.

p. cm.

Includes bibliographical references and index.

ISBN-13: 978-0-8131-2416-2 (hardcover : alk. paper)

ISBN-10: 0-8131-2416-6 (hardcover : alk. paper)

1. United States—History—1961–1969—Biography. 2. Political activists—United States—Interviews. 3. Interviews—United States. 4. Oral history. 5. Counterculture—United States—History—20th century. 6. Protest movements—United States—History—20th century. 7. United States—Social conditions—1960–1980. 8. United States—Politics and government—1961–1963. 9. United States—Politics and government—1963–1969. I. Title.

E840.6.K57 2006

303.48'4092273—dc22

[B]

2006011831

Manufactured in the United States of America.

 Member of the Association of American University Presses

For the younger generation of my family:

my daughter, Elizabeth, and my niece and

nephews, Brittany, Evan, and Jared,

in the hope they'll make their own wise choices

and live righteous lives.

But mostly for Sue, with love and a wink.

When they said, "Sit down," I stood up.

—Bruce Springsteen, "Growin' Up"

Contents

Generation on Fire

Introduction

In 1998, Tom Brokaw wrote a best-selling book about Americans who came of age in the 1930s. Because so many of them survived the hardships of the Depression only to risk their lives in World War II, Brokaw called the book *The Greatest Generation*.

Brokaw was right to herald the enormous courage of America's World War II vets. Once the war was over, however, many settled into lives of conformity and comfort, paying little heed to the specters of poverty, racism, and McCarthyism that haunted the country. But it was the children of Brokaw's "greatest" generation—the so-called baby boomers who came of age in the 1960s—who fought and sacrificed to compel a reluctant nation to make good on its promise of "life, liberty, and the pursuit of happiness" for every citizen. This book is a tribute to those Americans who stood up and said no to war, greed, racism, sexism, homophobia, pollution, censorship, lame music, and bad haircuts. All too often they had to wage these battles against their families, their neighbors, and their government, often at the risk of their own safety.

Rebellion, of course, is as American as a Fourth of July picnic. Without rebellion, there would be no progress. Those long-haired radicals named Washington, Jefferson, Adams, and Franklin recognized this over two hundred years ago when they rose up against King George and demanded their independence. In the 1960s, antiwar activists believed they were acting in that same patriotic tradition when they demanded that President Lyndon Johnson and, later, Richard Nixon end the war in Vietnam.

Think about it this way: if not for the activists of the 1960s, the first black person might still be waiting to enroll in the University of Mississippi. You or your sister might not be able to have children because of a botched back-alley abortion. Someone you love might have been the twenty-thousandth American to die in Vietnam.

Nor is this just ancient history. In the wake of the 2000 presidential election controversy, the tragedy of September 11, increased erosion of civil liberties, and a war over the now admittedly false claim that Iraq had weapons of mass destruction, the need to ask questions and speak out is as important as it has ever been.

Newspapers are filled with stories indicating that the spirit of the 1960s is thriving today. The World Wide Web is an electronic version of the old underground newspapers. Antiglobalization protesters and Greenpeace activists make headlines by borrowing the tactics that many of their parents used so effectively to help stop the war in Vietnam.

The 1960s also live on in the conservative backlash against so-called liberal values. The decade scared the daylights out of the industrial, military, political, and religious elite of America—and for good reason. Profit margins were threatened when corporations could no longer dump industrial waste with impunity; in Vietnam the military suddenly found itself forced to act with more restraint than it was accustomed to; and religious leaders were taken aback when young people began taking the motto "Make love, not war" literally. The '60s also lay siege to the moral police, who believed that sex before marriage was immoral, use of drugs a crime, profanity an offense, and different ways of thinking a danger. Mostly, the 1960s proved that in the face of widespread protest and discontent, even the most entrenched aspects of American life and thought are not immune to change. For those in power, that remains a terrifying prospect. That's why, forty years later, the establishment is still fighting back. Laws have been passed limiting free speech on the Internet and curtailing a woman's access to abortion. Congress has reinstated draft registration and the death penalty; and because so many elected officials receive campaign contributions from major corporations, they are inclined to serve those interests rather than the citizens they were elected to represent. Perhaps most frightening of all, in 2000, politicians, not the voters, decided who would be the next President of the United States.

Eternal vigilance, as our Founding Fathers knew, is the price of liberty.

My first book, You Must Remember This, was an oral history about life in Manhattan from the 1890s to World War II. I talked to people in their eighties and nineties, and even centenarians, about what the Big Apple was like when they were young. Former bootleggers, jazz musicians, World War I veterans, even the last farmer in Manhattan—almost all were great fun to talk to. By the time I interviewed them, you'd never know that many of them had been real tough guys (or women), far stronger than I ever was. I remember one tiny ninety-year-old woman telling me about her union battles. "I beat up a lot of scabs," she said with pride.

That book hinged on the value of community. My next project, The Box, focused on creativity. Using the history of television as a backdrop, it told the story about what happens when creative and commercial visions collide. Again I met people who were long into retirement. Many of them told similar stories about being in the lab or on the set, attempting to do things that hadn't been done before. Some supervisor would invariably say, "That won't work" or "It's impossible," but through cleverness and determination my subjects would prove those in authority to be wrong.

With this book I intended to focus on responsibility. I also wanted to write a personal book about the decade that shaped my own life. I was fifteen years old on May 4, 1970, when four students at Ohio's Kent State University were shot and killed by National Guardsmen for exercising their right of free speech. The next day in my Long Island high school, there was a riot when jocks chanted, "Kill the Jews," attacking a group of long-haired students (many of them Jews) who were attempting to lower the flag on the front lawn as a protest against the killings at Kent State. The jocks, who mirrored the thinking of most of the country, insisted the shootings were justified ("The kids weren't in class"; "They were throwing rocks") and defended the freedoms the flag symbolized by beating up those who disagreed with them.

I was a ninth grader in junior high at the time. We learned what had happened when a freshman football player walked into my classroom and gleefully exclaimed, "The Jews tried to take the flag down and the jocks killed them!"

I'd like to say that my friends and I confronted the football player and set him straight. But we didn't. We shrank from saying anything, because we were small and he and his buddies were big. The next day we held a rally to protest what had happened at Kent State, but for me it wasn't enough. I was ashamed of my own fear.

In formulating the idea for this book, I decided to focus on people in the 1960s who believed they had an obligation to make the world a better place. Specifically, I wanted to find the people who had what I didn't have—the courage to stand up and be heard, to say no to the things that were wrong.

What unites the people who tell their stories in these pages is that they were—and still are—rebels who stood up and said no, sometimes when theirs was the only dissenting voice. That simple, courageous act of refusing to go along brought about much positive change in America, demonstrating yet again that progress occurs when people think for themselves.

The stories in this book also help explode at least one enduring myth of the

1960s: that the former '60s radicals are now SUV-driving stockbrokers who long ago traded in their principles for a six-figure salary. That's certainly not what I found to be the case with the people in these pages, or with the others I met while conducting my research. Every one of the individuals you'll meet here are still doing interesting things—still making a contribution, in one way or another, to causes larger than themselves. That doesn't mean, of course, that everyone from the '60s has traveled the same road since then; but I think it's safe to generalize that those who were truly committed to the cause of change, those who didn't glom onto it simply because those around them did, in one way or another continue to live an ethical life.

The courageous acts of the people in these pages often had far-reaching consequences. When Freedom Rider Bernard LaFayette stepped off a bus into the hands of a white mob, he gave strength to a whole generation of African-Americans to stand up for their civil rights. When two priests, Daniel and Philip Berrigan, helped found the antiwar movement, they were opposed by their own church, but by holding on to their convictions, they gave moral authority to the movement that helped bring an end to the Vietnam War.

When Frank Kameny decided he had had enough harassment at the hands of the government simply because he was homosexual, he helped bring about changes that opened the closet doors for succeeding generations of gay men and lesbians.

Of course, not every decision or stance these individuals took changed the world. Sometimes people just changed their own world. It may have been a young child fending off an abusive father, a gay man stepping out of the closet, or a football player standing up to his coach. Sometimes the most courageous acts are simply those that get you through the day.

Because these activists of the 1960s were young and human, they sometimes made mistakes. You may not agree with everything they did, but as you read their stories, I hope you will come to understand and admire them, and possibly recognize yourself in their struggles to learn who they were and what place they were meant to assume in the world.

None of these individuals was ultimately afraid to be "different." I found it fascinating how time and again people told me they believed they were all alone until they stumbled across an affinity group of outcasts just like themselves in college or elsewhere, and that invariably these fellow rejects made for the most interesting, challenging, and enjoyable company and gave those whom I interviewed the courage to be themselves.

The people profiled here were not chosen because they were the most courageous members of the '60s generation. Mostly, they are simply thoughtful individuals who represent a cross section of '60s activism. But each did something special to warrant inclusion here. Some came from progressive backgrounds, while others were born into families where little was expected or offered in the way of encouragement to better themselves. They traveled a long emotional and intellectual road to step out of the mold that formed them. For that reason alone, I was filled with admiration. Each has a great story, with a lot to say not only about '60s activism but also about his or her own personal development.

Of those I spoke with, no one was more naturally inclined to question authority than Paul Krassner, whose combination of contrarian instincts and sense of fun were obvious even when he was just six years old. Though he earned his fame as a satirist, his impact would not have been as strong if he had not also been a terrific investigative journalist. But what struck me about Paul—and this is true of most of the other people I interviewed for this book— was that, despite his ardent criticism of American society and politics, he is at heart a patriot. The ubiquitous bumper stickers of the 1960s that declared "America, love it or leave it" missed the point. You could love what America stood for but detest its actions.

Not all endings are happy ones. Allison Krause and three of her classmates at Kent State were killed for exercising their right to protest. Allison's death was devastating, but it's a story that must be told. America is a great country, but it's an imperfect one, and the deaths of Allison Krause, and people like her, remind us that there is still work to be done. Allison should be remembered not just as a name in the history books, but as a person, so that we might better understand what was lost when her life was snuffed out.

All of these stories are personal. For that reason, this book isn't your usual history of the '60s. Sometimes the best way to tell a very big story is to tell a very small one.

Bernard LaFayette
Freedom Rider

The Freedom Rides may have been the most selfless event in American history. On May 4, 1961, seven blacks and six whites boarded buses in Washington, D.C., fully aware of the brutal fate that awaited them at their destination down South.

And that was the idea. The civil rights group CORE had organized the rides, figuring if the riders were beaten, or even killed, the publicity would pressure the government to enforce the rights of Negroes to travel freely on interstate buses. That right had recently been guaranteed by the U.S. Supreme Court in *Boynton v. Virginia*, but the federal government refused to enforce the ruling.

The trip proceeded with only minor incidents until the riders reached Alabama. In Anniston, the riders in one of the buses barely escaped with their lives when the bus was burned by a mob. The second bus made it to the station in Birmingham, but when the riders disembarked, they, and members of the press who were there to record the event, were beaten brutally by a white mob. The beatings were so severe that several of the riders never recovered.

At that point, CORE halted the effort, fearing the riders wouldn't survive the rest of the trip to Louisiana, but a group of divinity students in Nashville refused to back down. Trained in nonviolent civil disobedience by the Reverend James Lawson, they were concerned that halting the rides would send a signal that the movement would surrender in the face of violence. On their own, they vowed to continue the journey to New Orleans, no matter the cost. They paid a severe price for their determination and courage.

One of those remarkable students was twenty-year-old Bernard LaFayette.

Where did he find the strength to act the way he did? What made this young man so determined, so sure he could succeed, and so pure of motive that he would not try to meet violence with violence? What is the nonviolent philosophy, and how can one sustain it under such awful circumstances?

Bernard LaFayette's office is on the second floor of the University of Rhode Island's multicultural center. The room is so spare, his bookshelves are cardboard boxes that sit on the floor. From this small space, LaFayette organizes nonviolent centers in Rhode Island and throughout the world. His students seem to be getting the message. They are bright-eyed and fun, and they treat him with genuine reverence. This amuses him to no end. "They call me Granddad," he says with a laugh.

Growing up in Tampa, you learned early on that there was an invisible line that was always there, and you didn't cross it. Whenever you heard of a lynching or a beating, you knew that it could happen to you simply because you were Negro. All Negroes had, in a sense, a bullseye on their backs, so, for example, you didn't have eye contact with a white girl. All a white had to do was say, "He insulted me," or "He stuck his tongue at me." You could get lynched for that. As a result, you walked along many times, particularly if you were alone, as an invisible person, hoping you would not draw attention from anyone. You were also never sure about whether you would be accepted or rejected. You were always surprised if you were treated with any kindness, particularly by strangers.

Many times a white guy would say to me, "What are you looking at?" He didn't have anything to do, so he entertained himself by picking on a little black kid.

"Nothin'."

"Oh, you call me nothin'?"

The other rule was if you drew the attention of a white person in any kind of negative way, run. We always practiced running. I mean like fast as you can, as straight home as you can get. That was your only hope of escaping.

One day, I was by myself on the sidewalk, kicking this can. I kicked the can, and I accidentally hit this man in the head. There were two other men, and one of them started running at me. I took off and ran to my front door. My grandmother happened to be standing there. She unlatched it, and I ran in. She latched it back, because the guy was right on the porch. My grandmother grabbed me, and she stomped on the floor and yelled at me.

It was all a big act. She never touched me, but when the guy walked away he was satisfied that I had been punished. Then she started to laugh.

I learned about the problems Negroes faced very early on. We would travel to different church meetings, and we had to relieve ourselves on the highway at night because we couldn't use the restrooms, even when we stopped to get gas. If you asked, they would say, "We don't have any, for you." Sometimes they would let you go around the back into the woods. It was very demeaning for your sisters and your mother and your grandmother. We had to stand and watch with our backs turned to make sure nobody came around back there.

When I was seven, there was an incident with a trolley that I'll never forget. You would enter the front door of a trolley, put your money into the slot, and then Negroes had to leave and enter the side door to sit in the back. Sometimes, the guy would let up the steps and close the door and take off with your money, so you'd have to run. If more than one person was there, the other would hold the door. Hopefully, the driver wouldn't take off and drag you along.

This time, the driver took off after my grandmother put her money in, and she fell running after the trolley. I was a little bit ahead of her, and I was caught in between trying to run and hold the door and trying to come back to get her. She couldn't get up. She was heavyset, and the heel of her shoe had caught in the cobblestone when she was trying to run, and there she was plumb on the streets, by the tracks, and cars were coming, too. I couldn't pick her up, and she was in pain. I had a deep feeling in my inside, and I said to myself, "When I get grown, I'm gonna do something about this."

I got to Nashville in 1958 to go to the American Baptist Theological Seminary. John Lewis, who is now a congressman, was my roommate. He was a year ahead of me, and he'd go to these meetings about nonviolence led by James Lawson, a Methodist minister at Vanderbilt. I didn't have time. Besides my academic work, I worked as a janitor. I also would go down at noon and wash dishes at one of the restaurants. I'd get free lunch and be paid maybe five dollars for an hour, which was pretty good.

John kept talking to me about it. "Why don't you come down and just see what it's like?"

I said, "OK, I'll go with you this time." No sooner than I got there and found out what was going on that I said, "Hey, this is what I need to do."

I was fearful about getting involved because it was almost a violation of the commitment my parents had made to sacrifice and send me to school,

Seven-year-old Bernard
LaFayette in Tampa,
Florida. (Courtesy of
Bernard LaFayette)

although I worked and paid for most of my education. This was not part of their expectations, and they were depending on me as an only child.

On the other hand, I also felt a sense of responsibility to work for this change so that my grandmother would enjoy it before she would die. After a while, I decided that it was my responsibility to join. The tragedy was she died while I was going through these classes. She never lived to see me get involved.

Jim Lawson started the workshops in the fall of '59. Part of Lawson's lessons included the philosophy of Gandhi and Martin Luther King and the scriptural basis for love and forgiveness. I'm convinced that we ultimately succeeded because of the training, and today I'm still doing that training because I've seen it work over and over again, while I've seen violence get nowhere.

Physically, nonviolence is no problem. If someone spits on you, you wipe it off. It's not going to kill you. They can hit you. It's possible they can hurt you, but what was really at stake was not so much in being able to endure the physical attack; the real question was how would you feel on the inside about that person and about yourself.

One of the problems in dealing with nonviolence is a tendency to feel helpless and weak, because we're taught culturally that fighting back and attacking is a position of strength. It's the weak who get trampled or beaten.

Nonviolence requires a different perception. You have to look at yourself and the other person and understand why these conditions exist in general and specifically why that person is behaving in a negative way. That's where the discipline comes in.

But then, a person with a good heart and is willing and committed gets the hell beat out of him with seemingly no results. That happened a lot in the '60s, and you'd ask yourself, "Why am I doing this?"

The answer is: it works in the long run. Others see the bandages and get stirred up and want to do something about it. What do we want them to do, simply raise some money and go to court? No, we want them to join us, and many of them did.

We knew it could have stopped the movement if we had quit. Suppose during the first Freedom Ride when the bus was burned and the people were pulled off and beaten, they would have not gone on? In fact, that's what happened. Those of us in Nashville who had been trained not to do that responded differently. When we got out of jail in Nashville because of the sit-ins, we went back and sat in again. That's a difference between a nonviolent protest and a nonviolent movement.

The other struggle is to fight the perceptions that the other person has of you. He thinks you are wrong, that you are out of place, that you are doing this to harm white folk. You have to respond to their hatred with the greatest amount of love.

How can you fight back with love when the perpetrator is practicing violence against you? How can you communicate to that person that you care about him as an individual human being? That's the fight. You have to be trained to do that.

I'm being honest with you when I say this: none of us expected to live to be twenty-five years old, particularly with the kind of behavior we were involved in. That was part of the understanding. You can't practice nonviolence being afraid to die, and the training frees you from that fear.

When the students in Greensboro started their sit-in, one of the chaplains there called Jim Lawson and said, "What can you do in support?" so we had a sympathy march downtown. Of course, no sooner than we got outside, we said, "Sympathy? We got the same problem." So we said, "We got to start doing what they're doing."

In one of our first sit-ins at McClellan's, a white demonstrator, Paul LaPrad, was pulled off his stool and beaten. Then the police arrested him. Soon, we were all arrested. When we sat on those stools, we knew we had crossed a line. That was an act of defiance. As the police arrested us and took us out, I instructed students who couldn't get in to tell the others to come. Sure enough, they started arresting everyone who was on the street.

In jail, it was euphoria. We felt we had joined a whole class of people who had proceeded us who had gone to jail for their beliefs, like King and Gandhi. We were now part of a train of history going to a glorious destination, not knowing what our fate would be.

The community brought down food and sandwiches, and we sang freedom songs at night. All the students at the college who didn't come to the demonstration came down and demanded to be arrested, but the police said, "There's no more room. We'd like to arrest you, but what are we going to do?"

. The cells were made for eight people each, but we had around thirty or so in each cell. After we were arraigned we refused bond. After they found us guilty and fined us $50 we refused to pay, even though it was clear they were trying to get us to leave. They couldn't believe it. "These people are crazy. They want to stay in jail."

They put us in the workhouse. They sent us out to shovel snow off the parking lot. People came out of the buildings to scoff at us, but we were having so much fun it took the enjoyment out of it for them. The warden wanted to humiliate, but this was the thing we learned about nonviolence: it's not what you have to do, it's the attitude that you take towards it. Transforming is what it's about, and we transformed it.

We maintained a schedule. We had devotion before breakfast. After lunch, we had choir hour and a silent period. The jailers came to respect us because of our discipline, and the way we were respectful to them. They used to sneak inside and listen to us sing.

We had seminary students give sermons. Students who were in chemistry gave us chemistry lessons. There were lessons in biology, math, and English. After dinner we had entertainment. Some of the clowns would get up and tell jokes. We even created songs about the jailers, saying how great they were and how glad we were that they were protecting us.

Because of our conduct we were able to change their attitudes toward us. When we finally left, the warden stood by the entryway and shook hands with each of us. He said, "You're the best prisoners I've ever had. I'll see you again."

We promised him he would because the next week we were going back to the lunch counter.

When we sat in, we always wore suits and ties because one of the first things we had to do was change images. We were appealing to white America to condemn the practice of segregation, and one way we did this was by contrasting our appearance with the hoodlums, who were dressed in black jackets and ducktail haircuts. Policemen were swinging billy clubs at women who had high heel shoes on. That made it difficult for people to identify with our opponents.

We were also intent on desegregating the counters at the bus stations. I was beaten badly at an all night sit-in at the Trailways station. There were about ten of us there. Around four that morning, we decided to go home because we had made our point. I went out to a phone booth to call the dormitory so they could send some cars to pick us up. While I was on the phone, a cab driver kicked the door open, put a headlock over me and dragged me outside. About twelve drivers started to beat me up. They knocked me down, kicked me against the wall. I had about three ribs cracked. Fortunately, I didn't lose any teeth.

Every time they knocked me down, I would get up, brush off my coat, and then they would knock me down again. But I figured out how to roll with the punches rather than try to block them, so I would tumble around and get back up on my feet. It happened so much [laughs] that once when I got back up again, I said, "Just a minute," and started cleaning up again. Because I wasn't resisting, it weakened their resolve. I just stood there looking at them. Finally, I said, "If you gentlemen are through, I need to make a phone call." I started walking straight through them, and they separated. As I got to the phone, the police rushed in and arrested me for fighting.

Sometimes we were beaten coming back from a demonstration. People would throw bricks and bottles and pull you off the back of the line and stomp you on the ground. One time, Jim Lawson and I were at the end of a long line returning from a demonstration when this motorcycle guy named Danny spat on Jim. Jim asked him, "Do you have a handkerchief?"

This guy reached into his pocket and pulled out his handkerchief. Jim wiped himself off and handed it back, and then he started a conversation about bikes and hot rods. Jim knew about these things, and instead of this guy doing what he came to do, here he was in this discussion, and he walked with us almost to the church. What Jim was in effect saying was, "I reject the idea of you looking at me as a potential victim. I am a person, and I'm going to treat you like a person, and instead search for common ground rather than set up these barriers."

We never saw Danny again at any demonstrations, and he had been the main one who had been creating problems for us at the lunch counters.

We were also boycotting the department stores and the dime stores. At Harvey's department store, our boycott was 98 percent effective. We made an appointment to meet with the store manager. Our group was sitting in downstairs while upstairs we were negotiating in his office. We sat there looking at him, and he said, "I know what you're thinking. I've already decided I'm going to desegregate our counter."

He said he was going to do it by himself, but we knew he'd be ostracized and run out of town, so that wasn't enough. Our goal was to win our opponents over, not just to desegregate the lunch counters. We convinced him to go to the Chamber of Commerce and work on them.

We intensified the sit-ins, and blanketed the entire downtown. Someone firebombed the house of our attorney, so we organized a march downtown to protest. We had a couple thousand people descend onto the steps of City Hall. When the mayor came out, Diane Nash asked him, "Do you think it's morally right for someone to discriminate against a customer solely on the basis of race?"

He said it was not morally right. Then she asked him, "Is it your desire that the merchants downtown serve everybody on an equal basis?"

He said, "Yes, it's my desire."

This came out in the headlines, and that's what happened. No new city ordinance was passed. The merchants got together and decided. He formed a biracial committee. They said if there were thirty seats at the lunch counter, the first ten would be for whites, the middle integrated, and the next ten for blacks. We said no, and they gave in.

By the end of that spring, we were on to the Freedom Rides.

In 1960, John Lewis was with the original group that left Washington. When CORE canceled the rest of the trip, he returned to Nashville. We all talked about it, and Diane and John and the rest of us decided that if CORE was not going to continue the Freedom Rides, we would. The next leg was supposed to be from Birmingham to Montgomery, Alabama. James Farmer of CORE tried to discourage us. He said it was too dangerous, but if we went, he would support us.

We had to sneak into Birmingham early in the morning because word had gotten out that we were coming to town. We went to the bus station, but every time we attempted to get on the bus, the bus drivers wouldn't drive. They knew what happened in Anniston. One driver said, "I got one life to live, and I'm not going to give it to the NAACP or CORE."

We couldn't find a bus to take us, so we spent the night in the station. The Klan showed up to scare us. The Imperial Wizard wore a black robe. He was a little guy. There were about eight or ten of them in their robes and hoods. They would step on our feet and throw water on us, call us niggers and the whites nigger lovers. The policemen didn't do anything.

Finally, we got a bus to take us to Montgomery. I sat near the front. There were also some civilians on the bus. One was a black guy who was sitting in the back. [Laughs.] He said, "Momma said there'd be days like this." That was a popular song then.

There were troopers on the bus, and police cars behind us and on the side with sirens and lights. From Birmingham to Montgomery in those days was about ninety-five minutes. We made it a lot faster. They were driving at high speed because they were afraid of snipers. We had no idea whether we would still be alive at the end of the day, but we were going to take it to the end, whatever it was going to be. Our only consolation was we had our best buddies with us, so if we were going to die, at least we would be together.

When we got to the city limits, it was eerie. The streets we went down were empty. We learned later that they blocked them off. We were supposed to get picked up by some local citizens in private cars, but when we pulled in, they weren't there. The bus door opened, and we saw a mob run through the doors of the station. At first, they ignored us and went straight for the reporters, photographers, and cameramen. They knocked them down, hit them in the face, smashed their cameras. When we saw that, we said, "OK, we know they're coming at us next, so let's get off the bus now."

I wanted to get the five or six women with us into the cab. They made it, but when the white women got in, the black driver jumped out. It was a rule that black cabdrivers could not drive white people, and they especially could not be caught driving white women. He was shaking all over. I said, "Take the black women. Let somebody survive the situation to tell the story." But the black women said no: "We're not going to leave them here." Here a huge mob is beating people, and I'm trying to be practical. [Laughs.] So I suggested we lock arms and wait. We did and began to sing "We Shall Overcome," fully prepared to die at that moment.

As soon as the mob was finished with the reporters, they came after us. They were older people. Some of them were women with gray hair. Some were wearing overalls. They were brought in by the busloads off the farms. They started swinging ax handles and shovels at us—farm tools, Coca-Cola crates, anything they could get their hands on.

They were screaming and yelling like a pack of wild animals. I got kicked in the ribs with boots. John was hit across the head with a crate. It cut his head wide open. Suddenly, a courageous Alabama state trooper [a white man named Earl Mann] fired a shot in the air. That quieted the mob down, and sometime after that they dispersed. John was taken to the hospital along with William Barbee and Jim Zwerg, a white man. Barbee never really recovered. He is dead now. Zwerg was beaten worst of all. I was fortunate. I only had three ribs cracked.

That night, we had a mass meeting at the church. The sheriff showed up to arrest us for disturbing the peace and inciting a riot. We knew they were coming, so we put on choir robes and hid out among the chorus, and they never found us. But there was a mob outside, screaming and hollering, and throwing bricks and bottles through plate glass windows, and tear gas. That went on all night.

I thought they were going to burn the church down with us inside. We were on the phone with Robert Kennedy, but there wasn't much he could do. Finally they brought in federal troops to pick us up in convoy trucks around four in the morning. When I got on the truck, an old woman said to me, "Are you a Freedom Rider?" I said yes, and she whispered, "You go home with me."

She was a poor elderly lady, but she sent me to bed and stayed up all night looking out the front window. It was a heckuva day.

The next morning, I went to the hospital to see Barbee and Zwerg. Barbee was wrapped up in bandages, his face all swollen. He looked at me and said, "Good brother, when are we going to Jackson?"

I said, "You're not going to Jackson. You're staying in the hospital."

But that moment, if there were any questions about whether we were going to Jackson, Mississippi, they were answered. We had to go.

We knew that every move we made could be our last. There was really nothing the federal government could do to protect us. A deal was worked out for us to ride the bus. Again, there were troopers on the bus and on the side and helicopters. At the state line, the Alabama troopers turned us over to the Mississippi troopers.

It was my first time going to Mississippi, which was like another country. In Mississippi, they would say, "You can't think of no federal government down here. We're gonna do things our way."

Everything in Mississippi was controlled, iron clad, from the top down. Medgar Evers's killer was an elected official. Herbert Lee was killed by a state legislator. Schwerner, Chaney, and Goodman were killed by a sheriff.

When we crossed the state line, there were two huge billboards. The first one said, "Welcome to the Magnolia State, Mississippi." The next sign said, "Prepare to meet thy God." [Laughs.]

I wasn't sure if I would get out of Alabama. I knew I wouldn't get out of Mississippi. Inside the bus was eerie and quiet. Out the window, we saw this moss hanging from the trees, and we wondered what stories they could tell.

Finally we got to the bus station. We filed out of the bus into the white waiting room. The police were prepared. There was no mob, no Klan. I went straight to the rest room, and when I was inside a cop came inside and said

"Move on." I said, "I can't right now," so he arrested me for disorderly conduct for disobeying the orders of a police officer. We were put in a paddy wagon. A couple of days later, we were tried and convicted.

One of the things we expected to happen was that students from all over the South would come and join us, but no one did. The worst thing was when the governor was quoted on the front page of the newspaper that he applauded his "Nigroes" for not following those outside agitators. That was a constant theme in Mississippi—outside agitators. The real story was people were intimidated. If something was done to you, nothing would be done about it.

Stokely Carmichael was my cellmate in county jail. We stayed up all night arguing about violence versus nonviolence. He was for self-defense. He said if a person wasn't willing to defend himself, he wasn't willing to live and deserved to die. I said that was nothing new, and that's what's wrong with the world now. Retaliation was not related to change. If you want change, you have to have a better example and a more noble approach.

He said, "What about your own life?"

I said, "If it's for the cause, then no one is taking my life. I give my life by choice to what I believe in, and if you are violent there is no guarantee that you are going to survive. Actually, the chances of you being killed by being violent are probably greater because you are perceived as a threat or a greater threat."

We never agreed, but we stayed friendly. When he later made his black power speech, I asked him, "What's your point about black power?"

He surprised me, because he looked at me and smiled. "Look at the reaction of white folks. It's very interesting." What he was basically saying to me was that he appreciated agitating white folks. [Laughs.]

We were in four different jails over thirty-nine days in Mississippi. In one place, they put us in a row of cells and gave us these old prison uniforms. Mine was peppered with holes in the back. I figured out that somebody who was wearing the uniform had been shot in the back with a shotgun. We had to look out the windows and see the graves.

Then, just to amuse themselves, they began to interrogate and beat us. We found out that they wanted the person they interrogated to use the word "sir": "yes, sir, no sir." The warden was behind the desk, the person being interrogated was sitting on the other side, and there was a row of about five officers. If someone didn't say "yes, sir" or "no, sir," they would beat him, or take his chair from under him, knock him to the floor and kick him.

They went down the line of cells. As the word came down, we all decided not to say "sir," and everyone was beaten. C. T. Vivian had gotten hit with a leather-covered blackjack, and there was blood all over his face.

Two of us were in the last cell, and we weren't beaten. My cellmate was Leroy Wright. Leroy was tall, strapping, and very mean-looking and not totally nonviolent. When the warden asked him a question, Leroy stood up and started flailing around. That meant they were going to have to fight, and those guys didn't want to fight. They had beaten up so many people they were exhausted, so they sent him back.

Then they got me in the chair. I didn't know if I would survive a beating, so when they asked me a question designed to get a yes or no answer, I avoided it. "Are you from Nashville?"

"That's correct."

They were immediately puzzled, because usually it would take one question to beat somebody.

"Have you ever been in the Navy?"

"I've never been in the Navy."

I would either say, "That's correct" or repeat what they said.

They said, "You're a smart nigger, aren't you?"

"I don't think of myself in that way at all."

They kept trying, but I would never say yes or no until they finally just said, "Get the hell out of here."

The next day we were moved to a brand-new jail called Parchman, a maximum security prison. They gave us new uniforms that were the wrong size. It was all part of a plan to humiliate us. Every so often, they would hose us down with cold water for their entertainment.

Finally, we decided to get bailed out. There was no discussion about continuing the ride to New Orleans. But when James Bevel and I were released, we decided to stay in Mississippi. We remembered what the governor said about his Negroes, and we had to find out what was happening.

We started to organize, and the response was great. In two weeks, we had put forty-two people in jail. They would go down to the bus station and sit in the white station. We would call the media first. Then we would call the FBI and then we'd call the local police, and we'd let them know how many people we were bringing down and what time they were expected to arrive. That gave us protection.

Then one day, the police arrested us because there were some juveniles in the group we had taken down. We spent ten days waiting for trial in their drunk tank. It was the worst jail experience I've ever had: no bed, no blanket, no mattress. We slept on the hard, cold concrete floor. The toilet was a hole in the floor. I didn't take a shower for ten days, longest I've ever been without one in my life.

We were facing the very real possibility of several years in jail, but we defended ourselves. There was no jury, so Bevel preached the judge in hell. [Laughs.] Bevel was so eloquent, you could almost see the flames leaping around the judge's robe. At one point, he choked on his chewing tobacco. The judge gave us a two-year suspended sentence, but we had to leave town. That was in October. On November 1, the Interstate Commerce Commission ruling went into effect, barring discrimination against interstate passengers.

Next, I wanted to work on my own project. We had gotten a grant from the Voter Education Project of the Southern Regional Council. They funded these voter registration projects. I think they paid $30 a week. Big-time money. They had scratched Selma off the map, because they said the black folks there were too afraid and the white folks too mean.

I said, "I'll try it."

On my first trip to Selma, I found that everything they said was true.

When they thought that the Freedom Riders might stop in Selma, they deputized every white male over twenty-one and told them to go down and meet us at the bus station. There were about 2,000 people down there, ready to attack the bus. That's why we bypassed Selma. Those people were ready to fight the Civil War again.

The tool they used to keep things as they were was fear. According to the law you needed at least ten people to sign a petition, asking the Board of Education to integrate. In Selma, when they submitted the ten names, the only response was threats, to the point where they got every person to withdraw their name except one—a federal postal employee. Everyone else was run out of town.

The white officials followed me everywhere to see what I was up to. I found a small group of people, maybe eight, who were willing to work on voter registration. I called them "The I Ain't Scared Group" after they were all threatened with arrest but stuck with it anyway.

We opened a voter registration clinic to help people fill out the forms to take the literacy test. Then we started looking to have places for mass meetings. The ministers were afraid. They didn't want their churches to be burned down or blown up. Everywhere we went, people were afraid to get involved. People had lost good jobs, and they had families to take care of.

How do you break that cycle of fear? We started with our small group, and slowly we got people coming into the clinics and then going down to register to vote. You could only register twice a month. The first time they went, they were turned away.

The Justice Department filed suit against them for refusing people, so what they did was to allow people to fill out the forms, but then they would fail them. You had five to eight pages of stuff you had to fill out, and they would ask you a whole bunch of questions. "Have you ever been guilty of moral interpetude [sic]?"

They would fail you for that. You had to have a voucher, a registered voter who said that was where you lived and you were OK and you weren't a carpetbagger who had come in to vote. It was hard to find a registered voter who would vouch for you.

The clincher was you had to read a section of the Constitution, the one that the registrar would select for you, and interpret that to his satisfaction. It was unbelievable. How could you pass? He would just say, "No, you didn't interpret that right."

They would keep them out in the rain. "The voting place is closed today." They would push people back, knock 'em down, and charge them with resisting arrest, put you in jail.

Then they started doing interesting things, like they would pass one or two people, and sometimes the person they would pass couldn't read or write. Then a schoolteacher would be blocked. The registrar would say, "We got people registered. If you pass the test you can be registered."

It was discouraging, so we had mass meetings. At the first mass meeting, the sheriff brought in his posse. They carried table legs from the local table company. They busted the taillights on our cars. That way, when we drove off we would be given tickets for driving with a broken taillight.

The thing that saved us in that situation, and this is why I hold to the beliefs I have regarding white southerners and even white segregationists that not all of them are evil. In this case, a white man came forth and said, "All right, boys, get back on the truck and get out of here." He was not part of law enforcement. He was the high school football coach. He had more authority than the sheriff. They turned around and got back on the truck. If it wasn't for him, there would have been a riot. The black people would have fought back, and we would have had law enforcement beating down people who were rioting.

I was there about six months, and we started to gather steam. We had people who were trying to register to vote for the first time in fifty years. We had an organized youth group. They started having meetings and singing songs, and they would go down and have sit-ins.

All through that period, black people told me I was being watched. Then the night Medgar Evers was killed, that's when I was attacked. It was part of a plan.

I was driving home one night when I saw a guy bent over the hood of his car, and there was another behind the wheel. They were white, but I lived on the border of a white neighborhood, so it was not unusual to see whites on our street.

I got out of my car, and I heard footsteps behind me. I said to myself, "Oh, well, this is it." I turned around to face my assailant. This guy was huge. He said to me with a deep southern drawl, "How much you charge me, buddy, to give me a push?"

I was so relieved I said I wouldn't charge anything. I jumped in the car, and I pulled up behind him to match the bumpers.

I said, "Do they match?"

He went and talked to the other guy, and then he motioned over to me. "Maybe you better come out and take a look."

I jumped out of the car and bent over to take a look. That's when he clubbed me in front of the head. At first, I didn't know what it was he hit me with. Then I saw it was the butt of a gun.

I stumbled back and fell to the street. I got up very quickly, but he hit me again. The third time, he jumped up in the air and came down on top of my head. I couldn't see him, because the blood was coming down into my eyes.

The last hit was devastating, but after I got back on my feet, he started backing up. Now, he pointed the gun at me. At that point, I yelled out to my neighbor. "Red!"

Red was my self-appointed bodyguard. He lived upstairs from me. He immediately came out on the porch, pointing his rife at the guy. I yelled, "Don't shoot." I knew if he shot that guy, he would have gone to jail. I only wanted a witness to see what happened. But when the guy saw Red, he jumped into his car and took off.

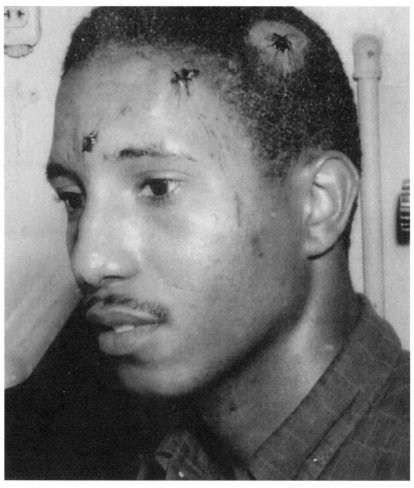

Bernard LaFayette after a near-fatal beating in Selma, Alabama, in June 1963.
(Courtesy of Bernard LaFayette)

Red took me to the hospital, and they stitched me up and kept me overnight. Later, I learned from the FBI there was a conspiracy that was spun in New Orleans to knock off three civil rights leaders, Medgar Evers in Mississippi, Ben Elton Cox in Shreveport, Louisiana, and me. Cox had left town and was away, but they killed Medgar Evers. My wife was his secretary. She called me that night to tell me what happened. The next day, I went right back to work. I wanted to make a point that I wouldn't be intimidated.

Meanwhile, the number of people we were able to get to vote picked up.

One reason was we got people from Bogachida, which was an all-black community across the creek. They were very independent people who were known to be militant. Sometimes, blacks who were running from white folk after committing some kind of offense could make it across the creek to Bogachida. The whites were not anxious to chase them in there, because the people there were known to shoot back.

I got a lot of those people to come and attempt to register. When the blacks in Selma saw that, they said, "Well, if they're going to go register to vote, then I better go and register."

I stayed in Selma until the fall of 1963, when I went back to school By then, SNCC [the Student Nonviolent Coordinating Committee] had sent other people down, and the core group was able to handle things. I went back to college, but I stayed involved in the movement. In 1967, Martin Luther King appointed me as National Program Director of the Poor People's Campaign. I was twenty-seven years old.

What they were trying to do was make poverty visible. All of the superhighways passed the local towns, so people never saw the poverty and the poor housing conditions. While petitions had been made and people talked about statistics, there was no face with the statistics, so King said, "What we'll do is gather up all these people and take them to Washington on mule trains and wagon trains and show them these are human beings. They can testify and let them talk to their congressman."

I had first met Dr. King in 1960 at a workshop in Miami, Florida, that CORE organized. When he gave a talk about nonviolence, most people went off swimming, but I stayed there with him, so he and I had this long, private conversation. I was still trying to develop my philosophy. He talked about the New Testament concept of love, and I came to understand it a little bit more. We also talked about pacifism. It was interesting, because while he believed in nonviolence, he was not a pacifist. He was very approachable, but he didn't look at you when he was talking to you. He was always looking around. Even when I worked with him later, I remember he didn't look at you right in the eye. Still, he was great fun. He told jokes all the time. In those days, the only way you could get from one city to another was by car, and those trips with him were a riot. He would keep everybody in stitches, the way he would mimic the slow drawl of the older preachers.

In April 1968 we went to Memphis because the sanitation workers were on strike there. The movement was kind of waning then. They thought if King went there it would get some media coverage and motivate the people to continue the strike.

I was with him the night before he died. It was raining like cats and dogs that night. He was tired and was already in his pajamas when Ralph Abernathy called to tell him to get dressed and come to a mass meeting.

Martin said, "I'm tired," but Abernathy kept pushing him. Finally, King said, "Well, Ralph, if you think I oughta get up outta the bed as hard as it's raining and come out there to that church, then that's what I'm gonna do. If you think that's what I should do, that's what I'm gonna do."

He was reluctant, but of course he went out there and made one of the best speeches he ever made in his life. That's when he said, "I've been to the mountaintop. And I don't mind. Like anybody, I would like to live a long life. Longevity has its place. But I'm not concerned about that now." At the end he said, "I'm happy tonight. I'm not worried about anything. I'm not fearing any man. Mine eyes have seen the glory of the coming of the Lord."

The next morning, he was kind of down. The press was tearing him up over the nonviolence issue. He said to us, "No matter what you do, don't abandon nonviolence. We're in a period of violence here, but it's gonna run its course. When it's over with, people are going to be ready for nonviolence, because they'll see you cannot bring changes with violence."

I got on the plane and went to Washington, and while I was flying to Washington, he was killed.

I have continued to follow his path. These days, I set up training schools for nonviolence. Our goal here is to make Rhode Island a nonviolent state. We are organizing and mobilizing people to appreciate nonviolence from the ground up. We've got policemen, schoolteachers, kids, mental health professionals. We have a 160-hour certification program where we train them to be trainers. Then they go out and train other people.

We're setting up nonviolent centers around the country and around the world, in Colombia, South Africa, Haiti. We have one in Michigan, another in Florida. We take on these experiments, like in Colombia, where 35,000 people are killed each year. Most of them are being killed by neighbors. They have no tools to solve conflict other than what they have traditionally done. Everybody agrees this is not the way to do things, even the gangs. They want to see their grandchildren live. "Could you help us?" So we trained their leadership and gave them a sense of hope.

I have a lot of hope for other reasons, too. Today you see blacks on city

Bernard LaFayette, still spreading the gospel of nonviolence, 2003.
(Courtesy of Bernard LaFayette)

council, as school principals, doing voter education, in positions of administration. You see black mayors and chiefs of police. The mayor of Selma is black. I've had occasion to go to back to the bus station in Nashville. We have a home in Tuskegee, and I go to Montgomery all the time. I don't think about it all when I go to the bus station.

I have met young people who don't believe the stories I have to tell. [*Laughs.*] If you tell someone there were segregated parks, "What do you mean, you can't walk through a park?" They couldn't believe such a condition existed. Four restrooms? Why would they have four restrooms? That's about as dumb as they could imagine, so some things have changed.

Bob Zellner
The Traitor

Bob Zellner is living testimony to the fact that not every white Southerner was racist. Time and again Zellner, as a young member of SNCC, risked his life so that people other than himself could enjoy their civil rights. That he managed to survive so many attempts on his life can be attributed to luck—and a lot of bad marksmanship.

These days Zellner lives in an old farmhouse in Sag Harbor, New York. The first thing a visitor notices is the plethora of American flags around the property, which occasions some surprise, since it was the apathy of the federal government in the face of brutal oppression that caused so many problems for Zellner and SNCC.

He comes to the door on this summer morning in a bathrobe and two-day growth of beard. He is solidly built, with a warm smile and a southern accent as thick as Tupelo honey.

I get a tour of the house. In the living room is an old family picture. Bob points a finger at each of the men in the photo. "He is a Klan member. He is a Klan member." He points to another man sporting a tie with an unusual design. "My father said it was pretty dumb to be a member of the Klan and wear a target on your chest."

How was it that the son and grandson of Ku Klux Klan members got involved with the civil rights movement? Zellner brews a cup of coffee, and we set up the tape recorder in his backyard so I could hear the answer. Before we start, he holds out his arm for me to see. It is grotesquely misshapen, the product of his most recent confrontation with the police. He explains that developers were moving in on some sacred land on the nearby Shinnecock Indian reservation. He was stating their case to an officer when he was grabbed from behind and beaten to the ground. Then, reminiscent of numerous incidents from the civil rights movement, Bob was handcuffed and charged with resisting arrest. The incident was captured on camera, and a lawsuit is pending. With a smile, Bob quotes the great Yankee philosopher Yogi Berra: "It's déjà vu all over again."

My father was a preacher man in the Methodist Church. I was named for Bob Jones, the ultraconservative preacher. My mother and dad both graduated from Bob Jones College, and Bob Jones performed their wedding ceremony. In fact, my dad went to Europe in the Second World War with Bob Jones on a cockamamy scheme to save the Jews of Europe by converting 'em all to Christianity.

My father had been in the Klan in Birmingham. His father had been in the Klan. His three brothers and his sisters were all very active Klan people. He eventually left the Klan on principle. What happened with my father was when he went to Europe, he began to work with the Jewish underground, and he came into conflict with the Nazis, who were his ideological soulmates, but he began to identify with the Jews, not the Nazis. Also, while he was there, he met up with a group of black gospel singers from the South. They were together for months. They talked about the same kind of food and they liked the same hymns and music. Years later, he said to me, "Bob, something very disconcerting began to happen to me. One day I forgot they were black."

He said it ruined him as a Klansman. My mother was quite happy about it. She cut up all his white robes and made shirts for us boys. We were five little boys running around in South Alabama with white shirts made out of Klan robes. [*Laughs.*]

He truly changed. He began to see black people differently, Jews differently, the mission of the church differently. He became active in the Southern Conference Educational Fund, which prepared the ground for the civil rights movement.

I grew up in a house on three acres of land. The cook lived through the woods in a field in a cluster of little houses they called "the nigger quarter."

It's amazing how southerners grow up with that word. We would go over and play with them, or sometimes she would bring them over to the house to play with us. We didn't see any difference between us and those kids, but there came a time, and in the South this was around puberty, when if you had interracial playmates, you don't play together anymore. Nobody ever said not to, you just gradually stopped.

I heard lynching stories, but they were something that adults talked about. Then, years later, I'd meet someone who would open a drawer and take out a dried-up preserved finger and say, "This is from the lynching of . . ."

Early on, I was interested in the contradictions about race. As a young teenager, I worked in a country store in East Bruton, Alabama, way out in the piney woods. My boss said one day, "You can't do that, Bob."

"What did I do?"

"You said 'No, ma'am' and 'Yes, sir' to those people that were just in the store."

"Well, I've been taught to be very polite to older people."

"Well, it's all right if just you and I are in here, but if any white people are in here, you can't say that to colored people."

I did say "sir," but I would say it quietly. Still, I was very puzzled about what he said to me. He wasn't upset for himself. This was another thing I learned about southerners. They will teach you these racist things, not for themselves, but as a protection to yourself, so they say.

When I was in high school in 1955, everybody was talking about Autherine Lucy, the first black student at the University of Alabama. I said, "I think it's a good idea."

Immediately, my friends started whispering, "Don't let anybody hear you say that. We're not going to hurt you. We know you're crazy, but other people may not and they will hurt you." I never wanted to fight, but it turned out that I was a very good fighter. I was very tough, and that saved my life over and again years later.

In high school, there was a serious attempt to recruit me to the Ku Klux Klan. I was out with people in this fraternity, and someone said, "Let's go nigger knockin'."

I was immediately very uncomfortable, but also I was in this peer group, so I said, "Oh, yeah, let's go nigger knocking."

The idea was to go and do random violence to black people, throw bottles at them, hit them with a brick, hit them with a rod that they would hold out the door as they went speeding past, and it would slash people.

Then they would say, "You want to do it?" That was a way to find out who had real hate in their heart. I said, "No."

"What's wrong?"

So I did my little bit of violence, which I am very ashamed about. A person was coming by, and I kind of lofted a biscuit in the direction of the person. That was the extent of my ability to do violence to an anonymous person simply because they were black, so luckily I failed the test.

I went to Huntingdon College in Montgomery, Alabama, from '57 to '61. Those were the boycott years in Montgomery when I met Martin Luther King and Rosa Parks. That was my undoing right there.

Before we even met Dr. King, some of us secretly took up a collection on campus for him and Reverend Abernathy, because at one point their cars and houses and everything were all confiscated. We circulated a letter in support. Everyone was afraid to sign it, so they said, "You sign it for the committee." It said, "We want you to know that not all white people in Alabama feel the same way." Years later, a reporter told me, "Reverend Abernathy still has your letter. He's unfolded it and showed it to so many people it's in four parts now."

My senior year I was in a sociology course called "Race Relations." We went to the Klan and got their literature. We went to the White Citizens Council and got their literature. Then five of us told our professor we wanted to go to King's organization. Our professor stiffened up. "Well, that won't be necessary. I'm sure you have enough research."

We argued. "We're here at a four-year liberal arts school in favor of the best education; we don't feel we can be educated unless we go and talk to Martin Luther King."

"If you meet with Martin Luther King and the Klan finds out, they'll beat you up, and that'll be a breach of the peace, and you'll be arrested."

"Why wouldn't they arrest the Klansman?"

"Oh, there's too many of them."

We went around and around until finally we said, "We're going anyway."

We figured out the best way to meet King was to go to the federal court where at that time he was involved in a famous libel case. At recess, he was standing in the hall. The five of us kind of meekly approached him. I said, "Dr. King, I'm Bob Zellner from Huntingdon College. We're writing a paper, and we wonder if we can talk to you."

"Great, great to have some students from Huntingdon College."

This was a terrible taboo to begin with, but the main taboo was shaking hands. It's hard to believe that this would be one of the main things that all the hangers-on at the court were saying [in an exaggerated southern accent]: "They went right up there and shook hands with that nigger right here in the courthouse, oh my God."

When we later told the professor that we had met Dr. King, he immediately wanted to know if we were standing up. I said, "Yeah, we were standing up."

"You didn't sit down?"

"Why was it important?"

"Well, if you sit down you can be arrested, but you can stand up."

We met [King] again in his office. He said there was going to be a series of mass meetings for the anniversary of the bus boycott. We said we wanted to come.

"Well, you're certainly welcome, but you're likely to be arrested."

We said we wanted to come anyway. Sure enough, the police surrounded the church. They had all our names. I got an A on the paper, but the five of us were asked to leave school. I refused, and I stayed, but the Klan burned crosses around our dormitory, and we were called into the office of the attorney general, who said we had fallen under the communist influence.

At some point, I told Martin King that my interest in the movement was more than academic.

He suggested I go to the Highlander Folk School to learn more about the movement. The Highlander School was run by Myles Horton, a white guy from the mountains of Tennessee who went to the Union Theological Seminary and fell under the influence of some very progressive folk. He wanted to teach, but in a very untraditional manner. He wanted to teach adult education among basically illiterate folk and get them to share knowledge and work collectively on practical problems.

The school was always integrated, which created problems. Once the state destroyed it and it had to be moved. When I went there, one of my duties was lifeguard at the lake. We had two or three rules: you had to swim with a buddy and respond to a buddy count; and you had to get out of the water if there was any lightning—or any shooting. We didn't have that much lightning, but people across the lake liked to shoot at us, so everybody would have to get out and stand behind trees. "Everybody out, they're starting to shoot!"

Myles would work on labor issues with both blacks and whites. Once someone asked him how he got these people to sit down together, and Miles said, "It wasn't all that complex. We had three steps to approach this problem. We prepared the food, we put it on the table, and we rang the dinner bell."

Highlander was the most amazing experience of my life. I met the students who had conducted the first sit-ins in Greensboro, North Carolina. They were my age, and they were going against the authority, against the power. They were all so well dressed in their trench coats, I thought, "Boy, these people must be rich." I couldn't afford a trench coat. They had books and were so dignified. For a young white southerner to see these young black southerners who I had lost all contact with at an early age, doing these famous things, I was so full of admiration. I just knew there was nothing for me to do but be a rebel from then on.

I was still a student at Huntingdon when the Freedom Rides came through in the spring of '61. That probably had more impact on me than anything else.

We agreed that if there was going to be so much violence that people were going to be killed that we would try to nonviolently intervene to save lives. The streets were all blocked off, so by the time we were able to get to the bus station, they had already been beaten. There were cameras and blood all over; people laying on the streets. The suitcases had gaping holes in 'em, and the mob was putting it all into a big pile along with school books. They were throwing them into a fire and kind of dancing. It reminded me of the book burning rituals of Nazi Germany.

Then we found out the Freedom Riders had been taken to St. Jude Hospital. I saw Jim Zwerg and John Lewis and William Barbee, who were just beaten horrendously. I had met them before, but now they were almost unrecognizable. I remember saying to John Lewis or William Barbee, "Well, your Freedom Ride is over," and I was struck by what he said. "Oh, no, as soon as we can walk, we're going back to the bus."

I said, "My God, you're gonna be killed."

"We know that. But this can't be stopped."

[Tears form in his eyes. He looks down and shakes his head.]

I could never be normal after that. I had to get into that movement that would have young people so courageous that they would literally sacrifice their lives.

That fall I was hired by SNCC to travel to white southern campuses and tell them about what SNCC was doing. I thought I was joining an ongoing outfit, but I realized when I got there that I was considered one of the fifteen original staff members. I spent most of my time around the office reading, learning all I could. After a few weeks, Jim Foreman, who was my boss, said, "If you're gonna do this, you really have to learn what's going on, so you're going to go to the staff meeting tomorrow in McComb."

Bob Zellner as a SNCC organizer in Atlanta, 1962.
(Courtesy of Danny Lyon, Magnum Photos)

I said, "You mean Mississippi?"

I was from Alabama and I was afraid to go to Mississippi, and I was white. We left the next day by car. I was the only white person in there, so at night I could sit up, but during the day I would have to hide by laying on the floorboard of the car. When we'd stop for gas I'd have to be completely covered up. They'd bring me an RC Cola and a moon pie when they stopped, but I couldn't get out at a gas station even to take a leak. For that, they'd have to pull over on the side of the road, and I'd go in the bushes.

At the meeting, I met most of the original members of SNCC for the first time. They were just as curious about me as I was about them, but they were all very welcoming. People took me aside to discuss what the situation was. They said it was really rough. One familiar face was Bernard LaFayette, one of the Nashville Freedom Riders, who had a wry sense of humor. When I told him what I was up to, he grinned at me and shook his head. "The white people are going to string you up, boy." He also said, "They're gonna be on your ass like white on rice." Of course he was right.

We started the meeting with a song. Singing was always very, very important to the nonviolent movement. For people bent on murder, it is very difficult for them to do that in the presence of nonresisting, powerfully singing people. I remember some songs that would start out very timidly in very tense situations, and then as the singing gained strength it gained power, and then it gave strength and power back to the people who were singing.

We started that meeting singing "Woke Up This Morning with My Mind on Freedom." It immediately became one of my favorite songs. Then Jim Foreman started off the meeting. He introduced everyone around the circle. Then he said, "This is Zellner, Bob Zellner. I have to tell you his daddy was a Klansman, his granddaddy was a Klansman. But I don't think he is." Then he shoved his hand out and said, "Just kidding, just kidding." [*Laughs.*]

Then he said, "I know that some of you here have never had a chance to be this close to a real peckerwood [*laughs*], so we're really gonna get to know each other well. I want you to know that I've talked to him for a couple of hours, and we're gonna work together. We'll start out anyway."

Soon after we began, we heard people singing "We Shall Overcome" from down the street. It was a bunch of high school kids who had been expelled from school for a series of sit-ins to desegregate the bus station, some lunch counters, and the local library. Many of them had been in jail for thirty-five days, and they were just sixteen years old.

They came upstairs, and it was decided we would march immediately across town. As we marched, there was a lot of jeering, but it began to get very nasty when we were stopped at City Hall by a big mob. A group of Klansmen gathered around me and started swinging at me. Bob Moses and Chuck McDew, who hadn't been arrested, came over and, in the nonviolent tradition, surrounded me to absorb some of this punishment. Then the police came over and hit them in the heads with billy sticks and blackjacks and took them off.

By then, I moved to the City Hall steps. I heard someone yell, "Bring him out here and we'll kill him," and they started carrying me out. I realized if they carried me away they would kill me. Somehow, I grabbed onto the City Hall railing. I was in shape, and when you are fighting for your life you have superhuman strength, so I was able to hold on.

One guy got so frustrated that he came over the back of my head as I was holding on and started putting his fingers into my eye sockets to try and get ahold of my eyeball. He actually pushed it out onto my cheekbone by looping his finger in the muscle behind it with his thumb and forefinger. I would pay attention to that while I was paying attention to everything else. Just as he was about to get ahold of my eyeball I would move in such a way that it would pop back into my eye socket. As the muscle pulled it back in, it would actually make a thunk, and I remember thinking, "Boy, that's a tough little muscle there, that eyeball."

I kept trying to work my way up the steps. Finally I got to the top. Then someone kicked me in the head. I remember the rail getting slippery with my own blood. That's when I thought, "This is the way I die."

The next thing I knew I was being dragged into the town hall, and the chief of police was screaming at me right into my face, "I ought to let 'em have ya. I ought to let 'em kill ya."

Well, he did. The mob filled into city hall, and they grabbed me, put me in a car, and drove out to the country, saying they were gonna hang me. They kept shouting at me and called me a "nigger-lovin' communist Jew motherfucker from New York."

I said to them, this car of big old guys, farmers, pulpwood cutters, tough as nails, I said, "Well, now nine out of ten is not bad, but I want you to know I'm not from New York." I had an Alabama accent at that time that would cut leather.

I wanted them to know that as a southerner I wasn't afraid of them and that I was as mean and tough as anybody there. I picked out the biggest one and said, "You are a yellow-belly, cowardly scum motherfucker, and I can whip you. You just get everybody out of here, and it'll be just me and you. Let's be gentlemanly about it, let everybody else stay out of it, and I'll whip your damn ass."

"Oh, my, this sumbitch is crazy."

Then they started arguing among themselves. They were trying to figure out a way to get out of hanging me. We got to a cow pasture, and went through these gates, and there was a huge group of people waiting for an old-fashioned lynching, but they ended up taking me instead to a jail in a town called Magnolia.

The sheriff is there, and there is a mob out in the yard. One of them said, "We're just waiting until dark. We'll get you then." The jail was like a little wooden cabin. I kept saying, "It's just my luck, the first time I'm ever in jail, and they can push this thing over with a pickup truck." I wanted a good strong jail.

A black prisoner brought me about six or seven real thin mattresses and started stuffing them in between the bars. He said, "They're getting gasoline together, and they're gonna come in here and try to burn you. If they get in here, stay in the corner and cover up with these mattresses."

Then what happened was the incredible heroism of Jack Young, who was one of two African-American lawyers in the whole state of Mississippi. He came to the jail in the middle of that crowd and bailed me out. He could have been killed right there himself.

He took me back to McComb, and from there we went immediately to Jackson. I was more terrified probably than I ever knew. Most of us were. One of the things that it did do to me was it made it a lot easier later on to do even more dangerous things, because I figured that every day I had after October fourth was extra.

After I got back to Atlanta, I started organizing on college campuses. Sometimes Chuck McDew and I would go from McComb to New Orleans to organize down there. Dion Diamond, SNCC's field secretary, had been arrested in Baton Rouge for organizing demonstrations. So one day on our way to New Orleans, we stopped off in Baton Rouge to see Dion. At the jail, they told us, "You can't see him. Our nigger day is not until Thursday."

We said, "Can we leave him some toothpaste and some books and stuff?"

They said OK, so we walked out to a drugstore. By the time we got back, they had surrounded the place with an army, and arrested us on charges of criminal anarchy. They said "on or about the twenty-third day of December 1961, Chuck McDew and Robert Zellner entered the parish of East Baton Rouge and did attempt with force of arms to attempt to overthrow the East Baton Rouge Parish, the State of Louisiana, and the United States of America."

They said we had incited war.

We were both tortured in jail. At first it was sleep deprivation. [He takes a deep breath.] Even if I tried to sleep sitting up, they would throw water on me, beat me on the bottom of the feet, threaten me with knives. To this day, if I'm asleep and you inadvertently touch my foot, I attack.

When I complained to my lawyer, they put us in the sweatbox. The sweatbox can kill you. It's a tiny cell with a slit at the bottom. Through that slit, they blast you with heat from a furnace. You can't even lay down, the cell is so small. After two or three days, I told Chuck, who was next door to me, "Chuck, I can't take it anymore."

He said, "See if you can take it a little while longer, because otherwise they're gonna really hurt you."

"At this point, I don't care if they kill me."

I started screaming until finally they opened the door and they pulled their guns and said, "We're gonna kill you."

I said, "That'll be a relief to me. You gotta kill me or let me out of here, both of us, because as long as I can scream, I will scream."

All this time, they were bringing tourists through. They would open this little slit, and they would point out McDew and say, "That's our black communist in there." Then they would look at me, and they would say, "That's our white communist."

I remember one little girl said to Chuck, "Say something in Communist." [Laughs.] Chuck, who had converted to Judaism, said in Yiddish, "Kish meir ein tuchis"—kiss my ass.

I was in jail about thirty-five days. Many of us think that there are war criminals down there and they are still alive. I used to think that maybe they led miserable lives, except maybe the ones who were murderers, but I don't think they ever drew an uncomfortable breath. Like Byron de la Beckwith said after he killed Medgar Evers, "Shooting that nigger was no more painful than my wife in labor pains."

There were plenty of people who wanted to kill me. I was shot at when I was still at Huntingdon. I was standing at the window when a bullet came through the glass. Soon I was shot at so many times that I got to recognize the sound of a bullet that comes very, very close to your head. It's more of a feel than it is a sound. If you hear it, it's not the one that you have to worry about. [Laughs.]

When we started the staff in the fall of '61, the idea was to go into communities and burrow in for the long haul of organizing. In Albany, Georgia, I was arrested and put on an all-black gang. I think their attitude was "If you're gonna be a nigger lover, you're gonna go work with the niggers." It wasn't a problem for me. Those guys were great—no matter how bad or mean they were, they knew every last detail about the movement and were sympathetic. I was glad to be outside and working, and what happened was the trustees in the jail would tell somebody from the local community where we were gonna be working, and they'd come by and throw stuff out of their cars—chewing gum, toothpaste, chewing tobacco, cigarettes, so we all had a tremendous supply of that stuff to share with everybody.

After I was released, I was given my own organizing project in Talladega, Alabama. It began when Foreman told me to go over there and speak at the convocation of an all-black college. I got a really good response. Afterward, I found out that they all thought I was a light-skinned Negro. One young woman came up to me at one of the workshops and said, "Bob, when Verna introduced you to speak, I thought you were a white guy."

"What made you think that?"

"Well, you look as white as anybody I've ever seen."

"Well, people have said that. How did you know that I wasn't white?"

"The way you talk, and you're a SNCC guy. And when you smiled, I saw your dimples. White people don't have dimples."

It was very touching later, because she came to me later on and said, "Bob, I found out you're white."

Then she asked me some interesting questions. First, she wanted to know if she could smell my hair. I leaned over, and she smelled my scalp. Then she exclaimed, "That doesn't smell like chicken feathers! I thought all white people's hair smelled like chicken feathers."

She had all these ideas. She said she originally thought we put something on to make ourselves lighter. She said, "I know now it doesn't rub off, but for a long time I thought it did." She said her Dad was a high school principal and she was raised in a middle-class home, "but we just have all these things that we think about white people, and I'm finding out that almost none of them are true." [*Laughs.*]

I said, "White southerners are raised with just as many misapprehensions about black people, and none of them are true. In the end, we're just people, that's all we are."

The students were the main support for this small town, and it was just egregious segregation. They were needed as customers, but they couldn't sit down at the lunch counter, so they sat in. The town responded with fire hoses and dogs.

At one march, the police were pushing us along. This one guy behind me kept prodding me with his nightstick, and there was something so sharp it was ripping my shirt apart and tearing my back up. I didn't want to cause anybody any alarm, so I just gritted my teeth and decided, as long as he doesn't kill me I'll be all right. We walked back almost a half a mile to campus. As soon as they pushed us back through the main gate of the campus, everybody, including the girls, started pulling their shirts up, and it turned out every cop there had taken a pocket knife blade and sharpened it like a razor and embedded it into their nightsticks.

That same year, we had some of our worst experiences. In Danville, Virginia, there was an effort to integrate the library and the lunch counters. It got very violent. The town had a furniture factory, and the sheriff deputized the factory workers, who were all given table legs, which they beat us with.

In one march, out of 125 people with us, 90 were hospitalized. We tried to get press coverage, but the sheriff had his thugs beat the reporters and take their equipment. I had my camera, so I went up to take pictures. The police chief said, "OK, Zellner, you don't value that camera very much." He took the camera from around my neck and threw it down and smashed it into the ground. Then he opened the back, took out the film and said, "Now, anybody else want to take pictures?"

Then he arrested me, and he arrested Reverend McGee, who was leading the march. But they didn't take us away. Instead, they said, "Watch."

That's when they turned on the fire hose and started beating people. The cops stood there with their guns drawn at us, and they said, "McGee, your wife is out there, what kind of man are you? Aren't you going to help her? Zellner, your girlfriend is out there. Aren't you going to help her?" And they literally washed her under a car. Then, when she started to climb out, they hit her on the head with a table leg. A woman.

That night in the hospital, women arrived with their breasts split completely open, noses split, eyes knocked out, ears ripped off. Somehow, we got a film of it. A local guy had a movie camera and took film at the hospital of the staff sewing up person after person after person.

I and a few others were charged under the John Brown statute, inciting the black population into acts of war against the white population. We took sanctuary in a local church, thinking they wouldn't come after us, but we also had to get that film to the networks. We decided we would try and get out of the church in the dark of night, find a place to meet, and then get a car to Washington. So at two or three o'clock in the morning, we crept out to the back of the church and were about to go down this deep ravine into the gully when the cops turned the spotlights on us and just started shooting.

We took off for the church door, and fortunately someone opened it. We zipped inside, and they bolted the doors again, but at least we were able to give the film to some woman who put it in her dress and took it away. She was able to get it out.

The next morning they broke the door down and took us off to jail. It was a very serious charge, but it could not stand up in court, and they knew it, so they reduced it to something else, like disorderly conduct or disturbing the peace. Over the course of that summer we were arrested five or six times. We would have parties in people's backyards as a way of relieving stress and keeping everybody's spirits together. If the police found out where we were, they would surround the place to catch all the SNCC people and put them in jail. If you ran, they would shoot at you.

This one night, they surrounded a party and surprised us out of the blue by shooting at us. The amazing thing was that more people weren't killed. Everybody ran. I ran two or three houses down, and went into a house, and everybody jumped into closets and climbed under beds and everything, but the woman of the house, seeing me, was terrified. She said, "Oh, you can't stay here. Everybody else can be passed off as a relative from the neighborhood. I hate to do this, but you've gotta go."

I said, "OK, but the police are in the backyard. Can you let me out the front?"

When I went out the door, she slammed the door behind me, and the cops turned the spotlight on the porch and started shooting at me right away. It was like shooting fish in a barrel. I was there on the porch with this big spotlight, and the bullets were flying all over the place, so I ran down to the end of the porch and just leaped into the darkness.

On the left hand side of the building, out of sight from the police where they would be coming from, was a huge pile of brambles: bushes, briar stickers, and God knows what else was in there, snakes, broken glass, rusty nails. I thought my only chance was to dive into there.

By the time they came around I was settled into the pile and quiet. They shined lights directly at me in the pile. They searched the whole back. Some of them ran off into the woods behind the house. "He went this way."

It seemed like I was in there an hour or so. Then, after everything got completely dark and they were all gone, I heard a little tiny voice, "Psst, hey mister, hey mister."

"What."

"Mr. Bob, they're all gone. Come follow me," so I climbed out of there, and this little kid took me through the woods to somebody else's house that he knew, and he called somebody to come and retrieve me.

I was committed to nonviolence, but after a while, I did question it. Even by '64 there was some degree of disillusionment settling in with the death of the civil rights workers and with the unrelenting brutality that we faced for a number of years and the basic indifference of the federal government. The hypocrisy of the government, still putting themselves up as the leader of the free world, the bastion of democracy. We couldn't stand hypocrisy. We got along better with the Klan and the killers and the terrorists, because they made no bones about what they were doing.

The Kennedys could have said, "Look, there's laws against killing people for wanting to register to vote. I'm gonna put you in jail, George Wallace. We're not gonna pussyfoot around with you if you stand in the courthouse door against a court order."

People see JFK as a hero. Not in my book. The real American heroes were people like Medgar Evers and Fannie Lou Hamer, who paid their lives for freedom.

You could understand how people would get angry. I've been beaten, shot at, cattle prodded, had hoses turned on me. When they would turn the water against you, the force of it is so strong, it would knock the windows out. It just knocks you all over the place. It slides you along and skins you up, and it's cold. The water is so hard it can break your bones. It can wash you into a brick wall or a pole or some kind of metal.

The cattle prodding happened during the William Moore march in 1963. Moore was a postman from Baltimore. He decided that he would walk from Chattanooga, Tennessee, to Jackson, Mississippi, to deliver a letter to Governor Ross Barnett, saying he didn't agree with segregation. When he got to Alabama, near Anniston, the same spot where the Freedom Riders were attacked, he was shot and killed as he walked along with a little sandwich board on him. The front of it said, "Eat at Joe's." The back said, "Both black and white."

It was decided that a group from CORE and SNCC, which had been the two main organizations in the Freedom Ride, would try and complete William Moore's march. I think there were five or six people from SNCC and five or six people from CORE. We would be walking in Tennessee, Georgia, Alabama, and Mississippi. The whole distance was 400 miles.

When we got to Alabama, Sam Shaara put on the sign that Bill Moore had worn. The road went into a little bit of a valley, and behind the fence on both sides of the road were huge crowds of people. Most of them were Klansmen, rednecks or hecklers. The police stuck cattle prods against us, which have a high energy charge and burns you and causes you to go into spasms. It feels like being hit by lightning. It's one of the worst pains you can imagine. When they used the electrical charge, the crowd just went into a frenzy. They thought it was the greatest thing on earth. Of course, we were arrested for disturbing the peace. We were in jail for thirty-five days.

In '64, we began screening people for the Mississippi summer project. The rationale behind sending white volunteers to Mississippi for the summer was that if black people were brutalized and arrested, the country didn't care, but if it happened that the white son of a congressman or a lawyer gets arrested, beaten, or god forbid killed, then they will demand that the government do something about it.

Well, that's exactly what happened with Schwerner, Chaney, and Goodman.

The three went to Mississippi to investigate a church burning on a Sunday. It was a policy that if someone went out into the field, there was a call time when you had to call in, and they didn't. So our Jackson office knew within an hour that something was up.

What we were trying to do in the initial hours—and if they had done it, it would have saved their lives—was to get someone from the Justice Department or the FBI to call the jail in Philadelphia, Mississippi. The idea is whether or not you know they are there, you assume the attitude that you know they are. You want the jailers to know that you know they are there. If they're not, then there's nothing lost, but if they are, then it could have given them enough pause so that somebody could have gotten to them before they were taken off that night to be murdered.

Neither the Justice Department nor the FBI would make the call. They said they have to be missing twenty-four hours before they could assume that anything bad has happened to them, and we went over with them time and time again, but they refused.

We had a meeting, and it was decided I would go down there with Mickey [Schwerner]'s wife, Rita. Most everybody knew very early on in their bones that they were dead, but when I was with Rita I held out hope that we could find that they weren't dead, that maybe they had been kidnapped.

At one or two o'clock in the morning, we drove into Neshoba County. We went to the church that had burned. By this time, we had been noted by the Klan, and they laid an ambush for us. They left the road down to the church clear, but as I pulled into the churchyard, I spotted a whole bunch of pickup trucks lined up on the road just beyond the church.

When I saw the silhouettes of guns and men, I swung around the circular driveway and just continued on out. Of course the pickup trucks fell in behind us. There was also a lawyer in our car. He kept saying, "Why don't you stop and talk to them? Maybe they just want to talk."

I said, "No." [Laughs.]

They blocked the road in front of us with a pickup truck. I knew there were piney woods on both sides of the road, and there was a slight possibility I would be able to go off the road and get around that truck, but I also knew they all had pickup trucks that were much bigger than my Corvair.

I kept my speed up as much as I possibly could and picked my spot across the ditch. I got across the ditch fast enough to crash through a row of bushes. Then I picked my spots between the trees in the hope that I wouldn't get wedged. I took pieces of the car off getting through the trees. They didn't think I would get around but, by golly, I did.

When I got to the road, they started shouting to get the truck out of the way. Then the race began back into Philadelphia [Mississippi]. I knew the motel where the press and the FBI were staying. I figured if I drove straight to the FBI, I had the best chance. If they had gotten us, there would have just been three more victims, but we managed to get to the motel before they cut us off.

We knocked on the door and a little crew-cut red-headed FBI guy opened the door, and he looked up and said, "Zellner, my God, do you wanna get us all killed?"

I introduced Rita, and I told him what happened. He wouldn't arrest those guys, telling us the only thing he could do was call Sheriff Rainey, who was one of the murderers. Rainey and his deputy, Price, came down, and we insisted on seeing the burned-out car.

"I'll take you to the car, but after that I'll escort you to the city limits and you're on your own." He escorted us to the car, but we still had to get out of town by ourselves. It was like running a gauntlet. They had lined the roads. They threw bottles, bricks, and pipes and everything at the car, but at least they weren't dead set on killing us at that point, and we made it.

Over the next ten days we went from Rainey and Price at the county level to the governor to President Johnson for help, and we got absolutely none at all. At the governor's mansion, nobody would even tell us where he was. We were about to leave when Governor [Paul] Johnson and George Wallace pulled up and got out of the car, followed by a lot of press and policemen. We just fell in with the crowd. As we got to the top of the steps, one of the newsmen asked them about the missing civil rights workers. Johnson said, "Well, Governor Wallace and I are the only ones who know where they are, and we're not saying." He laughed and made a big joke out of it. I stuck my hand out and said, "Governor Johnson." Of course, any politician will always stick his hand out. I grabbed it with both of mine just as Wallace looked around and saw me. When he did, he ran into the house and slammed the door.

I introduced myself and Rita to the governor. He began bucking like a fish on the line, trying to get away from me, but I was holding him with both my hands. Finally, the police pounced on me and broke me loose from him, and he ran into the mansion and slammed the door.

Before we met President Johnson, we had a fairly long meeting with Nicholas Katzenbach, who was the acting attorney general. We asked him about Buford Posey, who was the Mississippian who had given the FBI some information to the effect that someone had seen three men shot and killed and then buried in a dam. Of course the FBI shared the information with the murderers. At the time we were speaking to Katzenbach, we told him Posey was sitting in his house in Mississippi with a shotgun across his lap, and he knew he had to leave. We wanted assurance that he would be able to get out of Mississippi alive. Katzenbach's response with his little cold eyes was, "Well, we've lost witnesses before."

Finally they took us to President Johnson. He came out of this door, and he immediately reached for Rita's hand and said, "I'm so pleased to meet you." It was obvious he had no idea why we were there. Rita explained that this was not a social visit, that we saw no evidence of any large-scale search, even though the news was full of servicemen tramping through jungles looking for the bodies. We also had no evidence of any concern about possibly saving the people if they were still alive.

He said, "I'm terribly sorry that you feel that way, but I have an important meeting of the National Security Council, and I have to leave." He turned on his heels and left.

Then we got about a half-hour lecture from Pierre Salinger about how you don't treat the President of the United States that way. In fact, we also said to Katzenbach that we saw no evidence of a search, and he looked at Rita and said, "What makes you qualified to run a search of this magnitude?"

She said, "The only thing I can think of is I can't be bought off by southern politicians."

As you know, the three bodies were found in a dam a month later.

Despite the disappearances, the Mississippi Summer project went on. I went to Greenwood, Mississippi, to help register voters. When I got there,

Stokely Carmichael was project director, but he was constantly being called away to deal with other problems, so I was asked to come in and coordinate the volunteer effort.

I got along fine with Stokely. We were very close friends. I think I was the only white speaker at his memorial service, and I think I was followed to the podium by Louis Farrakhan. Stokely was always very independent minded. He was a born star, very charismatic, and personally appealing and funny. Because I was there before he came South, I helped him get his sea legs and showed him how to operate without getting killed right away.

What Stokely would do that others wouldn't was tear down the legitimacy of the lawmen by confronting them. He would call the sheriff a fat, tobacco-chewin', white imbecile, cracker, redneck peckerwood. Any one of those might get him killed in certain situations, but Stokely was willing to die, and what he was doing of course with his great grin was delegitimizing them as a source of terror by saying in effect, "We're not scared of you."

Still, Greenwood was pretty vicious. There was a lot of bloodshed there. That's where Byron de la Beckwith, Medgar Evers's killer, was from. He was the local hero and was famous for driving around town in his car, which had seat covers made of Confederate flags and with gun racks in the back.

The pickup with the gun rack in the back became a symbol because of the redneck factor. Usually, it was a pickup with the gun rack in the back, and the CB whip antenna. When we saw them, we knew we were being tracked by organized Klan, heavily armed and with the latest in communications equipment.

But Greenwood was also home of a tough black family named McGee. There were three brothers, Clarence, Jake, and Silas, and Mrs. McGee was just about as fierce as they come. One time the cops arrested Jake, so I went and got his mother and took her to the jail. Jake was in another room with the police chief and a volunteer lawyer. Mrs. McGee walks over to the door and puts her hand on the doorknob when one of the local cops says, "You can't go in there."

She says, "Oh, yes, I can, they're talking about my son, Jake. I'm coming to get him out of jail." But the guy steps between her and the door, knocks her hand off the door knob and says, "You can't go in there."

In a split second, Mrs. McGee hit him right over the eye so fast, it knocked him out. He was unconscious before he even began to fall, but still she wasn't content with that one blow. She took advantage of the situation and hit him again and again.

Do you know they didn't arrest her. When I tried to figure out why, the lawyer said, "She had beat that poor bastard so badly that nobody wanted to say that Mrs. McGee was arrested for knocking out the cop."

Part of voter registration work was to develop a propaganda campaign locally and nationally that would put pressure on the local government, so at least the police would be neutral. Even that was an advance, because that meant that if someone tried to register to vote he might not be beaten by cops or the local thugs.

We would sign people up and organize them in groups to go to the registrar. We'd make sure they'd have food and a place to park if they needed it. Sometimes the registrar would force them to stand in line literally for days. We kept records of who applied, how many times they applied. Each registrar would have rules about if I turned you down today, you can't attempt again for ninety days. All of those things were in violation of federal law, so you had to document those things. Eventually, after the Voting Rights Act of 1965, they appointed federal registrars and put these hard-core areas under federal trusteeship.

I look back on Mississippi Summer as a great success. It accomplished what we set out to do. It broke the back of massive resistance in the south. One of the things it did was bring hundreds of students, mainly white and mainly middle class, from colleges and universities all around the country to the South. When they went home, it was like a tremendous seed-pod explosion of people who had had this searing experience in Mississippi, and that steeled them as organizers and gave them a lifelong Holy Grail of social action and involvement. You had people like Mario Savio going back to Berkeley and starting the Free Speech movement. A lot of empowering movements came out of the civil rights movement. Some of them went into the Cesar Chavez farm worker organizing, labor union organizing. A number of them became the presidents of international unions. The women's movement was stimulated tremendously. Many women in SNCC played leadership roles: Anne Braden, Fannie Lou Hamer, Majeska Simpkins, Diane Nash, who was one of the premier leaders and founders of SNCC, Joanne Grant. Ruby Dora Smith Robinson was our boss, and she ruled with an iron hand.

But there was also a lot of cynicism after 1964. By 1964, people had already been on the front lines for two, three, or four years. They had been beaten and battered. There were a lot of deaths, a lot of trauma. We didn't understand battle fatigue at that time, but it was a problem.

In 1965, Dottie and I were in Atlanta when tensions between blacks and whites were getting worse. I felt bad about it because everybody would go out of their way to say to Dottie and me, "You know, when we're talking about white people, we're not talking about you."

I would have to say, "Well, I'm white people, so you are talking about me."

We now know, through testimony and the release of government documents, that a lot of the problems and internal dissension that eventually destroyed the organization were fomented by the FBI with its COINTELPRO program. They would use informers, anonymous calls, or anonymous letters to make accusations against certain leaders and make those accusations seem like they were coming from another leader.

There is some evidence that some of the people who expressed the strongest antiwhite views were FBI informers. Sometimes you would know who the agents were, but it could also tear the organization apart trying to guess.

In 1965, SNCC voted to become all black. Their reasoning was that it would be more effective in northern urban areas. What organizing did they ever do in northern urban areas? None.

By then, Dottie and I had developed the proposal for the GROW project, which stood for Grass Roots Organizing Work. The idea was to organize poor southern whites, which was a terrifying prospect because we were going to the people who had been shooting at us and beating us all those years. How do you do it without them stringing you up?

We didn't know the answer, but we were determined to try it. We wanted to do it as a SNCC project, but there was a very emotional meeting at the SNCC office, and the board said only if we accepted second-class status within the organization. I said that wasn't acceptable. I had been on the staff since 1961. It was my life, my existence. It was my total identity.

So now we were on our own, but we got funding from elsewhere, and the GROW project turned out to be an enormous success. The breakthrough came one day a guy came through who told us he had been to a union hall in Laurel, Mississippi, where they were on strike at Masonite. He said about 20 to 30 percent of the people in the hall were black, and the rest white. We drove up there and told them we wanted to meet the president of their union, and we set up a meeting for the next week. In the meantime, we talked to the head of the AFL-CIO in Mississippi. He told us that there were a lot of Klan people in the union, people who knew who I was.

He said, "There's some real bad Klan guys in there. They're all friends of

Bowers, who killed your guys in '64. Be very careful with a guy named Herbert Ishey. He's one of their executioners, and he's very active in the union."

Well, we went down the next week and met first with their lawyer. He said he knew that we felt that black people and white people needed to get together. He wasn't too thrilled about that, but he said, "The people over in the union hall, they need all the help they can get. I've called 'em up, and they're waiting for you now. Go over and talk to them, and be sure to talk to a guy named Herbert Ishey."

We go over there. This time, a lot of union guys are standing out in front, and they're very quiet. They're very white. They take us down all these halls into a room, and there's about twenty guys sitting around this big oval table. We're introduced to Mr. Jolly, the union president, and I introduced us, and I said, "We all worked for the Southern Conference Educational Fund and we all worked for SNCC, Mr. Jolly. We've all been in jail and we've been charged with everything from trying to overthrow the government to being communists, and we just want you to know who we are and where we're coming from. We have a project called GROW, and we feel that working people, black and white, need to get together and work together."

Well, he introduced us to the people at the table, and the last guy he introduced me to was the guy sitting next to me, a great big beefy guy with a cigar box in front of him. He kept flipping the lid, and there was something very heavy and blue and metallic in there, and he said, "And this is Herbert Ishey."

Ishey raised his fist and he hit the table and he said, "Goddammit, I don't care who you are. We need help from wherever we can get it. You think you're the only ones who have trouble with the FBI? They call us Kluxers. We don't care. Commies or Kluxers, we need to get together."

I ended up staying with Herbert Ishey probably more than anyone else in Laurel. He completely turned around. Two years later, he wound up running for office in Laurel on the same ticket as Susan Ruffin, who was the leader of the civil rights office in Laurel.

We started having working-class rallies. We'd have 1,400 to 2,000 people out in a cow pasture, black and white, old Mississippi rednecks with whip antennas and Wallace stickers on their trucks standing next to black folks talking about the power structure. And they got it. We said, "You don't gain from segregation, you lose from segregation. You have poorer schools, poorer work conditions, health care, housing, all that you lose. When you get together, that's when you win."

During the strike at Masonite, we were trying to keep the pulpwood out of the plant. The train crews wouldn't take the pulpwood as long as there was a picket line there, so we had to keep the picket line up twenty-four hours a day. One morning about 2:30, I went down with coffee and doughnuts down to the picket line, and three great big white burly woodcutters said, "Come here, Bob, we want to talk to you about something," so I walked over where they were, and they said, "We want to talk to you about this communist thing."

"What about it?"

"Come with us."

They started walking down this dirt road, and I know that a guard had been killed down that road about two weeks before, but I knew I had to go, even if I didn't know what, if anything, might happen to me. Anyway, I took a walk with them down there, and they stopped and were smoking cigarettes and chewing tobacco.

So I said, "What about this communist thing?"

I knew it was bugging them a little bit. The papers were full of accusations that we were communists.

They said, "Well, we looked it up."

"What'd you find out?"

"Well, as far as we can tell we are one."

"What was it that it said?"

"That everybody share and share alike and that everybody's equal, and that's what we come to. We've decided that's the only way to do it so, by golly, if that's a communist then I guess we are one."

That's how we just took that anticommunist red baiting away from the company as a tactic against us. We told the men, "No matter if you are a communist or a Klansman, your behavior is what counts. If you're gonna have a strong union, you're gonna have black and white in there. You know you don't want black people crossing the picket lines, but that means you can't have segregated drinking fountains and bathrooms and lockers the way you had before. You can't have segregated seniority lists. You gotta do more than you ever expected to do, but when you do that, then you have strength and they can't beat you." And they didn't.

Following that plan, the project was very successful. We kept it going until about 1980, and then we came North. I got my Ph.D. I lecture. I also do contracting. I've run for office several times out here, and I'm still active.

Bob Zellner, 2003. (Courtesy of Bob Zellner)

There was some estrangement from a few individuals of SNCC over the years. Now, when we get together, the years and months fall aside, and we are SNCC again.

I never had an opportunity to confront my tormentors. I feel a lot more personally insulted about people who should have been supportive and weren't. I often think back on the people at Huntingdon College. This is a Christian institution. These are all people who are supposedly role models for young people, but I never had a single one of 'em take me aside and say, "Maybe I don't agree entirely with what you are doing, but I think you have a right to do it. I know it's a lot of strain, and if you ever need to talk to anybody about it, come talk to me."

I probably resent those people more than the Klansmen and the Governor Wallaces of the world. I do have a kind of abstract bitterness about some of the people who were murderers, and they may well have been my murderer if one of those shots had connected or when they took me out to the woods to hang me. I know that nothing ever would have happened to them.

I don't consider myself a hero. Medgar Evers, Amzie Moore, Fannie Hamer, E. W. Steptoe and Herbert Lee, those people who had fought the lonely battles for so many years. They were heroes.

Amzie wrote a book about SNCC. He wrote about the SNCC kids, saying, "How gladly they took their place at the head of the line. How tall they stood. How fearlessly they stood against the power. Gunmen and wheelmen from way, way back, strong stone killers did not frighten them. How gladly they stood."

We reached a point where we didn't mind dying. We were ready to die, and that gave us a power that was invincible. Crazy brave is a very powerful state. In a philosophical sense, it's difficult to live until you're willing to die. The worst kind of way to live is in fear. You can have reasonable fear. That's OK if you know it's not going to stop you from whatever needs doing. That makes for a powerful person and a powerful way of living.

Gloria Richardson Dandridge The Militant

Cambridge isn't just any place, it's a people making progress.
—1961 road sign welcoming visitors to Cambridge, Maryland

There is an amazing photograph that is reprinted in many histories of the civil rights movement. It shows a middle-aged woman in a white shirt and jeans, glaring at a National Guardsman who has leveled his bayonet directly across her chest. But it's her left hand that tells you everything you need to know. It isn't raised in surrender or fear. It is simply pushing the rifle aside. The anger on the woman's face is palpable; so is the courage. You know who is going to win this fight.

The photo says a lot about Gloria Richardson, who was forty-one years old in 1963 when she led the fight against segregation in Cambridge, Maryland. It was a battle that made headlines across the country, mostly because the black citizens of Cambridge were decidedly *non*-nonviolent. When the whites attacked, they fought back—and scared the daylights out of white America.

Ironically, the photograph was taken in June 1963 at the height of the Kennedy administration's "Camelot" period, supposedly one of the most peaceful and affluent periods in American history.

That was true—unless you read the newspaper.

While the war in Vietnam was rapidly escalating, at home the civil rights movement was exploding throughout the South. In the summer of 1963, photographs and film footage of Sheriff Bull Connor unleashing his dogs and fire hoses on civil rights protesters in Birmingham, Alabama, caused an international fury.

But the protests weren't only in big cities. That summer, Somerville, Tennessee, county officials used fire hoses to end a protest against a segregated drugstore. In Danville, Virginia, police fired on activists who had gathered at a local party.

The summer of '63 was also when Cambridge, Maryland, population 13,000, occupied the front pages with stories that read like Civil War battles. Only a few years before, an ABC News documentary on Cambridge portrayed a town that was "a model city in terms of interracial relations."

What happened? Why was this small town suddenly attracting the attention of the White House? And who was this seemingly intractable woman who had little use for Martin Luther King and who had no trouble telling the President of the United States literally to go to hell?

A *New York Times* profile of her written that summer noted that among white members of the Cambridge community, Mrs. Richardson is "widely characterized . . . by unprintable epithets."

Richardson clearly wasn't cut from the same cloth as other civil rights leaders. First, she was a woman at a time when most women hardly left the kitchen, much less stared down armed soldiers. Second, unlike the leaders of the nonviolent protest movement, she had no problem with blacks defending themselves any way they had to. Richardson was what was called in the '60s a "militant"—a description that often sent shivers down the backs of even liberal whites who were infinitely more comfortable with a Martin Luther King or Ralph Abernathy, who were perceived as nonthreatening. She had no interest in projecting a sympathetic image. What she cared about was winning for her people the rights guaranteed them in the Constitution, and she wasn't going to settle for less.

As I enter her Manhattan apartment building, I can't wait to find out more about Gloria Richardson. But mostly, I want to ask her about that photograph. This woman, who in 1963 was one of the most feared people in America, now looks like a kindly old grandmother. That turns out to be almost accurate. She's a kindly old great-grandmother, but a thoroughly modern one. Her apartment is filled with books. CNN is on the TV, and a computer sits by her door. She tells me that if she had the time, she'd spend nearly all of it on the Web.

Though her hair is gray and thinning, it's not hard to see the person in that photograph. There is one way the picture does not do her justice. Because it's a moment frozen in time, it does not reveal her sunniness, her light laughter, or her eyes that brighten with merriment as she marvels at her own chutzpah in telling an armed National Guardsman where he could stick his bayonet.

Gloria Richardson leading the fight against segregation in Cambridge, Maryland in 1963.
(Courtesy of Blackstar Photos)

Yes, that picture. I had been inside a little shoeshine place talking to General Gelston, the head of the National Guard unit in town when I heard this bang. We thought it was bullets, so we went crashing out of there. When I got out in front to see what was happening, this Guard charged me. I was furious, so I pushed his rifle away and cursed at him. I was thinking, "What on earth do they think they were doing?"

In retrospect, I think, "Was I crazy?"

A few days later, I was called to a meeting at the Justice Department, and they were furious with me. They just wanted us to be quiet, and they would solve all our problems. Well, we weren't going to do that, and they didn't like it one bit.

My family goes back to the early 1800s in Dorchester County, Maryland. Until segregation, there was a lot of intermixing. My grandfather had a Dutch middle name. The judge that fined us a penny for demonstrating in 1963 was related to my grandfather. In fact, they were almost identical.

After segregation, there was only one black police officer in Cambridge. He could only arrest black folks. There was one black city councilman, who would only represent black folks who were confined to the Second Ward.

Blacks had been voting in Cambridge since the 1850s, but Cambridge was totally segregated until World War II, when blacks started making more money. After that, they could go into the stores and buy things. Still, you couldn't sit in most of the restaurants; you had to go into the back door and take stuff home. The Fire Department built a pool with town money. In the winter it was a skating rink, but the black kids weren't allowed to use it.

The city hospital had one maternity room, and if somebody else was in that room a black couldn't go in there, which meant they had no place to go.

I had an uncle who was a Harvard graduate. He died in his twenties, because he got sick and the hospital in town wouldn't take him.

We were aware of the injustice of it, but my parents' attitude was that you should fight against racism, but you should also use your talents to go as far as you could. We didn't necessarily focus on achieving in the white structure. There was a whole society of black culture to succeed in, with our own lawyers and professors and businessmen.

I was a rebellious child. I remember a beating I got from my father when I was four or five. My mother had asked me to go get the mop at the top of the steps. I told her I didn't feel like it. When he came home, I got whipped.

After he started, he asked me, "Will you do that again?"

"Yes."

I said it twice before I gave up. Then I said, "No." And he said, "Oh, yes, you will."

As a teenager I was good, but I remember throwing a book at a teacher. A big boy had taken my books, and the teacher said, "Well, you shouldn't get so upset." So I threw this book at her. She had to chase me all around the school.

I was brought up to slug it out in terms of what I thought or felt with anybody. I think I turned out like a lot of women in Cambridge. They did their cooking and their ironing, but I don't remember any of them walking two steps behind anybody, and I think the men knew that. Later, most of the members of our civil rights group were women. Some of them were old ladies. When we were attacked at demonstrations, they were the ones throwing stones back at the whites.

I graduated Howard University in Washington in '42 and went to work for a couple of years in the federal government. Then my grandmother got sick and said I should come home. But the only thing in Cambridge besides menial work that I could have done was teach, which I hated. I had a degree in sociology, but the Department of Social Services wouldn't hire black social workers. I ended up getting married, and I was a housewife for twelve or thirteen years.

The main employer in town was the Philips Packing Company, which canned tomatoes and corn. They hired blacks for the lowest jobs. The work was pretty much seasonal, which meant during the winter people relied on handouts from the company for food. It was just like being on a plantation. When the Freedom Riders came into town, Cambridge had upwards of a 40 percent unemployment rate for blacks. The average income was $800 or $900 a year for blacks.

The Freedom Riders came in '61. Charles Cornish, our black councilman, was an Uncle Tom. He tried to discourage them by saying that everything in town was desegregated. He had four buses, and most of his livelihood depended on his contract with the Board of Education. When the TV network did a documentary on Cambridge in 1961, Cornish was the one who told them, "Our blacks are happy."

Donna Richardson Oronge (Gloria's daughter, who was fifteen years old at the time of the Cambridge uprising): "We weren't happy. Sometimes we tried to make fun of segregation, but we were definitely angry about it. We couldn't swim at the pool and only in one little section of the beach where you had really bad jellyfish. We had to sit upstairs in the movie theater. We couldn't even go downstairs to buy popcorn. The usher would have to buy it for us. Sometimes we would spit on the people downstairs and throw soda and popcorn. It was our way of getting even."

Gloria Richardson: The protests started with a knock on my door. It was these two fellows from SNCC. They said, "Do you know any young people who could act as guides for tomorrow for a demonstration?"

Donna and her friends were baking cookies. I said, "You can go back and ask them," so they did and they all said yes. SNCC trained them on nonviolent precepts and how to position their bodies. Donna became one of the captains. I didn't want to go on the picket line at first because I didn't think I could follow the nonviolence thing. It turned out I tried to trip somebody that passed by me, and Donna put me off the line. [*Laughs.*]

At the time, Cambridge was the center for Dorchester County. On weekends, everybody came in, black and white, to shop. After the picketing began, those places were empty. White folks wanted to avoid trouble, and the black folks started going to other places to shop, like Salisbury, which had desegregated before the Cambridge movement began. Some of the banks were even threatening to close because they had lost so many deposits from their business customers. That's when the ministers stepped in. By and large, most of the ministers in Cambridge didn't want to do anything with the demonstrations. I had one minister tell me, "What do you want me to do, be like Martin Luther King?" The only reason they opened their churches to us was that their congregants who were involved told them, "We are coming to services, but we're not putting any money into the collection plate unless you let us in here."

By then we had formed a civil rights committee. Our main activities were voter registration and information, and a survey to prioritize our demands. Once that was done, we took our demands to the City Council. We wanted an end to segregation in the schools, and we wanted public accommodations opened to us. We wanted a low-income housing project they opposed, but we also wanted them to pass a housing code. That really infuriated them. But most of the blacks in town were living in what they called "chicken coops." They didn't have hot water, and they had to use outhouses.

We also demanded they put a black person into the state employment office so we'd know what the jobs were. We wanted the post office to hire black mailmen. We wanted them to force storekeepers and banks on the main street, Race Street, to hire blacks.

We didn't think they would agree, but we were not asking for anything that was not supposedly guaranteed you as a citizen. Eventually, we did get what we wanted, but only because we took to the street.

Then came the night in May 1963 when everybody in the community got behind us for good. What happened was my mother and I and Donna went to Dizzyland's because my mother refused to believe that a second-rate cubbyhole of a restaurant like that would refuse to serve her. She said, "You're going to have to prove that to me," so we [went] inside and sat down to order a Coke and a hamburger. The owner said, "We don't want you in here."

We said, "Well, we're gonna sit here."

He called the police. They came and read us the trespass law. We said, "We'll still sit there," so they took us to jail.

That was the first time my mother was ever arrested, and she was indignant. Also, they took the mattresses away in jail, and she didn't like that because she couldn't sleep on the wires of the frame.

Usually, when the kids were jailed, the authorities would tell them to go home, and generally they'd refused to leave, because we wanted to pack the jails, figuring if they had no more room, they couldn't keep arresting people.

This time the kids left. We were so disgusted with them. We didn't know that they went home and got their toothbrushes and changed into jeans. Then they went and laid down in the theaters until the police came.

Donna Richardson Oronge: "They literally dragged us down the street and put us in the police car and locked us up."

Gloria Richardson: The police were brutal. They piled six or seven people on top of each other in one police car. The people who saw that went back to the black community and told them. It was like Paul Revere, with people knocking on the doors of their neighbors. Around twelve o'clock at night in the jail, you could just hear this roar. It got closer and closer, and we realized that nearly the whole community was converging on the jail, either by car or on foot. They were mad, and they started marching around the courthouse, around and around until the police started arresting them. Afterward, the lawn was full of knives and things. The people dropped them there so they wouldn't be arrested with weapons.

About sixty of us stayed in jail until the judge tried all of us together. We were found guilty of disorderly conduct, but he fined us a penny each and suspended the sentence.

It started to get even more nasty after that. We would have a demonstration, and the whites would jeer and throw eggs and rocks at us. Sometimes they threw lit cigarettes. At night, they would throw Molotov cocktails at the houses in the black community. Every night, we had to patrol out there and listen for gunshots. Then, we'd go to the area and make sure everybody was OK. We knew the fire department ambulance wouldn't go in there to get anybody out if they were hurt. I was just lucky I wasn't killed.

At one point, the judge tried to intercede with the whites, so we agreed to halt the demonstrations while he tried to negotiate. His position was that some of our demands were not unreasonable. But the whites wouldn't budge. Then one night Dinez White, who was fifteen years old, was arrested for praying in front of a bowling alley. She was tried and convicted of juvenile delinquency, and they ended up sending her away for a year to a juvenile detention center. Robert Kennedy finally got her out.

People were so mad that she was arrested that they went back into the streets. From then on, we were constantly rallying. When the police realized they couldn't control us, the state police brought in their K-9 dogs. They'd let the dog snarl at you during a demonstration, and then they'd bring the dogs around the houses of black people to search for guns.

Most of the men who were protecting the community were World War II and Korean vets, so they were prepared to do anything they needed to do. Other people told us, "We aren't nonviolent, and if they don't want to give it up this way, we'll see that they give it up our way."

They were very tough.

Around that time, Malcolm X said if the state government and the federal government and the city government do not protect you in your home, then you go into your house and protect it yourself. The press asked me what I thought about it, and I said I agreed. I wasn't committed to nonviolence. It was just a good model, but it didn't upset me if sometimes that model broke. I thought violence was the only thing they listened to.

Birmingham was happening at the same time. We sent packages of red pepper down to Martin and Andrew Young to keep the dogs away from them, but they wouldn't use them, because that wasn't "nonviolent."

We used it, so when the dogs came up to us, they would stop in their tracks and start whining. The white people didn't know that we had put the red pepper around our pants cuffs. The whites were more scared of us when we would get down to pray than when we would just be walking along because they thought we had some kind of extra supernatural power. They didn't know about the pepper.

On June 12, there was a riot on Race Street, which was the dividing line in town between the white and black sections. Two whites were shot. That's when the National Guard came in. They had men stationed on the corners; jeeps were patrolling. They even brought in tanks.

White folks were furious because they thought the Guard were there to protect us, so at first they spit on them and threw stones, just like they did to the press. Many of the blacks welcomed them. The black ladies would even go out and give them lemonade while they were standing out there in the hot sun.

General Gelston turned out to be pretty fair. When he found out they were beating people in jail unnecessarily, he put his guards over there. The white folks hated that, and they actually tried to get him decommissioned. He later claimed that anybody who stayed in Cambridge for a short time would become an integrationist because of the way the blacks were treated.

Still, we had to disobey him. We weren't supposed to demonstrate while we were under martial law, but we did. As the protests continued, Cambridge, being so close to Washington, became an embarrassment to the Kennedys.

Gloria Richardson greeting Malcolm X in 1964. Between them is comedian Dick Gregory. (Courtesy of Gloria Richardson Dandridge)

Things like this happened in Alabama; they weren't supposed to happen so close to the Mason-Dixon Line.

There was a fellow from Cambridge named Maceo Hubbard, who worked in the Civil Service Division of the Justice Department. The Kennedys sent him to talk to my mother. Then he called me at my uncle's house to say the Kennedys were disappointed because we didn't stop our demonstrating. That's when I told him he could tell Robert Kennedy and the President to go to hell, that I was not afraid of them. Hubbard also offered me a job with the government, but I knew it was a bribe, and I turned it down.

Then Gelston told me that Robert Kennedy wanted me to meet him in Washington. When I got to his office, there was this man at the door wearing khakis and with his shirtsleeves rolled up. I thought it was the janitor. I just said hello to the man and sat down. Then, when I saw him go behind the desk, I realized it was him.

He told me I was being too recalcitrant and that I would have to learn to negotiate. My point was, "Fine. If you want to settle it, get an agreement on paper."

Before we left Cambridge, we had heard this story about people who went to the White House for tea and cookies and then gave away everything, so when he took us into the other room to talk, we made sure we refused everything they offered. We wouldn't even take their lemonade.

I told him about the survey that had been done of Cambridge by students at Swarthmore, that the survey showed that the extent of poverty in Cambridge was enormous. I said if he didn't understand what we were trying to do from a civil rights point of view, he should understand it on the basis of the poverty. He said I should send the survey to him, which I did. I think it changed his attitude.

He pressured me to accept a plan that the mayor [of] Cambridge had come up with to have a referendum in town on desegregating public accommodations. Their idea was the people of the town would vote on whether or not to end segregation. I was denounced for this everywhere, but I refused. In the first place we had veterans who had been overseas to fight for democracy. They didn't know why there had to be a vote about whether they could go into a restaurant. Why would we agree to submit to have our civil rights granted by vote when they were ours already, according to the Constitution?

We went back, and the demonstrations continued, and the tension just got worse. Two cars full of white men came through the neighborhood, shooting. The first time they drove through, nobody was sure what was happening. After a while, the blacks realized, "There's somebody out there shooting at us."

Even people who thought we were crazy for being in the movement began taking out their guns. When the whites turned up the street again, I ran outside and hid behind a telephone pole, thinking that that was going to save me. It was a whole long street with little houses, and from where I was standing, I could hear, click, click, click, click, all along the block. The blacks were ready. When the whites started shooting again, from every window on the block, people shot back. They shot the cars right out from under them. Guns were going off all over. It was like a war.

When we woke up the next morning, you could smell the cordite, and the neighborhood was still filled with smoke. A couple of the whites reported that they were hit by gunfire. It turned out that the whites in the car shooting at us were Guardsmen and they got court-martialed.

I got called back to Washington. This time I had to have a police escort because the Klan was threatening to kill us. We were there for three days. I wanted to make sure any agreement included a promise to desegregate the schools. Robert Kennedy wanted me to accept the referendum. He told me I had to be a statesman like Martin Luther King. I said, "I'm a woman. I can't be a statesman."

So I stayed in the anteroom and watched the TV in there while the secretaries typed and retyped drafts until I got what I wanted. In the end, I signed the agreement even though it provided for a referendum, because I got the other points I wanted, and I decided I wouldn't support the referendum anyhow. None of the whites from Cambridge were there during the negotiations. On the morning we came to an agreement with the Kennedys, the mayor was just ordered to come up and sign. The mayor just thought we were awful, but Robert Kennedy told him that if he didn't sign they would not get any funds from the Party in the next election. No one else had ever gotten such an agreement from the whites who governed a town.

When we went home, there was a lot of pressure on me to support the referendum, which was scheduled for that fall, but I wouldn't do it. The ministers came, and I would sit there and tell them, "I have already stated I never said I would support the referendum."

The referendum only covered places like restaurants anyway, and on our survey of what the people wanted, that was at the bottom. Other things, like the low-income housing, which was promised in the agreement, were much more important.

That was the summer of King's "I Have a Dream" speech in Washington, D.C. At first, I was excluded from speaking because SCLC and the NAACP decided that because of the violence in Cambridge I was an embarrassment to the movement. Then they decided they couldn't avoid having me up there, so they called me and they asked me. Then they said, "Please don't wear jeans."

I always wore jeans, because you never knew when you were going to be arrested or what was going to happen in the street, and in jeans you could run if you had to. I had to run around the Eastern Shore looking for a jeans skirt. They were hard to find in those days.

I was going to tell people to sit here until the civil rights law was passed, but all I got to say was "Hello," before someone from the NAACP took the mike away. Then, just before Martin spoke, the marshals took me and Lena Horne off the platform, saying it was too big a crowd. They took us home in a taxi. I didn't really care. I heard his speech in a taxi going home. He was always a great speaker, but I didn't trust him.

I'll tell you why. When SNCC first came in, there were a whole lot of community meetings, and they suggested that King come in to speak to us to kick off the organizing effort. He wrote back, saying he was really busy, that it would cost $3,000, and that we should contact him in a couple of years.

In a way that was good, because it meant that we had to do it ourselves. But in '63 when everything heated up, he announced he was coming to Cambridge to see what was going on. When we heard that, we held a press conference to say we would meet him halfway across the bridge and turn him right around. What was he going to do, now that we had done everything ourselves? He was going to come in and play big shot? We wanted no part of that. I think a couple of days later, he announced he had the flu or something and couldn't come.

Then I really didn't like him after September. The vote was coming up, and they went through all these little hooks to get me to meet with Martin. There was a Frank Sinatra and Lena Horne concert in New York. I was invited, but it turned out that the only reason they asked me was so I would be seated in a booth with Martin and he could give me a lecture on how they were drumming for the vote in the South, and here I was going to boycott a vote. I said, "I'm not going to agree with you, and if I had known this is what the setup was I wouldn't have come."

Then I told him it wasn't his affair, and I just got up and left.

The referendum did lose, and I was blamed. Yes, we boycotted, and yes we lost, but when the civil rights bill passed, it became irrelevant anyway. Once the restaurants opened up, the people tested them to make sure they were open to them, and then they didn't go anymore.

I left Cambridge and came up to New York in '65 because I got married. I had a hard time finding work because the regular civil rights people would not hire me. I think the government told them to stay away from me. I finally got a job with one of the antipoverty programs in Harlem. I did it for about six years until the program was closed down.

Now I work for the Department of Aging. I manage contracts for senior centers. We contract out to nonprofit groups to run senior centers. They give a variety of services. I'll think about retiring in a few years. Initially, I didn't have enough pension time, but I do now.

When I'd go back to Cambridge in the '60s, I was followed by the police. Now I go back about once a year to visit friends, and I still have a cousin there.

Gloria Richardson today. (Courtesy of Gloria Richardson Dandridge)

I think the whites still remember me. For the longest time when I'd go back, I wouldn't go downtown. I do it now if I'm with somebody. It's more integrated now. Some blacks live in the white area, but not many. We've had a black president of City Council. The last one was a woman who came out of the movement.

I know I was one of the few women to lead a movement like that, but I don't think of it in terms of being a woman. I think of it in terms of being a person. And what we did wasn't liberal or conservative, it was just right. But I know they think a woman shouldn't be doing what I did. They also didn't like it because we were demanding and not asking. That wasn't ladylike.

If there is any lesson to come out of Cambridge, it's that community organizing can work. Great speeches may motivate you, but if you're gonna mount a campaign that works in the long haul, you need community organizers, and you need to have people who understand how to do that kind of work.

I think also Cambridge showed you could achieve anything you want if you are determined. There was a moment when the Guard put on their bayonets to intimidate the people, but the people went right up against them. Instead, the Guard got scared. We weren't going to take it anymore, and they knew there were a lot of people who felt that way.

Paul Krassner
The Realist

J. Edgar Hoover thought Paul Krassner was such a danger to America that he tried to arrange a hit on him. Yet the only weapon that Krassner ever wielded was his manual typewriter. As editor of The Realist, one of the most influential underground newspapers; as a contributor to such mischievous magazines as Mad magazine, and as a popular humorist whose main targets were hypocrisy and government heavy-handedness, Krassner has made questioning authority his life's work. He fearlessly challenged government policy at a time when McCarthyism still had a grip on the country. He openly discussed sexuality at a time when the TV networks refused to show Elvis Presley's swiveling hips on the air; and, with his friend Lenny Bruce, he challenged Americans to take their First Amendment freedoms more seriously. And that was only what he did in the 1950s. In the 1960s, he really got going.

For his trouble, Krassner was wiretapped, followed, beaten, and even targeted for death by an FBI sting operation. Hoover evidently didn't have much of a sense of humor. He certainly wasn't amused when Krassner sent him one of The Realist's classic "Fuck Communism" posters.

"I couldn't imagine he'd disagree with the sentiment," Krassner suggested innocently in the living room of his Venice, California, home.

It's hard to imagine that the person sitting opposite me in a T-shirt, jeans, and running shoes, his face framed by black curly hair, is nearly seventy years old. Adding to the incongruity is the mischievous grin that seems to perpetually light Krassner's face. But then you notice the bad limp and the twisted way he must sit, the result of a beating he received at the hands of San Francisco police in 1979, and you realize that he has paid a severe price for his irreverence.

To prepare for the interview, I read and reread his autobiography, *Confessions of a Raving, Unconfined Nut*. Never was research so much fun. The book makes it clear that Krassner didn't come by his rebellion by reading the newspaper or a dog-eared copy of Karl Marx. It's simply his nature. I wanted to hear about how that rebellious energy became his life's work, and how it tapped into the particular energy of the 1960s, leaving behind a powerful legacy that is still felt today.

Like many journalists, Paul is a patient and generous interview subject who knows how to tell a story. He is also a warm host, and his rollicking stories make the day pass quickly, with only brief breaks for Paul to indulge a toke or two. British critic Malcolm Muggeridge once wrote, "By its nature humor is anarchistic, and it may well be that those who seek to suppress or limit laughter are more dangerous than all the subversive conspiracies which the FBI ever has or ever will uncover. Laughter, in fact, is the most effective of all subversive conspiracies, and it operates on our side."

If that's the case, you're about to hear from Public Enemy Number One.

Getting circumcised as an infant had a huge impact on my life. The person who performs the circumcision is called a *moyel*. That's Hebrew for kosher butcher or surgeon without a license. He left a kind of flap on my foreskin, and it was uncomfortable.

I would constantly have my hands in my pockets trying to separate the flap from my scrotum. My parents decided I was playing with myself, and they got me all kinds of toys. One of them was a violin, and I was OK at it. In fact, I was a child prodigy. I ended up playing in Carnegie Hall at the age of six—the youngest person ever to play there—all because of this extra flap of foreskin.

But the violin didn't give me pleasure. Making people laugh gave me pleasure. I learned that while I was performing a Vivaldi concerto at Carnegie Hall. While I was playing, my leg started to itch, and I scratched it with my other leg, and the audience laughed. I liked that. Ever since then, I've always been curious about what makes people break through their conditioning. It might be called rebellion, but to me it's really recapturing who you are.

I always thought for myself. My parents thought it was strange that they had to come to school almost every term. When I was seven years old, a kid got in trouble for exposing himself to the class and got sent to reform school.

I thought the punishment didn't quite fit the crime. Why don't they talk to this kid and see what made him do that?

So I got in front of my class and unzipped my fly to reveal a drawing of a penis that I had done. The class laughed. The teacher didn't know what to do with me, because I wasn't exposing myself, I was exposing a picture of myself.

I did that intuitively. When I think back on it, I think what an outrageous thing for a kid to do, and that kid was me. It seems like there was a kind of a personal destiny in progress.

Here's another example. The movie *Intermezzo* was the first film I saw. The theme song in that was a violin song, "Intermezzo." I fell in love with it, and I went back to my teacher and said, "I want to learn how to play the song." He wanted me to play Vivaldi and Mendelssohn. "That's not right for you."

I was shocked. I realized, without having the vocabulary to express it—and this was true of so many grown-ups and people in authority—that they wanted to mold you in their image. To me, it was like a declaration of cultural war. When he died I bought the sheet music, taught it to myself, played it for my parents, and then chucked my violin career.

I grew up in Astoria, Queens.

Early on, my brother and I used to tell irreverent jokes at the table. I remember one. "If your mother and father had a fight, who would you stick up for?" The answer was, "My father, because he stuck it up for me." I got slapped for that. That was also a lesson. What we thought was funny, others didn't.

I was the All-American boy in those days. I'd get on my bicycle Sunday mornings in my baseball uniform and with my dog, Skippy, in the basket, deliver papers, hoping to be an FBI agent when I grew up. I've never lost that idealism, but the innocence was lost a long time ago.

I was such a patriot, but one of the first disillusioning events in my life happened in grade school. I had to do a report on a political candidate. I picked Vito Marcantonio, who at that time was running for mayor. The only thing I knew about him was that my hero, Frank Sinatra, was supporting him, but my teacher said he was a Communist, and she called my parents.

I went through with my bar mitzvah to please my parents, but even then I couldn't accept the concept of God. We'd go to Coney Island, and I'd see so many people there, and I'd say to myself, "How can this God thing answer all the prayers of all the different people?"

During my freshman year at City College in New York, I was doing a paper in a Philosophy 101 class. I wanted to do a dialogue between Plato and an atheist. I looked in the phone book and there under "Atheism" was the American Association for the Advancement of Atheism. The group put out a magazine called *The Truth Seeker*. There was a notice in the magazine, advertising something called the Rationalist Forum, which had an "ism" night where people could come up and talk about any "ism." It could be humanism, communism, socialism—anyone could speak.

While I was there, someone mentioned *The Independent*, which was published by Lyle Stuart. Lyle had been a reporter, and he started the paper on a shoestring. *The Independent* advocated a rational way to deal with the world instead of superstition and supernaturalism. It was anticensorship, essentially. It ran stories on the falsity of the Bible and on population control. There were articles about cigarettes and cancer and alternative treatments for cancer. It also condemned Bell's telephone monopoly. This was in the early '50s when nobody else was talking about this stuff. He did a critical series on Walter Winchell, who was probably the most powerful columnist in America, and got beaten up by a couple of Winchell's goons. He exposed the Anti-Defamation League for printing anti-Semitic literature so they could then raise funds from their Jewish contributors. People connected to the ADL poured tar on his printing presses. Then, when he started publishing stuff about Nazis, his wife had a miscarriage because they received so many threats.

I went to Lyle's office to subscribe and I asked him if he needed any help and gave him my number. He called me up, and I started stuffing envelopes for him. I ended up becoming his apprentice and then the managing editor of the paper. *The Independent* was a combination of *Mad* magazine and the First Amendment, entertainment without compromise. I was totally in sync with what they were doing. All through college I had been in a daze, because I didn't know what I wanted to do with my life. Now I knew. I thought I would rather work there than the *New York Times*.

I wrote a humor column for the paper called "Freedom of Wit." It was about sick humor. I also wrote an article about the Army Loyalty Program. The attorney general had a list of some 600 organizations which were considered subversive. One of them was Nature Friends of America. If you were drafted, you had to swear that you were not a member of any of those groups. I felt I had the right to join a subversive organization. I was about to be drafted, so I decided to challenge it in court.

The idea was I would join a young socialist group, not because I was a socialist, but because I had a right to. But before I got to court, I got so nervous that I started picking at my face. It got so bad that I was classified 4F and got rejected, and that was the end of the suit because at that point I was not longer at risk to be drafted.

But then I got called again around 1958. By then, the Supreme Court had declared the Army Loyalty Program unconstitutional. The first time I was called, I was in effect trying to get into the army, but this time I wanted to get out, so I deliberately mutilated my face by poking my skin with a needle. They didn't want anybody that nuts in the army, so I got out of it.

I didn't want to go not because there was a war on. There wasn't one. I didn't want to give up my freedom, and if there was a war, I didn't want to kill anybody and I didn't want to be killed. Besides, I was working for an anticensorship paper at the time. I felt that I was already serving my country.

This is what crystallized the absurdity of the army for me: it was required that in your inspection kit, along with a razor and other things, you had to have a pack of cigarettes. Required! They must have had some kind of deal. The ultimate product placement. This was the perfect example of unnecessary authority.

We had a tiny little office on 42nd Street opposite Bryant Park. Bill Gaines, the publisher of Mad, was a subscriber and a friend of Lyle's. He was a lovable, playful man. The first time I went to his office, he was chasing his secretary around the office with a "Fragile" stamp that he wanted to put on her forehead. He later married her, so I guess this was part of their courtship ritual.

I was still living with my parents at the time, and Bill gave me the keys to his office, because I had no place to take a girl. I lost my virginity in the office of Mad, with Alfred E. Neuman smiling down on us.

The Realist came about in 1958 when Lyle bought an atheist publication called Progressive World. It had a mailing list of 6,000 and was run by an old couple. Lyle wanted some fresh blood managing it, and that was me.

I said, "Why me?"

"You're the only one who's neurotic enough to do it."

I got a bigger office and Lyle's lawyer on retainer for $15 a month. The paper had a columnist named Fred Worthheim, who was known as the Village Atheist in Albany, Georgia. We were corresponding about the magazine. I wanted to give it a new name, and he was the one who came up with The Realist.

We started out with a circulation of 600. Then we got to 1,000. I thought, a thousand, if I can only get to 3,000. Then we got to 3,000. At its peak in 1967, the circulation was like 100,000, and it had a lot of pass-on readership, so maybe it reached a million people.

From the very first issue, we started having fun. We pulled a wonderful hoax to satirize the oversensitivity of the TV networks to criticism. To give you an example of how scared they were, on one TV show there was a scene of a mixed-race couple. Some viewer called to complain, and the network actually flew an executive down to the guy's house to talk to him.

So to expose how afraid they were to have anything controversial or offensive on the air, we picked out one show on NBC called Masquerade Party. It was so innocuous and so unlikely to have anything offensive at all that it was perfect for the hoax. I asked readers to write in and complain about something on the program and how offended they were by it, but they were told not to mention anything specific.

They wrote to the sponsors, too, threatening to boycott them because of what they saw on the show. The networks figure that each letter they receive represents 10,000 letters that weren't sent, so you can imagine how anxious they were. I found out they watched films of the show, trying to figure out what it was that was so offensive. They even called people up to find out what offended them, and the people said, "You want me to say on the phone what offended me? I can't say that." In the end, NBC sent letters of apology even though they had no idea what they were apologizing for.

I started infiltrating my own paper with satirical articles, and I made sure to violate all the taboos I could think of, not just religious, but also political and sexual. I published an interview with Albert Ellis. He talked about the semantics of profanity. Ellis had this whole campaign that said since fucking is good if you get pissed off at somebody you should say "Unfuck you."

The printer got nervous about that. In those days, publications put dashes or asterisks for profanity. I thought, how could an anticensorship publication censor somebody? The printer wanted a note from my lawyer, so my lawyer on his $15 retainer wrote a note saying in view of the Supreme Court's definition of obscenity, it was legal.

One of the people I interviewed for the magazine was Lenny Bruce, who had a huge impact on my life. Lenny was a comedian who broke through the traditional material that comedians did. They would be doing jokes about their mothers-in-law, lady drivers, their wives' cooking, or airplane food. He started talking about Lyndon Johnson and the atomic bomb, about Kennedy's sexuality—the kinds of things that people actually talked about in their living rooms.

He got arrested many times for talking about that stuff on stage. He wasn't looking to get into trouble; he just wanted the freedom to talk on stage to people who paid to see him voluntarily with the same freedom he had at home. Nearly every comic today has that freedom, but few of them realize that it had to be earned, and he was the one who did it.

In Chicago, he said if we had lost World War II they would have strung Truman up by the balls just the way we had our Nuremberg Court. The police arrested him for saying that. On the police report, one of the charges was that he said, "Harry Truman strung up by the balls."

In Milwaukee, the cops came into the dressing room because he had said "son of a bitch." In Boston, I think he said Cardinal Cushing looked like Shirley Temple, and the cops came into his dressing room and said, "We don't want to hear you making fun of the Cardinal."

He was arrested so many times that after a while the police almost felt obligated to arrest him. As Lenny said, "If I get arrested in Town A, then Town B says, 'Oh, we can arrest him, too.' Then Town C says, 'If we don't arrest him, what kind of town are we?' "

He understood he was the pawn in their game, that they were just advancing their careers. I learned from a woman who dated Richard Kuh, the guy who prosecuted him in New York, that Kuh liked to play Lenny's albums. That's the level of hypocrisy that existed.

He was sentenced to four years in the workhouse in New York. He kept appealing it and appealing it. Finally, four years after he died, the Supreme Court ruled that his arrest was unconstitutional.

Lenny was a tragic figure in the sense of the loss of a personal friend but also in the sense of a person who had so much more to contribute and was denied that. I was there at his house, which had an iron gate inside a barbed wire fence, when the cops came in one night. He was shaving to go out, and they started talking to him.

He said to them, "You are on my property. Do you have a search warrant?" The cop took out a gun and said, "Here is my search warrant."

They weren't looking for anything. They were just hassling him. It was having an effect. He couldn't get work. He didn't have much money. He had heard that his house was being put in escrow. He was using drugs, and he overdosed and died, but someone said he was killed by an overdose of cops.

I got into trouble on a number of things I published, and there were all kinds of threats to take away my second-class mailing privileges and charge me with obscenity. With each one, I'd ask myself, "Am I willing to go to prison for this?"

Not that I wanted to. I didn't want to be a martyr, but I had faith I could fight it and win in court if necessary.

I thought I would go to jail when I wouldn't cooperate with the grand jury over the abortion issue. That was a big one. People don't realize what the times were like then. In the hospitals, they would only give you an abortion if an abortion had been botched by someone else, but the cops would be there in the hospital room telling the patient that she would not be allowed to get a painkiller until she revealed the name of the person who gave her the original abortion. It was incredible.

After I published stuff about abortion, I heard about a Dr. Spencer in Ashland, Pennsylvania. He was a humane physician who did abortions. People from all over the country went to see him. He was known as "The Saint."

The town not only tolerated him, it depended on him. From the dress shops to the motel to the restaurants to the bus company, he brought a lot of business to the community. Even the FBI and the church helped. FBI agents needed to arrange for abortions. So did local priests who had knocked up their housekeepers. He kept talking about the "hypocrisy, hypocrisy, hypocrisy," because he was at the center of the hypocrisy.

His office was plastered with all these pictures of people whose babies he had delivered, but these were people who had their babies when they wanted to. He said he performed abortions as a service, sometimes charging as little as $5. To give you another example of his character, in this little coal town that he lived in, African Americans were not allowed to stay in the motel, so he built an overnight room for them at his clinic. He went down in the coal mines to treat people there. He was a heroic figure and truly humble.

After I published the interview, I began to get calls from scared female voices who wanted abortions. It was preposterous that they would come to me, the editor of a satirical magazine, but they did. I had nurses come to me because they couldn't get help in their own hospitals. I heard from people of all ages from all walks of life who wanted to find him, and he gave me permission to refer them to him.

It was amazing how many people needed help. For a while, I thought my phone was being tapped. I spoke to an operator, and she asked me why I thought so. I explained it to her, and she said, "Oh, I can use a doctor like that." So I helped her.

I was threatened with arrest, and I got called before two district attorneys. My attorney countersued, saying they were denying my First Amendment rights. It wasn't a crime to give someone a doctor's phone number. The lawsuit was in process when we agreed that since the women's groups were fighting it we should turn it over to them, and it was continued by them. Because of that suit, the abortion laws in New York State were declared unconstitutional in 1970.

I got into trouble for other things. Several times I had trouble finding printers for things I wanted to publish. When I got married in 1963, John Francis Putnam, the art director of *Mad*, gave us a housewarming gift, a beautiful red, white, and blue poster that said, "Fuck Communism."

It played the Cold War mentality of "Fuck Communism" flush against their conservatism about language. I wanted to have it printed in *The Realist*, but the printer refused to do it. Finally I decided it would make a better poster, because I didn't have color in *The Realist*. I had to try a few places before I could get it done, but I finally found a place that would do it, and I sold them by mail order.

Postal officials threatened to charge me with sending obscene mail. I also had trouble with the "Disneyland Memorial Orgy" poster, which showed Minnie Mouse and Goofy having intercourse on a huge combination bed and cash register. The Prince was trying on Cinderella's glass slipper as he was peeking up her skirt. Tinkerbell was doing a striptease, and you could see Pinnochio's nose getting longer and harder.

A Maryland distributor took out the [Disney] centerfold, and Disney talked about suing me, but in the end they decided they didn't want to call attention to it.

The Disneyland was the centerfold in the same issue that had "the parts left out of the Kennedy book," which raised a huge fuss and was my biggest-selling issue. That came about because there had been an approved biography of John F. Kennedy by William Manchester. It was about the assassination mostly and was called *Death of a President*.

Then, in 1967, the publisher announced there was going to be a delay on the book because there were certain parts that Jackie Kennedy and Bobby Kennedy didn't want in. There were front-page stories about it. Everybody was speculating, "What can it be?"

Paul Krassner speaks at a New Year's celebration organized by the San Francisco Diggers in 1967. (Courtesy of Lisa Law)

I decided to write it myself and publish in *The Realist* "the parts left out of the Kennedy book."

I was careful to write in Manchester's style, so it would be completely credible. The heart of it was Jackie describing what she saw on Air Force One as she was accompanying her husband's body back from Dallas to Bethesda, Maryland. She described how she saw Johnson leaning over the casket; how she saw Johnson having intercourse with the corpse of Kennedy in the throat wound. The purpose of it was to enlarge the entry wound from the grassy knoll to make it appear as if it were the exit wound from the Texas Book Depository. The idea was he was doing this to cover up the fact that more than one gunman shot Kennedy.

One of my points was people would not have believed it at all if they didn't think that Johnson was actually capable of doing something like this, and I guess they did think he was capable of it, because a lot of people believed they were actually reading Manchester's words. It in effect forced them to believe that the leader of the Western world was a raving, unconfined nut, which is what the FBI called me.

The imagery was so powerful that more than thirty years later I still hear from people who believe it happened. Recently, a twenty-five-year-old woman told me this story about what Johnson supposedly did, not knowing that I had written it, and she believed it to be literally true. I guess with the stuff that happens nowadays, it's not so far-fetched.

Of course I had trouble getting it printed. My own printer, whom I had been with for ten years, wouldn't print it. He said he talked to his wife about it. She was a constitutional lawyer, and she said she consulted with her professors, and they said the First Amendment wouldn't apply to this. Even the Communist Party printer wouldn't touch it. For two months, I searched until I found someone in Brooklyn who simply said, "Why not?"

These days, you can print anything you want with a computer and a copy machine, but it's still a fight. I wrote a book called *Pot Stories for the Soul*. It was a Book of the Month Club selection. The first printer wouldn't do it. They went to Korea to find a printer. No one there would do it because it was about marijuana. Another printer wouldn't do it, not because of the marijuana, but because it had profanity in it.

When the "Manchester" piece was printed, there was a lot of outrage. The FBI sent a poison pen letter to *Life* magazine. They didn't do it on their stationery. The letter was from someone they named Howard Rasmussen, from the Brooklyn College School of General Studies. He said, "To call Krassner a social rebel is far too cute. He is a raving, unconfined nut." The letter was in my FBI file. That's what I called my autobiography: *Confessions of a Raving, Unconfined Nut.*

But the FBI also did something that was much more dangerous. They were trying to create tension between blacks and Jews, and they distributed a poster in the black community, which was in the form of a swastika, and there were photos in each square of the swastika of Jerry Rubin, Abbie Hoffman, Mark Rudd, and myself, and the headline was "Lampshades, Lampshades, Lampshades. They have always been oppressing the black community. These Jewish leaders should be eliminated."

In 1963 or '64, when LSD was still legal, I assigned a writer named Robert Anton Wilson to go to Millbrook in upstate New York where Timothy Leary was doing LSD research. LSD was invented by a Swiss chemist, and the CIA used it in the 1950s as a truth serum. They also experimented with it to see if they could use it to program people, but it backfired when kids started using it to deprogram themselves from the culture. Wilson wrote a front-page article on this new drug called "Timothy Leary and his Psychological H-Bomb."

Leary and I talked about his slogan, "Turn on, tune in, drop out." He said it was misunderstood. You don't want the lawyer who is defending you to drop out or your doctor to drop out. He meant it more on a psychic level, that you drop out of the value system that is so inhumane.

He said, "The changes in the culture start with yourself." I learned to agree with that. Wanting to save the world is formidable. Start with yourself and if others are doing it too, it's like heat molecules linking up to each other. It happened on a mass level in the 1960s.

When people started dropping out in the '60s, they set up what became the counterculture. To get by, they did crafts. They made candles. They shared cars instead of getting insurance. There's a thought that there was a conspiracy against the counterculture because the counterculture had economic implications. If everyone dropped out, the government and a lot of powerful businesses would have suffered. That's what the government's campaign against John Lennon was all about. Richard Nixon was afraid he would lead millions of kids into the counterculture. When I was at Woodstock, people in the Criminal Intelligence Division of the Army were there posing as photographers because they saw that these half a million kids weren't likely to be very good fighters in Vietnam. It was a huge threat to them.

That time in the mid-'60s when the counterculture was blooming was all very dreamlike. It was a wonderful time of experimentation and trial and error, and living an alternative. It was really an epidemic of idealism.

As the war escalated and as the civil rights struggle heated up, there was a kind of organic coalition of stoned hippies and political activists. They became the core of the Yippies—a name that I came up with.

I met Abbie Hoffman in '66 or '67. We would see each other at a lot of meetings. He was a reader of The Realist, so we knew of each other. His big legacy was that he proved that not only could you fight city hall but that you could fight it creatively. As Fidel Castro said, "We shall not die of fear, we shall die laughing." That was his style. He played the media. He knew what the media wanted, which was we were the bad boys, but if we gave good quotes, they would give us good publicity.

Abbie's idea was that the hippies could be a force that could be harnessed and could be educated into being more political. We went on a vacation together and we discussed that there had to be some demonstrations at the Chicago Democratic convention in 1968, but the idea was they had to be different. On the afternoon of December 31, 1967, a bunch of us were at Abbie and Anita's apartment. We were smoking marijuana and discussing some ideas for the Chicago convention. Our fantasy was to counter the convention of death with a festival of life. While the Democrats would present politicians giving speeches in the convention center, we would present rock bands playing in the park. There would be booths where young people could get information about drugs or alternatives to the draft.

Then we decided we needed a name, so that reporters could have a "who" for their journalistic who-what-when-where-why lead paragraphs. I felt a brainstorm coming on. I went into the bedroom and climbed up a ladder into the loft bed so I could concentrate.

What would be an appropriate word to signify the politicization of hippies? I started going through the alphabet: bippie . . . cippie . . . dippie . . . Finally, just as I was about to give up on that idea, along came "yippie"—it was perfect—a shout of joy!

Working backwards, Yippies could be derived from the initials Y.I.P. For which words could they form an acronym? Youth—this was essentially a movement of young people involved in a generational struggle. International—it was happening all over the world, from Mexico to France, from Germany to Japan. And Party—in both senses of the word. We would be a party and we would have a party.

There is a Trivial Pursuit game which has the question, "Who first suggested putting LSD into the water supply in Chicago in 1968?" and I'm the answer.

Before the convention, we had a meeting with one of the mayor's assistants to try and get a permit for the festival. I had this classic discussion with the mayor's assistant, a guy named Stahl. He said, "C'mon, what are you guys really gonna do?"

I said, "Did you see Wild in the Streets?"

That was a movie about teenagers putting LSD into the water supply and taking over the government. Mayor Daley ended up having National Guardsmen stationed around the reservoirs.

The city of Chicago decided there would be a hippie invasion of their city to spoil their party. Only a few months before King was killed, Daley had given the order to shoot to maim demonstrators, so I was afraid of what might happen at the convention. I wanted to warn people about the potential for violence, so I published an article by Abbie in which he said, "We've all been to police demonstrations before. We know there is police violence."

I was still under the impression, a false one, as it turned out, that the park where the demonstrators would gather to hear music and be together was going to be a kind of sanctuary, that the people who wanted to march could march and the people who wanted to confront could confront. We didn't know the police would come to the park, where we were just sitting, with tear gas and billy clubs.

Abbie, Anita, and I got there a few weeks early to get things ready. Then, one day I flew to the University of Kansas to speak. When I got back, I met up with Art Goldberg of *Ramparts* magazine. He was going to drive me back to the apartment where Abbie, Anita, and I were staying when a cop stopped us for long hair—no other reason. He searched the trunk, and then he saw Art's driver's license, which said Goldberg, and said something to the effect that "they should have put all of you in the ovens."

Those were the Chicago cops, but that delay could have saved my life, because the landlord of the building had been waiting on the porch with a gun, waiting to kill either Abbie or me. Finally, the cops got him, but if the anti-Semitic cop hadn't stopped us I might have gotten there just in time to be shot.

Right after we got to Chicago, we were getting into the car one afternoon, and we saw these two guys get into a car and follow us. It was clear they were cops. We approached them and they said they were local plainclothes cops and we were under surveillance twenty-four hours a day.

We talked back and forth for a while and gave them Yippie buttons so that if we lost them in a crowd, we could find them again. Then they asked us if we had eaten yet, because they had been following us all day and were getting hungry.

We said we were new in Chicago and didn't know of any good restaurants. Could they recommend any?

"Well, the Pickle Barrel in North Wellston has pretty good food," and the other cop said, "Yeah, and their prices are quite reasonable."

"What's the best way to get there?"

One of them said, "Follow us."

So we followed them, and we got to the restaurant and ate—at separate tables.

I had told Abbie how Lenny Bruce once used paper towels to spell the word "fuck" on his forehead. He said he did it because if they were going to photograph him getting arrested, that's what people would see in the picture. So Abbie had someone print "fuck" on his forehead in lipstick. Then he put his hat on to cover it.

That morning, the plainclothes cops who were following us were across the street, and Abbie went up to their car and said, "Top of the morning to you," and tipped his hat.

Then we went to have breakfast, and these guys must have tipped off the cops who arrested him, because we were sitting there eating breakfast and the cop came and said, "Take off your hat."

They wanted to arrest him, but Abbie said, "It's the duty of a revolutionist to finish breakfast."

When he was done, they took him off to jail, where he was beaten up pretty badly.

On Wednesday, the police rioted in Grant Park. They were provoked by Jerry Rubin's bodyguard, Robert Pierson, who took down the American flag and cursed at the cops. The police were just furious and started beating people up everywhere. It turned out later that Pierson was an undercover cop.

It was pure sadism. There was a National Guardsman with his bayonet pointed at me. He said, "You have to stop," but I just kept walking.

As I walked away, I wondered, "Is he going to stab me in the back with a bayonet?"

I didn't want to be a martyr, but I wanted to walk in the park, so I kept going. I was on the outskirts of the park, and a car tried to run me over, and to give you an idea of my level of violence, I kicked the tire. Then I met a reporter for *Newsweek* who said, "You better get off the streets, the cops are looking for you."

Anita and I then went and picked up Abbie, who was just getting out of jail. We got in a cab and laid down on the floor, and Anita sat up as if she were alone inside. We got a midnight flight to New York, and we were pretty glad to get out of there alive.

I think the convention inspired many people to become committed to the antiwar movement. So many people were radicalized by what happened at the convention. The slogan "The whole world is watching" was true. A lot of kids I've met who were fourteen years old then said it changed their perspective.

They were watching the convention on TV with their parents and they couldn't believe that the cops were just hitting kids indiscriminately.

The Realist hit its peak in '67 with "The Parts Left out of the Kennedy Book." I was still doing the occasional prank. During the Columbia student strike, Steve Post asked me to take over his show on WBAI one night. Marshall Efron was there, and we pretended to be students who had taken over the station, and I talked like this [in a whiny, nasally voice]: "The airwaves belong to the people."

Listeners actually called the cops, and the cops came. We explained to them what we were doing and that they could see we had nobody tied up or anything. When the cops left, I got on the air and said, "The cops just left. Boy, did we fool them."

And they came back.

By 1974, I ran out of money and taboos. Even at its peak, the magazine wasn't making much money because we carried no advertising, and I was constantly getting cheated by distributors. Also, I was a soft touch, and that didn't help my financial situation.

I resurrected The Realist in 1985. The Reagan administration had gotten reelected, so I had plenty of things to say. But in 2000, I decided to put it to pasture. I figured that all the taboos I had broken were now in mainstream awareness. With the Internet, there were not only professional satirical journals online, but there was also an outlet for individuals who were creative and irreverent. It didn't cost them any money, and they were able to reach people immediately. So The Realist had served its purpose.

Not that I'm no longer interested in issues. I am, and I'm still writing. I've also been publishing articles about what's happening to the environment. And there are so many people living in poverty. We're the greatest industrial nation in the world, and we're thirty-seventh on the list of health care. The priorities are just insane. In terms of my own career, I've accomplished what I set out to do, to speak freely without compromising. A by-product of that was that I served as role model for others to go out and do the same or to go out and do different but not be afraid.

Whatever my role was in helping to liberate communication, to that extent it was successful. I don't like everything I hear, but I just think, "Well, that's the risk of democracy."

People magazine says I was the father of the underground press. I sent them a telegram demanding a blood test. It started long before I did. There's a

Paul Krassner today—novelist, journalist, and stand-up comedian.
(Courtesy of Paul Krassner)

whole tradition, going from Lyle Stuart's *Independent* to I. F. Stone's *Weekly*, to George Seldes's *In Fact*, all the way back to Tom Paine and Ben Franklin. I'm sure when they had cave dwellings that when the adults were doing hiero-glyphics on the walls, there were some kids doing other stuff on some big boulder out in the field. That was the first underground press. It's the nature of evolution. There has always been a counterculture.

Being considered an elder statesman is amusing, but as long as I haven't compromised I don't feel I have sold out, and I haven't. It's outrageous, though, how much of the '60s have been co-opted. Now the Jimi Hendrix version of the "Star Spangled Banner" is used to advertise Pop-Tarts. When I heard that, I thought, that's it, the revolution is over. There's even a soft drink called Yippie.

The most important lesson of the '60s? Always put the vinyl curtain inside the tub when you're taking a shower and outside when you're taking a bath. OK, you want the real answer? It's question authority and think for yourself. To be suspicious of the government, to be suspicious of the media, to be suspicious of the corporations, that they don't have your best interest at heart.

Remember, the devil never sleeps.

Lee Weiner
The Revolutionary

Political types of the 1950s' generation might have challenged each other with "Name the Hollywood Ten."

In my youth—at the close of the 1960s—it was "Name the Chicago Eight."

When authorities in Chicago in 1969 prosecuted eight radicals on various charges, including conspiracy to cross state lines with intent to riot at the 1968 Chicago Democratic convention, it was as if a whole generation was being put on trial. Some of the defendants who were charged with conspiring together hardly knew each other, but the government seemed determined to find a cross section of the antiwar movement and make an example of them.

The group, with the exception of Bobby Seale (who had been in Chicago only briefly to make a quick speech), were the organizers of what had been intended to be a "Festival of Life" (in contrast with the deaths being suffered in Vietnam) outside the 1968 convention. There were several events planned, including a rock concert. The Yippies also intended to use the occasion to nominate their candidate, a pig, for president. But Chicago officials under the orders of Mayor Richard A. Daley refused to grant parade permits to the protesters or permission to sleep in the city's park. The organizers responded by saying they would go ahead with the festival anyway. The standoff resulted in a series of bloody confrontations between the two sides over a week, the worst being on the night of August 28, when, in full view of TV cameras (and demonstrators chanting "All the world is watching"), the Chicago police waded into a crowd of protesters with their billy clubs flying.

Although a government commission called the melee a "police riot," a grand jury sought to shift the blame to the protesters, and the eight were indicted on various charges in March 1969.

Little did the authorities know what they were getting themselves into. The defendants, led by Abbie Hoffman and Jerry Rubin, turned the courtroom into a veritable Marx Brothers set. For those watching on the sidelines, it was not only the greatest trial of the decade, it was also the most fun. It would have been even more so had the defendants not been facing years in prison if convicted.

Intending to display to the world their utter contempt for the charges against them and for the judge, Julius Hoffman, the defendants decided to undercut the government's case by ridiculing it. Abbie Hoffman repeatedly referred to him as "Julie." When the judge would frequently mispronounce their names, the defendants would respond with insults. They read and answered their mail at the defense table. They slept during testimony. They attempted to bring a cake into court to celebrate Bobby Seale's birthday.

Seale's situation wasn't so lighthearted. At the start of the trial, he requested a delay in the trial so that his lawyer, who was recovering from surgery, could represent him. This kind of request was routinely granted, but Hoffman refused. Seale, a member of the Black Panther Party, accused the judge of behaving like a slave owner. Hoffman responded by ordering court officers to bind Seale to a chair with a gag over his mouth. The sketches by courtroom artists of a black man gagged and bound to his seat shocked the world.

When Seale managed to slip the gag off his mouth and attempted to address the judge, the marshals restrained him. The defendants then jumped the marshals, and a full-scale brawl ensued. Seale's case was soon declared a mistrial and severed from the others, and the Chicago Eight became the Chicago Seven.

Having a last name that is all too frequently mangled, I found myself identifying with one of the defendants, Lee Weiner, who would object with increasing impatience each time the judge said *Wee*-ner as opposed to the correct *Wye*-ner. Another reason that Weiner intrigued me was that, of the seven defendants, Weiner and John Froines were probably the least well known. I've always had a special feeling for the underappreciated.

Photographs of Weiner from that time showed an intense man with black curly hair and a beard, not someone to be reckoned with lightly. I wondered what happened to him after the trial. I also wanted to know how he ended up there with the others. The charges against him involved espousing violence.

Did he? And what was it like to star in one of the most notorious political trials in the country's history? If you are a star of that magnitude, what do you do for an encore?

I ask around about Weiner's whereabouts. A friend tells me he's working in New York for the Anti-Defamation League, a Jewish organization that fights anti-Semitism around the world. I call the ADL and ask the operator for him. The next thing I hear is a voice on the phone, saying, "Lee Weiner."

I tell him about this project, and his first words are, "You've got to be kidding." Then he says he is in the middle of trying to explain his life to his fifteen-year-old, so why not. When we meet in the lobby of his office a few days later, I don't recognize the face. Thirty years is a long time for hair follicles. His are still there, but his hair is trimmed closely to his scalp and is gray. That is not to say I'm about to interview an old man. He's like a teenager sitting at his father's desk. He doesn't stop moving during the entire interview. He's answering the phone. He's kibitzing with coworkers. He's checking his e-mail. He's bouncing around in his seat. Imagine the Energizer bunny on atomic power. He's also warm and funny and still magnetic.

He speaks quickly—no surprise there; but rare is the question that receives a straight answer, not because he's ducking the truth but because to understand the truth, one must hear five other stories to understand the first one. Of course, the five other stories are equally fascinating, but each one of those generates a story or two. This is one of those interviews where I say a quiet word of thanks to the person who thought to put a rewind button on tape recorders. But it's a fun interview. Lee is a genuinely warm person. He laughs about the old days, his drug use, his buddies. He doesn't take himself too seriously, and he's a terrific storyteller. It's quickly apparent why he was a star.

Although he now works in a relatively conventional world, his political views haven't changed all that much. I ask him about working for such a mainstream organization. "I raise money to fight hate," he says with a shrug. "What's wrong with that?" He's married, for the third time, and lives in straitlaced Fairfield, Connecticut. "We're the diversity," he says with a laugh.

He's also a proud family man and doesn't hesitate to show off photos of his kids. One shows his twenty-one-year-old daughter, a cigarette in one hand, a megaphone in the other, leading a rally against sexual assault. She's a chip off the old block, and it makes the old block beam with pride.

For me, the 1950s were pizza places opening up and Elvis Presley on the jukebox and trying like mad to score with a girl. How did I get from that to sleeping with a shotgun at the side of my bed and thinking I was never going to live past thirty-five? The answer is one step at a time.

I grew up on the South Side of Chicago in back of a coal yard, just barely on the correct side of the tracks. I learned to fire a gun when I worked for a tailor in a black neighborhood. He did up the suits for pimps and ministers and kept a .45 in his cash drawer. When he had free time, we would go out in the back and shoot.

My parents tried hard to become middle class, but I grew up in back of a coal yard, just barely on the correct side of the tracks. This wasn't *Leave It to Beaver*. Houses? Give me a break. Nobody I knew lived in houses. My father left Northwestern University when his father died of lead poisoning—he was a painter—and my father went into the business to support the family. I still love the smell of wet paint. It reminds me of the times that I would I go where my father and his crews were working.

The painter's union was mob controlled. One of the guys he worked with was a crew chief named Al Coletta. Later, he and my father opened a bar on the West Side. He did pretty well with it. I later learned that they were doing numbers and gambling and taking bets out of the back room, and the "guys" decided that it would also be a good place to distribute dope. Neither Al nor my father thought that was a good idea at all, so they said no.

A few days later, two guys came in with shotguns. My father gets the message very quickly, and says, "Al, give him the money."

Al went to the cash register and brought up a .32 rather than the money and shot the guy in the face. He then chases the other guy down the street and shoots him. My father went home and said to my mother, "I told Al, 'You just bought the bar.'" And he went to work for his father-in-law, selling furniture.

My mother was a University of Chicago graduate. The day I walked my sister to kindergarten, my mother actually passed us on the street on the other side. She was that anxious to get out of the house and rejoin the world of the living. She was a schoolteacher and then a social worker. Her friends were either Communist Party members or sympathetic to the Party.

It was a wonderfully rich environment. I grew up watching my parents play poker with their friends, and half these guys were bookies who were running little operations out of their drug stores and candy shops. The other half were unemployed lefties and city social workers.

I was way different from the kids in my social group. I didn't give a shit about being a doctor. I was an unpleasant little bastard. I ran a gambling operation in high school. [*He pulls up his shirt.*] I got this knife wound when I went back to the theater a week after we threw somebody off the balcony.

I'm one of the few people who ever failed art in high school. The good news was I got to take art again, and in the industrial art course they had these huge drawers, and you could run a Twenty-Six game and a small roulette wheel in one of those drawers. The other good news was in South Shore High School very few people knew you played Twenty-Six with eleven dice, so I let them roll ten, and you could make out quite well.

But at the same time that I was fantasizing about living that Marlon Brando and James Dean life, I was also reading my mother's books by Hemingway, Sinclair Lewis, John Dos Passos, and everything else. I devoured science fiction like a fiend. I took four years of English and history and social sciences. Before classes started, I used to write quotes on the board and let the teacher guess who the quotes were from.

Still, when I graduated high school, nobody wanted to room with me at the University of Illinois, because their parents all said, "He's not gonna make it." They weren't half wrong.

I got to school in '57. There I was introduced to everything. It had a great library and great English graduate students. I read the Beat poets and loved them. I was reading Greeks for the first time. I met weird friends, people who just didn't fit in anywhere. We would have coffee down the stairs from the Y, across the street from the campus. Everybody down there looked weird. They wore political buttons and listened to folk music.

Kids have to take a lot more serious risks today to be considered weird. In those days, English majors were considered weird, as were people who weren't going to go to law school and who didn't belong to fraternities or sororities. Jews were considered weird.

This was how straight people were back then: There was a professor at the University of Illinois in '58 who wrote a letter to the university newspaper, suggesting that, well, if you are really mature and over twenty-one, and you're already engaged to get married, it wouldn't be a criminal act to consider the possibility of having some kind of sexual interaction.

They fired his ass.

So when "Mom's day" came, they invited all the parents down, and I jumped up on top of a car with a bullhorn to protest what happened. That was my first public demonstration. Within a couple of weeks, we were all in front of Woolworth's picketing for the sit-in movement. Nothing happened, but we all learned we could act politically, that part of our being was to act that way and that we were different from people who didn't. That notion, that government exists to make peoples' lives better, that's what I was led to believe America was about, and if it required something to move it in that direction, we goddamned well better do it.

After I graduated, I got into the sociology graduate school at the University of Chicago. I was going to be a sociologist. That seemed like a reasonable thing to do. I had gotten married. I was living in Glencoe, Illinois, where my first wife was teaching grammar school, and I was commuting to Chicago. I was supposed to do that every day.

Nah.

I ended up at the Oriental movie theater more often than not, trying to figure out, what the hell am I going to do? Then one day, I was on top of a double decker commuter train, pondering my fate at twenty-one years old. Down below were four guys in seats facing one another. They had a piece of cardboard, which they used as a table to play bridge, and I remember clear as a goddamned bell, some guy saying, "You know, I can't stand my job. I don't much like my wife and kids. I just love the train ride."

I thought to myself, "Oh, God, no way."

So I dropped out of school. My grandfather became worried that I was showing too much concern for the colored people, so he decided to give me and my wife a really super-duper present: he sent us to Israel for a year from 1961 to '62.

It didn't quite have the effect he intended. That's where I met Jerry Rubin, who would be indicted with me in 1969. I took a class in social justice, and I learned that social justice wasn't going to come out of a book or the university. When I came back, I knew what I wanted to do—change the fucking country. That meant working with people, so I became a social worker and a community organizer.

We all joined SDS. Its national headquarters were right by a McDonald's off 63rd Street on Chicago's South Side. That's where I met Tom Hayden, who would be another coconspirator in '68. We would get hamburgers and french fries and sit down on the lawn in front and talk about organizing and making the change happening. The goal was to give people power and control over their own lives.

But countercultural I was not. Here's an example. My hair was as short as it is now. I had black horn-rim glasses.

We had to cut a deal with the loan sharks because when we set up the first federally chartered credit union, that meant people didn't have to go to the loan sharks anymore, and that pissed them off. So we had this meeting with these guys in white shirts and white ties at this lonely little bar. There was a guy singing on the small stage, and we couldn't hear ourselves talk. I walked up to him and said, "We're fucking trying to talk. Take your fucking guitar and go away." He looked over and saw who was at the table with us and did. The singer was Arlo Guthrie.

In the Chicago ghettos of the 1960s, people were hungry and dirty. If you saw photos of them and put them up against black families in the South during the 1860s, there was the same bleakness. Through all this, you saw families struggling desperately to make their lives better. My job as an organizer was to help provide people with the tools they needed to do that.

We set up the first federally chartered credit union, so that people didn't have to go to the loan sharks anymore. We organized a tenant union and a welfare union. We fought for housing redevelopment without mass disloca- tion: same neighborhood, just better housing.

This was serious stuff, and so I learned serious skills. To get attention, we collected rats from basements and threw them into the reflecting pool near City Hall and got our asses arrested.

It's not for nothing that they later indicted me for teaching and demon- strating the use of incendiary devices. When you collect lots of garbage from a slum in a truck and stuff the office entranceway to the real estate agent who collects the rents, and things still don't change, how can you make a stronger point?

There was a sergeant in the Chicago police department, a youth officer. He was a big guy, and he carried a big gun. His gun was so big, it literally pulled him over to one side. He used to throw kids up against the wall all the fucking time.

How do you put a stop to that? You do it by fighting back.

In 1967, Martin Luther King came to Chicago, the most segregated city in America, to get the civil rights movement going in the North. He hoped his bravery and honesty would make it happen, but he didn't get much. I sat at the table with him along with other local activists, but we weren't into symbolic confrontations. We were at war. We wanted to win. What people needed were organizers and coldheartedness, and I was about as fucking coldhearted as you could get.

I was never interested in becoming a saint. I wanted to effect change. I thought long and hard about nonviolence, and I concluded that it's an effective tactic in some circumstances in some places for some period of time, but I don't believe major change occurs without violence.

That means if you decide you're just not going to take being mauled by the cops any more, you fight back. Suddenly you're not a victim anymore, and it feels good. Maybe some cops would then think about it. Stonewall is a good example. What would be a nonviolent response to being hassled by cops in your own goddamned bar? There wasn't one. They fought back and started a whole movement.

Even so, I began to lose faith in the outcome of what we were doing. I believed that the scope of the problems were such that they were not going to be addressed from the bottom up like that. I no longer thought that working within the system would succeed. I didn't know what the answer was. Mostly, I was burned out. Then King and Kennedy were killed. Nineteen sixty-eight was the only year I ever thought that a revolution in the United States might actually happen. As Abbie used to say about 1968, "They don't make years like that anymore."

It was simply staggering from beginning to end, leading up to the organizing and the convention. I had met Jerry Rubin in Israel. I met Abbie through Jerry in 1966. We were on the Lower East Side in Manhattan. He was a great guy. There we were, three loudmouth Jews, all crazy, doing drugs, just into loving our lives. My first wife hated it when I went to New York. She was right. Our marriage didn't last.

We all were changing. We were thinking and talking about revolution. It seemed doable, and if it meant I wasn't going to live past thirty-five, so be it. The realist school said we had to develop skills to allow us to survive, so that's why I learned about all sorts of unpleasant things, like guns and bombs, sabotage. We lived then, as we live now, in a very violent society, so it wasn't difficult to get weapons or find places to use them. But I taught people how to use weapons for self-defense. I didn't see myself as an assassin.

Was a lot of it fantasy? Oh, yeah. Was some of it real? Ask Fred Hampton. He was killed in his bed by the FBI. That's when I started to sleep with a shotgun under my bed. Would I have used it if someone came through my front door? Yeah. Was I a potential target? All of us were.

Lee Weiner photographed by
Chicago police in August 1968.
(Courtesy of Lee Weiner)

In the spring of 1968, Jerry and Rennie Davis came to me because they were organizing for the convention, and they needed help. It turned out that the demonstrations would be occurring in an area where I worked as a gang worker, and I knew the cops, and since I also knew something about self-defense, I helped organize the marshals.

We had maybe three goals for the demonstrations. The first was to show that there was enormous opposition to the war in Vietnam. We also wanted to demonstrate that in the midst of this ugliness was a movement committed to social justice and a new way of looking at relationships and people. The third thing was to have fun. It was fun. People were nice. People were lovely. Drugs were good. The politics were righteous. And the sense of moving forward to achieve economic and social justice was real. It was alive in the air. How could you not participate?

It became obvious early on that things would not go well. The first night, I was at the cop headquarters at the north end of the park. We hoped that they wouldn't be so foolish as to attack the protesters in the park. We said to them, "At least if you come in, come in from one direction, and me and my marshals will help move people out." But they came in swinging from several directions, so we had no choice but to fight.

What they actually said was that they were going to break our asses, so I went back and showed the poor kids how to defend themselves from a billy club with a rolled-up magazine. If you hold it up, you can block a club with it. So when the police attacked, they had their clubs, we had fists and rolled-up magazines. When they hit us, we hit back and turned and ran.

It got worse. Two days later, there was an afternoon rally in Grant Park. Rennie Davis was standing up front by the stage when he was attacked from behind by the cops and knocked unconscious. Some people tried to take down the American flag (one of them turned out to be an undercover cop), and the cops just came in a line. They upturned the chairs and attacked the demonstrators. My marshals tried to hold the lines, but we couldn't. I was attacked again. When they knocked us down, we got back up, until finally the cops pulled back.

Earlier in the week, I walked past the Hilton hotel and saw people constructing a wooden platform. I asked a guy what were they doing, and he said they were making a platform for TV cameras. That turned out to be helpful news. Now, we knew where the TV cameras were going to be, which meant we did not have to march all the way to the amphitheatre. We could achieve a public demonstration in front of those cameras, which was very, very important, because getting past the security around the amphitheatre would have been a job and a half.

That turned out to be the demonstration that was broadcast all over the world, with the TV cameras showing cops beating the kids and shoving them into vans and through the windows of restaurants. That's why people were yelling, "The whole world is watching," because it was, and what they saw was a display of tremendous state violence, and it was no longer undercover.

The National Guard and cops were out there, and they had jeeps with barbed-wire fronts to block a lot of brave people who wanted to express their sense of citizenship and their sense of anger at the way their government was acting. But rather than slink away and say, "Maybe we should go to court and argue for our constitutional rights," the protesters expressed their anger verbally, like citizens in a free country, and surged forward. It was honest rage. Then, as they surged forward, the cops attacked.

While it was going on, I went over to the steps of the Art Institute to catch my breath. I watched the crowd surging back and forth, and for a few moments that Wednesday night, August 28, while I was taking a break and smoking a joint, I was one of those who thought, "Jesus Christ, the revolution might fucking happen."

I think many of us believed that if people saw what was going on, they would rise up and smite the aggressor, and there would be revolution. I decided I wanted to become Minister of Justice and pick out the people who would have to go up against the wall. That seemed like a great after-the-revolution job. [Laughs.]

Well, they didn't quite rise up. After about twenty minutes, my dreams of a revolution passed, and the reality of the situation set back in. It was pretty bloody out there.

The next day, I met with some of my marshals in Grant Park. There were a lot of people with bandages on their heads. You could still smell the tear gas in the streets. I was angry. There was this sense that the city felt as if it was their streets, that this was their country. I didn't agree with that. It seemed to me the thing to do was symbolically show them they didn't control the streets, and I suggested what I thought was an appropriate response.

I went and got my car and found a parking space in an underground garage near Grant Park. Inside were a bunch of old Pepsi bottles, soap, and rags, and the car runs on gasoline. Yes, you could say explosives could be made from those materials. I left the car to go into the MOBE [Mobilization Against the War] office to see what was going on, and when I went back to my car, it wasn't there. It had been arrested.

I wasn't arrested, only my car was. I found out later that one of my marshals was a cop. It's an interesting question that if you take away all the cops who were demonstrators, how many demonstrators would be left?

After the convention, I started going to New York a lot more often, getting wilder with Abbie and Jerry. More drugs, more sex. The counterculture was blossoming, and I wanted to get to know what the new community was all about.

It was wonderful to be on the East Side of New York in 1968 and '69. There was music, drugs, sex, writing, poetry, music, making it, listening to it, trying to take care of one and other, trying to create new forms of living as a community. It was an amazing time.

A few months later, I opened the door of my apartment to see my mother-in-law, this little bit of a woman, Russian-born. I say, "Hi," and she says, "Aiiiiiii, Aiiiiiii."

"What's wrong? Are you all right?"

"Aiiiiiii."

This goes on for ten minutes. I can't figure out what the fuck is going on. She is walking around the apartment moaning. Then the telephone rings. It's the *New York Times*. Now I know what she was moaning about. That's how I found out I was indicted.

There were eight of us. I was surprised about Bobby Seale. He must have shown up at the demonstrations for an hour and a half. Abbie was a stand-in for the whole counterculture. Jerry was the hard edge; Rennie and Tom, SDS organizers; Dave Dellinger, pacifist, antiwar activist; me, the student; Froines, the academic. Typical sexists, there were no women indicted.

Tom was supposed to get the bail money, $10,000 apiece. That's eighty grand. I didn't trust him, so I called my dad, and I said, "Hey, Dad, I need a little help."

"What kind of help?"

"Tom is going to come up with the money, but I know I'm gonna draw the short straw when he comes up with sixty. I'm not a media star. I don't want to be a schnorrer, but I need eighty for everybody."

He hangs up. Ten minutes later he calls back and gives me the address of a law firm in Chicago. With hair like that [*spreads his arms around his head*], beard down to here, I go to this big law firm on LaSalle Street.

"Don't worry about a thing. Friends of your father are friends of ours. No problem."

The mob lawyers loved you if you gave the finger to the cops.

He goes to Bankers Trust. "How much do you need?" He pulls out the lock box, puts $20,000 in his pocket and hands me eighty. I was the richest hippie in Chicago. I had $40,000 folded into each back pocket of my jeans.

We got money from some strange places. I think even some movement-related bank robbers sent us funds. During the trial, my grandfather also offered financial help. I said, "Grandpa, that's gonna cost a lot of money."

"It's all right. Did any of those people kill anybody?"

"No."

"Do you like those boys?"

"I like them."

"OK, if you need anything, ask."

"OK."

I was charged with teaching and demonstrating the use of incendiary devices and using incendiary devices to disrupt interstate traffic. If I had blown up the underground garage on Michigan Avenue, it would have affected interstate traffic. It was much more grandiose sounding than I had molotov cocktails in my car and was going to set them off. Was it true that I was going to do it? Absolutely.

We constantly talked about how we would conduct ourselves at the trial. What was finally "decided" was that everybody would have their own trial, so there was not a single strategy proposed that was rejected. Abs wanted the country to go on trial. Tom wanted a hard, strong, focused defense; David wanted to have the moral issues on trial.

The conspiracy actually had an office in Chicago. We hired a tough, competent woman to run it. We were doing a lot of speaking and running around, and people were sending in money, so we needed someone to coordinate the plans and keep track of contributions and have a place to keep our files.

From day one we were stars, which meant we would have these big meetings in wealthy peoples' apartments, and Arthur Kinoy [a well-known civil liberties lawyer] would come. He thought it was the greatest thing in the world. "You're never going to go to jail."

He was wrong.

The trial for me is a kaleidoscope of imagery, drugs, sex, work, speeches, travel. Some of it was dreary. Our poor attorney Lenny Weinglass. One of the lies he kept trying to shove down the jurors' throats was that Lee Weiner had a long history as a nonviolent organizer. The prosecution offered a bunch of photographs to show the jury. As Lenny looked at them, he grimaced. It was a picture of me in a black headband and with a tough-looking face, about to knock down the cameraman. The photograph was sitting in a pile on our table, and when no one was looking, I took the picture and hid it under some papers in a book. Nobody noticed. The jury never saw the photo.

My mother came to the trial once. My father came once to try and convince me to go back to my wife and child, which was very odd since I was being shadowed by cops and I had hair down my back. Hello, Dad? I'm not going to be a nice middle-class kid anymore.

As the trial wound down, there was no question we would be put in jail. I ended up going, mostly for correcting my name. People always pronounced it *Wee*-ner. It's *Wye*-ner. When the judge would say *Wee*-ner, I would shout out, "It's *Wye*-ner," and he got pissed off and charged me with contempt, which was a perfect summary of my political stance. I was sentenced to two and a half months.

You have no idea how bad the food is in jail. It's indescribable. We go into federal lockup during the trial. We are allowed out of solitary to exercise at certain times. Tom Hayden is out in this passageway, practicing karate, and these two thugs, who were waiting to be transferred to a federal prison for interstate hijacking, say to him, "Hey, kid, what are you doing?"

"Practicing for the revolution."

One guy says, "This is the only kind of exercise you really need." [*Mimes pulling the trigger of a gun.*]

The other guy says, "No, you also need this." [*Mimes swinging a bat.*]

I laugh, and they turn to me. "You know what we're talkin' about, kid?"

"Of course. Breaking somebody's kneecaps."

"Yeah, yeah, how do you know?"

So we start talking, and one of them says, "How you doin' in here?"

"Starving to death."

"How do you know about this stuff?"

"My father worked with Al Coletta."

"Little Al? Jeez, kid, you're having a problem with food? No problem. We got a thing with the assistant warden, no sweat."

That night, when I pulled in my tray, I had rock cornish game hen with fucking wild rice.

Originally, we were split up in the Cook County Jail, and all of us did exactly the same thing. We were up on tables, yelling and screaming at the crowd. People wanted to hear our riffs about the system. These were guys who were totally beaten down. They wanted to know what was going on, and we were fucking stars.

The sheriff treated us badly. They cut our hair with great glee. The guards were guards. Some of them were nice. A year later I was back in Chicago in a bar, and some guy came over and asked me how my mother was. He was one of the guards. But after we got out of jail, essentially the tent was folded up and the circus went away. One day, I'm crossing the street on Michigan Avenue, and a cop says to me, "Hey, Lee, we haven't forgotten."

I went directly to a phone booth. I called up my dissertation advisor and said, "Get me a job out of Chicago."

I couldn't stay there. Don't forget, they killed Fred Hampton during the trial. I didn't want to sleep with a shotgun next to my bed anymore. I went to Rutgers in New Jersey and taught courses in social change. One of the things I talked about was how someone could move from nonviolent to violent behavior.

I would take them to demonstrations, and we went down to a demonstration in Washington, where they were blocking bridges, and the last time I saw this one student, he was standing on the front bumper of a city bus, holding on to the windshield wiper in his left hand, while with his right hand, he was happily spraying the front window of the bus and shouting to me, "Mr. Weiner, you're right, it's easy and fun!"

But it was a tough time. Politics hardened after the trial as the level of protest against the war got more determined and the government got more determined. Some people became desperate for models, and they looked to people like Mao. Others disappeared into the woodwork of New Mexico.

I remember being asked by the Weatherfolks to judge a friend of mine who wanted to maintain his apartment on the Upper West Side. It was rent controlled. They thought it was bourgeois behavior, but he wasn't going to give up the apartment. What if the revolution didn't happen? He had to defend himself in their court. I remember another argument over whether it was counterrevolutionary to enjoy a sunset. We were hard.

I'm not going to condemn the Weather Underground, but if in order to be recognized as a political actor in their eyes you have to carry around a gun, then you are not going to have a mass movement. And you're not going to have a democratic movement. There was also a lot of paranoia—for good reasons. We had a police agent in the collective where I lived. The FBI was across the street. Another time, someone saved my life once when a wacko sent a package of poisoned food from Bloomingdale's.

The political side of the movement was also burning up. People with organizational skills were being denounced left and right by people who were less experienced. I was still a quasi star in the movement. I was hip. I was invited to fancy parties where outside the elevator they decorated the hall with a Renoir. There really was a party like that. That's when I realized I wasn't going to be an on-the-street organizer. Such an event is so divorced from the real world, but there I was, making love to very rich, beautiful, svelte women in wonderful places and doing too many drugs. After a while, I began to feel I was losing my grip on who I was. At least I didn't end up being married to a movie star.

Then Abbie and Jerry said, "Come on, we're going to go to Miami. " They thought it was important to demonstrate at the 1972 political conventions. They were also isolated. Yippies were attacking Abbie. Abbie was attacking Jerry, so this was their last political gasp.

There were reasons to demonstrate. The war was still going on, but the convention was a real disaster. First of all, the biggest differences between '68 and '72 was now we had cachet. Do you know how we financed the demonstrations in Miami? We published an art portfolio of modern American artists.

It wasn't like we didn't believe in the values. We did, but we weren't living the life. We got rooms in a hotel. There were lots of women and drugs. I remember some drug dealer offered me a job. He had a lazy Susan, and every little compartment was a different drug.

I came back from Miami full of self-loathing and disgust with what I had become and for who my friends had become. I couldn't tolerate the bickering and the crap that was going on. It was not a life I wanted to hold onto. I wanted to make a new one, so I burned my telephone book, a page at a time, in a restaurant. I didn't want anything to do with anybody. Everyone was too nuts. It had all gone bad.

I went to work with drug addicts and prisoners as a consultant, running around the Bronx and Queens trying to do legitimate work. I was a social worker until 1976. Then a friend asked me to go to Ohio, because Jimmy Carter was in danger of losing the state. If he lost Ohio, he might not get the presidency. My friend said, "Nobody has to know who you are."

I said, "Great." I organized a few districts in Ohio, and Carter won the state, and he was elected president.

I got an invitation to go down to Washington to try and use the resources of the government to encourage local organizing. I did that for a couple of years. Then I got real concerned about the failure of people in progressive politics to have any kind of secure financial funding and support, so I began helping people develop the skills to get it. I worked on political campaigns for progressive organizations doing complicated work, data analysis. We were using computers early on. The Anti-Defamation League was one of my clients, and they asked me to join their staff in 1989.

It doesn't bother me in the least that I'm not on center stage any more. For

Lee Weiner in 2004 with his daughter, Zoe. (Courtesy of Lee Weiner)

Abs, it was absolutely devastating, but I do good work here. If I had a louder public persona, I wouldn't be able to do this work. When my wife asked me recently if I missed the old life, I said I missed the drugs, but other than that, I don't miss the politics. Doing this makes it OK for me.

I remember a time very, very clearly when I was an undergraduate at the University of Illinois in the very late '50s. I was with a friend, and we were wondering whether we could ever experience the adventure, the sense of meaning, that existed in the '30s when people became communists, fought for Spain, and organized unions. How little did we know that we would become exactly what we were hoping to be.

We continue to have problems with racism, bigotry, sexism, ageism. Those things need to be fought on a day-to-day basis, and that's what I do. The fact that these issues were raised in the '60s and brought to the table are very positive legacies of the decade. That and good music.

I still feel we were essentially correct back then. I think the circumstances for poor people are worse today. And I think they will get even worse. The marginalized communities, the poor and people of color, are more isolated from mainstream America than they have ever been. I still think violence will always have a place in social change, and I feel strongly it's acceptable in self-defense situations.

The drugs, sex, and rock and roll were great. The last half of the decade was a helluva lot more fun than the first half was, but that's also where we failed as organizers. The bombings, for example, were counterproductive, because they made it too hard for people to feel that they could be a part of it. If someone asked you, "Hey, come over. We're gonna listen to Pete Seeger and we're gonna make some bombs, and we're gonna blow up the fucking South Shore bank and take the money and give it to an outlaw group and sell meth on the side to be able to buy the weapons," you'd probably say, "I'd rather go to the movies."

I think the best and most important legacy of my generation was the notion of self-empowerment, that people could act with others to effect change. That was something that made sense to people like me, that you could go into a community as outsiders and start to organize.

That notion of being empowered and being a part of a movement for change is still current for many young people, but when people talk to me generally what they'll bemoan is the feeling that there is no great something to struggle for and that they are isolated, so therefore their individual actions can't make a difference. I tell them they are not alone. They just have to lead.

As for Chicago, I think there are a couple of lessons there, and they're contradictory. The first was that our democratically elected government was fully capable of, in the past and probably in the future, of using its resources to fight people politically opposed to it and to stifle dissent.

However, the second lesson is here I am. It's thirty-five years later. I have six kids, a house, a wife, a life. In other countries and other places, going against the government as notoriously as we did, we wouldn't be around. It's as simple as that.

The Constitution saved my ass. There are second acts in America.

Daniel Berrigan
Peace Preacher

When the radical priest come to get me released
We's all on the cover of Newsweek.
—Paul Simon, "Me and Julio down by the Schoolyard"

Shortly after lunchtime on May 17, 1968, the local draft board in suburban Catonsville, Maryland, came under attack from nine people, including two Jesuit priests armed with their faith and some homemade napalm. Their mission was to remove and destroy the board's files designating the young men most likely to be drafted and sent to Vietnam. The invaders managed to grab 378 such files. Then, after a mad dash down the stairs of the building to the parking lot, they placed the documents in a wire trash basket and set them on fire. It turned out that napalm, which was being used effectively by the American military to defoliate the jungles of Southeast Asia, worked quite nicely on paper and cardboard as well. And since the media had been alerted beforehand, the protest action was filmed and eventually broadcast around the world. The legend of the Catonsville Nine was born, and the Berrigan brothers had once again succeeded in pricking the conscience of America.

Daniel and Philip Berrigan had been tilting at windmills since the 1950s. Philip, a World War II combat veteran, was a longtime civil rights activist who had led some of the earliest desegregation battles in New Orleans. Both brothers intended to participate in the first Freedom Rides in 1961, but were prevented from doing so by their superiors in the Roman Catholic church, who feared retribution from pro-segregation whites.

The Berrigans couldn't understand a church that refused to back up its own teachings with action. If Isaiah decreed "Turn your swords into plowshares," that was enough for them to commit civil disobedience against nuclear weapons. If the Fifth Commandment said, "Thou shalt not kill," then killing—all killing—was wrong, they reasoned. This placed them at odds with powerful figures in the church, including New York's Cardinal Francis Joseph Spellman, a cold warrior who publicly supported the Vietnam War. The Berrigans replied by saying that as far as they knew, there were no exceptions made for killing Viet Cong. They refused to abide by what they saw as the church's political agenda or a government that was bent on war abroad and reluctant to enforce civil rights at home. And since they didn't think you could compromise with evil and that polite dissent was not an effective response, they chose confrontation. In New Orleans, Philip organized picket lines and voter registration efforts. In upstate New York, Daniel helped run a veritable underground railroad of draft evaders.

Their political activities put them squarely in the crosshairs of not only the church, but also J. Edgar Hoover and the Nixon administration, which feared that the Berrigans' moral leadership would exert a powerful influence among young people. Their fears were justified. The Berrigans' straightforward religious message, their utter decency, and their bravery in putting their own bodies on the line placed them among the most respected voices of opposition in the 1960s. There was also a bravado to them that was immensely appealing to young protesters, who, if not totally in tune with the Berrigans' squareness, could certainly identify with their derring-do.

Neither Richard Nixon nor J. Edgar Hoover could figure out how to deal with them. Nixon had made a career out of red-baiting his political enemies, but he couldn't exactly call the two priests "godless communists" and expect it to stick. The Berrigans made no bones that they took their cues from Jesus, not Marx. That's what made them so effective: the apolitical quality of their mission for peace and justice.

Hoover sent his agents to uncover sexual dirt on the priests. When that failed (although Philip did eventually marry a nun), he used an informer to persuade a Harrisburg, Pennsylvania, grand jury in 1971 to level more serious charges that the Berrigans plotted with an anarchist group to blow up the steam pipes under Washington, D.C., and kidnap Richard Nixon's chief foreign policy adviser, Henry Kissinger. Upon hearing the charges, Daniel, who was an unindicted coconspirator in the alleged plot, joked that it would have made more sense to blow up Henry Kissinger and kidnap the steam pipes.

The subsequent Harrisburg Seven case only added to the Berrigans'

Daniel Berrigan after his capture by FBI agents in 1970. (Courtesy of Bob Fitch)

legend. The case was declared a mistrial when the defense picked apart the informer's testimony and the jury deadlocked 10–2 for acquittal. Deeply embarrassed at not being able to get a guilty verdict in the heartland of Nixon's so-called "Silent Majority," the government dropped the charges.

Within a year, Hoover was dead. A year after that, Nixon resigned in disgrace following the release of tapes that depicted him attempting to cover up the circumstances surrounding the Watergate burglary.

Even now, Daniel Berrigan is still at it. (Philip, two years younger than Daniel, died in 2002.) An accomplished poet whose first volume of poetry won the prestigious Lamont Prize, he has published some fourteen books of poetry since. He also writes nonfiction and scholarly treatises on subjects that interest him. When he was asked by a newspaper reporter how things were going at the age of eighty, he replied, "Well, things are a little weird. I haven't been in jail for a while."

He lives in a large apartment house on Manhattan's Upper West Side and is wearing jeans and a pullover shirt as he greets me outside the elevator. He certainly doesn't look like an outlaw who was once on the FBI's Most Wanted List. He is tall and gaunt and looks mostly like he could use a Happy Meal or two.

Softspoken and modest, he suggests that his brother Philip would have been a better subject, and while the robust and dynamic Philip was the more natural leader, it seemed to me that the more retiring Daniel was the more interesting brother because he had more personal hurdles to overcome as a leader. What was at the roots of his determination? How much did it have to do with his family background? Even if the Berrigans' cause was just, why did they feel it was necessary to repeatedly break the law?

Berrigan has a sense of humor about his retiring demeanor. On the door of his apartment is a small sign that says, "Absence of charisma may be fatal." His apartment is filled with painting and statues, some religious, some political, some both, but the real treat is in the bathroom, which Berrigan has turned into a veritable art gallery of his activist career. The walls are covered with political posters announcing Berrigan appearances from the 1960s, '70s, '80s, and '90s, from the Catonsville Nine to the Plowshares Eight. There is even a nod to capitalism via a Ben & Jerry's poster of 1960s characters enjoying their favorite flavor of ice cream. Dan's flavor, according to the poster, is mocha fudge. He tells me the ad agency actually picked it. So much for truth in advertising.

My mother was born in Germany and came here as a child with her parents. They got what the government called a "land claim," forty acres in Minnesota. She was a young, beautiful milliner when my father roared into town, literally; he was a railroad engineer. They met at a dance.

We're still trying to figure him out. He was so complex; it's like unraveling an old sweater. He had a quick temper and could be very violent. I was the second youngest of six, and I think my mother realized that too much of him would really crush me, so she made sure I was out of the path of his temper as much as possible. I took a lot of refuge in books, which helped keep me out of his way.

My father was something, all right, but that had good and bad attached to it. My brothers all stood up to him, and they learned a great deal from him because he was an amazing workman. They learned everything he knew: carpentry, crop raising, animals.

Although he was not formally educated, he was an omnivorous reader and wrote a great deal of poetry. He taught us a lot about conscience and about doing what you believe in. He lived to see my brother and me in great trouble. In his Irish Catholic enclave, he and my mother went from honored parents of priests to being shunned because the priests were disgraced, but they stood very boldly through all that. My mother was interviewed for a documentary when I was underground, and she was asked point blank, "What do you think of these priests breaking the law?"

She looked quietly into the camera and said, "Well, it wasn't God's law they broke."

My parents never bought into the American dream. As Americans, we're sort of stuck in this competitiveness and accumulation of money and ego, but they had no sympathy for that. We were raised during the Great Depression. We didn't have much, but we had acreage and food from a big garden, a lot of which ended up at the neighbors, given away. That was just the way we grew up. The benefits of a family who had land and food belonged to others who had nothing. And it was very quietly done; it wasn't talked about.

There were always people around us who were hungry. Hoboes, who had gone on the road looking for work, would come by for a handout or to stay over. One of them put a mark on our barn, which we never noticed. That mark was a sign to other hoboes that you could get a meal and a night at our place, so they came, and some of them stayed quite a while. When they did come, my mom would take them in, put them at the table, and make a meal for them.

We didn't have a radio. My mother would make a weekly trek into town, and all of us would stop at the library to bring home books. The winter nights were all about reading and homework. When we started going to school in the city in Syracuse, then we got a kind of slap in the face because these other kids had spending money and movie money. That was the first time we had any idea that we were poorer than anyone else.

Starting in fourth grade I went to Catholic school. That was really a reign of terror until sixth grade. I had some very mean, sad people for teachers. It was just awful. My fifth-grade teacher was big on physical punishment. She would pull hair and pound you against the blackboard. In sixth grade, we were pals in the neighborhood with a young guy who delivered newspapers. Sometimes he would hold on to a little of the paper money and we would all have a hot dog or a soda. He would also skip school, and we would cover for him.

Our teacher discovered this deep, dark plot, and she humiliated me by writing a letter to my father, accusing my parents of teaching me to lie. I gave it to my mother instead of my father, because he would have beaten us. My mother got furious, not with us, but with the teacher, and she confronted her, telling her the letter was insulting and these were minor matters. The teacher backed down. That was a great lesson to me on how authority could be confronted.

Finally, in seventh grade I had a kind teacher. One day I was fooling around with the student in front of me. We had these ink bottles on our desks, and while jostling around, he elbowed the bottle and spilled ink all over my shirt. What was I going to do? Well, she told me to go out to the locker and take the shirt off, and she took it home during her lunch hour and washed it. What a lady!

My brother Philip and I were great boon companions, being the youngest and subject to unprovoked attacks from others. But from fourth grade on, I had another great friend. We used to talk a lot about what we wanted to do, and in high school we both decided to become Jesuits. I don't think I would have gone this way without him, but he was quite clear all along that he wanted to be a priest. He died four years ago as a Jesuit.

These was a long history of priests and nuns in my family. On my mother's side, there were several distinguished church people. My great-uncle and uncle were both rebel priests of a certain kind.

My friend and I decided we would send away to four orders to get their literature, so we had eight orders between us. Then, we would look at all this stuff and come to a decision as to which order we would join. A lot of them sent pamphlets that were very fancy—"Come and swim in our pool while you study"—but the Jesuits sent this cheap little booklet that had all the attraction of an Amtrak schedule. There wasn't a picture in it. It was just a very dry account of what would be a very long haul, "and if you're interested, here's the number." We were both taken by it, so when the time came, we said, "Let's try the Jesuits."

Giving up a family or relationships was certainly part of the package. One had to swallow hard and say yes, sure, and I did. I was already writing poetry. I wanted to do a lot of studying and live a life with books. I was also mesmerized by the fact that there were so many achievers in the Jesuits. I wanted to be one of them.

It turned out to be a very strange era for the Jesuit order that we started with. It was all about keeping clear of the real world. My four brothers were all in the Second World War at that time. Philip was a decorated soldier. Our only source of news was when they would post the front page of the *New York Times* on the bulletin board.

When I learned we had dropped the atomic bomb, I just couldn't believe it. I read a book by a British Catholic writer, Ronald Knox, about alternatives to the bomb. His thesis was that this was a monstrous crime and that if they wanted to use that thing, why didn't they shoot it off on some abandoned island and say, "This is what we can do." I just ate that book up. A year later, I was teaching in a high school. I tried to explain my thinking to the kids, but they were all hungry for more war and gave me a very tough time.

The church was very anticommunist, especially the crowd of old Jesuits around Fordham in New York City where I had moved. The great exception was Dorothy Day.

Dorothy was a person of uncommon courage and tolerance. As a young woman, she lived a very bohemian life in Greenwich Village and wrote for all sorts of leftist publications. She marched on Washington for women's rights and was arrested and spent time in jail. After she had an abortion, she decided to investigate the church, but she never lost her social passion. She had a real sense of the poor and a belief that the modern state was intent mainly on war making. It was a very new voice, and she was alone in the church for quite a while.

During the Depression, she fed thousands of hungry people and found housing for the homeless. She lived among them according to her convictions. She was always at the typewriter, and she put out a paper called *The Catholic Worker*. We got it at our home almost from the start, so she was very much a part of our growing up. We were really running a little adjunct Catholic Worker place ourselves.

When I started teaching in New York, I brought students over to the *Worker*. They were a ragtag community of volunteers who were living hand to mouth in poverty, like she did. I don't want to romanticize it all, because I found the *Worker* a very tough scene right from the start. It wasn't my cup of tea. It was too disorderly and chaotic and not very clean. Still, I was in awe of her.

I was very much influenced by her passion for social causes and her pacifism. In the '50s, the government started forcing people to take part in air raid drills. It was all this nonsense about shoveling people into subways as a rehearsal in case an atom bomb would be dropped on us. She refused to participate and got thirty days in jail. Then she went back and did it the next year and the next year until finally they abandoned them.

It took me a long time to come around to her views on killing. After all, I had four brothers who served in the war. Thomas Merton also helped change my view about killing. Merton, like Dorothy, had a very tumultuous youth. He had also fathered a child. The child perished with the mother in the bombing of London by the Nazis. Merton was a member of a Marxist group at Columbia. He was always interested in the compassionate aspect of Marxism. They never got together for meetings about Marxism without first visiting somebody who needed some help, and he was always insisting on that, that they put their theories to work and that politics should have a heart to it.

Then, through friends who were Catholics, he got interested in the church and was baptized at around age twenty. He became a Trappist monk, moved to an abbey in Kentucky where he published a best seller, *The Seven Storey Mountain*. In the late '50s, he wrote an article for Dorothy's paper on nuclear weapons and nuclear war that blew me away. I wrote him to say thank you and that reading it had been quite a moment for me, and he wrote back and said, "Why don't you come down?"

I did, and in 1965, we organized an ecumenical group called The Spiritual Roots of Resistance to come to the Abbey and talk about Vietnam and other issues. That retreat became a kind of landmark, because everybody who took part in it either died or went to jail.

He was reaching toward something deeper, especially in light of the darkness of nuclear weapons and the real possibility of nuclear war. We were growing out of a very dominant "just war" of the church theory, which had held sway since, God help us, Thomas Aquinas. That theory said there were certain conditions where the gospel could be squared with killing. I slowly began to see that that was all hogwash, and this became the essence of my work in the '60s and even up to today.

Actually, I had already started on that path. In 1953, I was in France around the time that the French army was being defeated by the Vietnamese at Dien Bien Phu. A group of French priests defied the Vatican and went to work in the mines and docks. These worker-priests were living with the poor, and the Vatican was furious. It wanted its clerics to be apart and isolated from the poor, and it immediately put a stop to what the priests were doing. So in France, I got this education about the evils of colonialism and at that same time a practical vision of what the church should be. That visit changed me forever.

By the '60s, both Phil and I were agitating against the war. I was counseling war resisters and also doing civil rights work. Soon the steam was gathering against me among the church hierarchy. One afternoon, a whole group of us clergy, Protestant and Catholic, put on our collars and went off to a vigil at the New York City Board of Education about segregation in the schools. As we stood there, a lieutenant came by, obviously an Irish Catholic. He was very friendly, shaking hands, but he wanted to know who I was.

Later, he got on the phone with my superiors and lied, saying that I had been fighting and I had struck him, and they believed him. I was put on house arrest and told if I wanted to go and do something like that again, I had to get explicit permission.

It got worse. The final straw was when we held a vigil in front of St. Patrick's Cathedral with banners and leaflets against the war, and whew, there was trouble. This was in 1964. It was unheard of in the church. Cardinal Spellman literally gave me a one-way ticket to Latin America. Why did I stick with the church? I had this sense of myself, which I think my parents had too, which not only said to follow your conscience, but also, "I haven't done anything wrong."

Meanwhile, I got more of an education while I was down there. The poverty I saw was overwhelming. In Lima, Peru, there was a city of slums burrowed into a mountain. Over 150,000 people lived in this mountain. I'll never forget as I was visiting there, this fellow said to me, bitterly about American aid, "Millions for Vietnam, and this is what we get." That had a huge impact on me.

Meanwhile, back in New York, all hell was breaking loose after they sent me out. I had a lot of friends in the city, and I told them the truth because everybody in the church was saying, "Oh, no, he's just on a short trip."

The real story finally came out in the press, and a group of Catholics took an ad out in the *Times*, asking, "Why has Berrigan been exiled?"

As a result, I got a telegram while I was in Peru. It just said, "Come on home."

When I came back, I started right in again. I spoke everywhere about Vietnam. I always knew my toughest audience would be Catholics, and it was. I just quoted the gospel, saying Catholics are not allowed to kill, which didn't go over at all.

Then I was asked by Cornell to conduct the religious affairs of the university, do some teaching, be available for all sorts of counseling and to encourage nonviolent noncooperation with the war. This was the summer of '67. I plunged into all sorts of activity, and I really loved it. Our office was buzzing with activity day and night. The coffeehouse was holding constant teach-ins and concerts and poetry readings. I immediately started counseling students who were facing the draft and being sent to Vietnam. They had several sharp alternatives. They could choose exile to Canada or Europe, or jail. There was a lot of anguish over this. There were young people whose parents were with them and young people whose parents were cutting them off.

I never told anyone what to do. I listened a great deal and gave them a lot of time and tried to assess their strength or lack thereof and just encouraged them to be very thoughtful about a very serious decision. I said whatever they chose, I would do whatever I could for them, whether it was getting them to Canada, Sweden, or getting them to trial, all of which we did. We had a kind of underground railroad going to Canada. It wasn't particularly difficult. Once they got there, a lot of them went to Europe.

I wasn't there two months before Cornell's president called me in. He was really a third-rate bureaucrat. I don't know how he ever got that position in the middle of the turmoil. I borrowed a suit jacket and went to see him. He was very ill at ease. He said he was getting flack from the rich alumni about this priest and he wanted me to write a letter to the alumni that he would sign, reassuring them that I was not a danger to the law and order.

I said, "What?"

"You write the letter, and if I like it, I'll sign it."

I wouldn't do it, of course. I thought the whole thing was ridiculous. During the meeting, he showed me a book he had written. It was only semi-literate. In it, he talked proudly about how he had basically sold the university to the government. I couldn't believe it. Cornell also had big buildings that [had been] put up by the Navy and the Army. They had the first cyclotron put up there, and it was all for military research to test atom bombs and things.

That generated huge protests. The students had set up a twenty-four-hour vigil, seven days a week in the big quadrangle, and as the weather got cold they had a tent out there. It was later vandalized and pitched over. The fraternities were boiling mad at the religious resistance. In '69 they fired Molotov cocktails at the chapel and set it on fire. We petitioned the trustees that instead of restoring the chapel, it should remain as it was, as a testimony about the war and that the million dollars be given to the poor of Ithaca, but they didn't want a burned-out chapel for their image.

Cornell was very fierce. In 1970, a group of black students took over the student union with bandoliers and weapons. That was terrifying. They had hostages in there. We arranged with the SDS and other groups to have a ring of people around that building night and day because the fraternities were threatening to go in there with their own guns. I think it went on for a week until they felt they made their point and came out.

Then one day I got a call from Tom Hayden. He had gotten word that as a goodwill gesture on the Tet holiday, Hanoi would release some captured American pilots. Hayden chose Howard Zinn [a writer and historian, author of *A People's History of the United States*] and myself to go and bring them back.

Zinn and I decided we wouldn't approach the United States government for help. We would go on our own. I started out on a night bus to New York from Ithaca and ended up sitting next to an old soldier. He was a member of the honor guard at funerals of GIs. He was dealing with all these deaths and folding the flag and handing it to the parents. The poor guy was in tears talking about it. If I needed a reason for my trip, that was it.

Zinn and I ended up stuck in Laos for over a week, because the Tet uprising had started in the South, and there was no way of getting to the North. Finally we got a call, "Rush to the airport, we're going," so we went. It was a dangerous flight because we had to fly over the demilitarized zone between North and South Vietnam. Once we got to Hanoi, we were under bombardment by American pilots practically every night. The Vietnamese were outraged that while we were their getting their boys out, the Americans were continually bombing.

We spent a lot of time in bomb shelters. We also spent days touring the city and the countryside, meeting with officials, church people, and others. They had created all these museums to the victims, which were very hard to go through. The Americans had developed these antipersonnel weapons, which were designed to do special damage to people. The museums showed entrails of children in jars and things like that.

Finally, after a week we were notified that we could meet the fliers. When we got there, this large hall was dense with media from all over the world. The North Vietnamese told the fliers they would be released only if they stated to the world that they would never return to bomb Vietnam.

Then we went to the airport. As it turned out, we only had about an hour on the flight with them. What struck me was their innocence. At that altitude and at that speed, they had no idea what they were doing. They never saw the results of their bombs.

After leaving Hanoi, we made a stop in Vientiane, Laos, to transfer to a bigger plane, but the ambassador to Laos, William Sullivan, came on board. Sullivan was Nixon's hit man. He had been ambassador to Iran where he was a friend of the shah. He had been ambassador to the Philippines, where he was a pal of Marcos. Both cruel, iron-fisted leaders. Sullivan ran the secret bombing of Laos for Nixon. He was an Irish Catholic. He kept calling me Father.

He said he had orders from the president to take the fliers. The youngest pilot was the only one who put up an argument. He still had some integrity, that kid. He said, "We made a promise to go home with these men."

Sullivan said, "Well, the buck stops here. Let's go."

He just took them off the plane. That was a pure Nixon ploy. He didn't want those fliers talking to us for fifteen hours about the war, and he was worried about the propaganda value the antiwar movement would get from their release.

Catonsville started one day in October 1967. I had just been released from prison for the antiwar demonstration at the Pentagon. I was in the car on the way to a Catholic Worker house to get some soup. The radio was on, and the newscaster was saying that four people had invaded the draft board in Baltimore, Maryland, and poured their blood on the files as a protest against the war.

I knew right away it was Phil.

I thought I better phone my mother to let her know what was happening. She was always so self-possessed. She said, "Let me get this straight: your brother is in and you're out?" [*Laughs.*]

He was out on personal recognizance awaiting trial when he decided to do it again, but this time he wanted me to join him. The idea was we would go into the draft board in Catonsville, Maryland, and use napalm, such as had been used against civilians in Vietnam, to burn the draft files and prevent boys from being drafted. I had to think about it. I knew if I did it, that academic life, life in my religious order, life in my family, life in the church, nothing would ever be the same. I would be facing a great deal of scorn and condemnation, not to mention years in prison.

We talked about it. I told him to give me twenty-four hours. I wanted to really simmer down and be alone, and then I would call him yes or no. Cornell was still in the midst of this turmoil, and I said to myself, "I can't just be counseling other people to be heroic, I better do something myself."

I thought about this young man. One day I had gotten a call that an eighteen-year-old Syracuse boy was so despairing over the war that he had drenched himself in kerosene and set himself on fire. He would die from the burns, but was still alive when I went to see him in the hospital. When I was with him, I could still smell his burning flesh, that same smell I remembered from Vietnam.

After thinking about that young man, I phoned Phil and told him yes. We formed with seven others the so-called Catonsville Nine. Just to make sure everybody was involved, we made the napalm together, like witches over the brew. We found the recipe in a handbook of the Green Berets. They have the material to make napalm anywhere in the jungle, so they could throw it on people. It was a very simple matter to turn ordinary material into this terrible adhesive burning product.

Catonsville was a working-class town. It was a good target also because lots of its boys were endangered. The draft board was a tawdry little shack of a place and fairly accessible. You entered through a staircase at the back. It was ironic, because the first floor was a Knights of Columbus hall. They are a very high-minded Catholic group.

The draft files were open for scrutiny by anybody who wanted to look at them, so we knew where they were. We walked in wearing our collars, and we took the 1A files, the ones that signaled the most likely to be drafted. While we went through the files and were loading them in a wastebasket, one of the woman in our group held a woman who was running the place in her chair. The women, of course, got very agitated. Later on at the trial, one of them, a Mrs. Murphy, referred to the files as "belonging to my boys." "They took the files of my boys," which I thought was a peculiar kind devotion.

We didn't want to set a fire in the building, so we took the files outside to the parking lot and set them on fire there.

In all, we took about 380 files. I still run into men who are in their fifties now, who were in those files, and they thank me. It took so long to reconstruct the files, it really did throw a wrench into their system of killing. Of course after we did it, this started all over the country—people were burning and shredding files all over the place. General Hershey, who ran the draft, appeared with me on a television program once. He was so furious he could hardly talk. He said they couldn't keep the war going very well because of what we had started. I just grinned from ear to ear.

We had notified some very responsible media, and it was all photographed, so we were arrested fairly promptly. We were put in a room in the local post office until they could get the FBI in. We were sitting there, kind of light-headed and relieved that we had done it, when this FBI agent who had previously arrested Phil came in. He saw Phil and said, "Christ, it's you again. I'm leaving the church."

We knew we'd be convicted, because everybody down there was connected with the military. The whole thing was over in four days, but the judge let us tell our story, which is what we wanted to do. The jury was out maybe an hour before they convicted us. I was sentenced to three years. Phil got six because he had the prior blood pouring.

We appealed, and after our last appeal failed, we were told to turn ourselves in. We met again, and some of us decided to do the jail term and some not. I decided I would go underground. My decision was really about the war, which was worse than ever in the spring of '70. In my mind, I compared going underground to military induction.

To go underground, I just went out a first floor window at Cornell. There were friends waiting in a car. They took me to someone's house way out in the country. I hung around for a week because there was going to be this enormous rally against the war and in support of me. I thought it would be great to appear suddenly in this throng, say some words and be seized by the FBI, who I knew would be all over the place.

But things turned out differently. It was an incredible scene. There was a huge crowd. The FBI was trying to dress and act like hippies to blend in, but you could tell them a mile away, because they all had wires coming out of their serapes, or whatever it was they were wearing. They were a scream.

I came in on a motorcycle and waited in the wings of this auditorium, while the Bread and Puppets did a magnificent mime of the Last Supper. Then, at the end of it, a rabbi announced the return of Elijah, who in Jewish tradition makes a return at the seder dinner during Passover. At that point, I sat down at the table, and the whole place exploded.

Then I got up and made my speech. When the lights went down, someone whispered in my ear, "Wanna get out of here?"

I said, "Oh, OK."

"Follow me."

He took my hand and put me under a puppet, and the puppets went out. The lights went on, and this FBI guy went after us, but he couldn't tell which puppet I was under, and so they got me into a car and off we went to someone's house.

This time I stayed underground. I kept busy writing and reading. I made a few public appearances while I was underground. I preached at a church near Philadelphia on a Sunday morning. Someone simply had asked the pastor if he would like me to speak. He readily agreed. I also appeared on a national television talk show on NBC. We did a whole hour in a motel about the war. The interview infuriated J. Edgar Hoover. He threatened NBC, and the interview nearly didn't get shown. We saw FBI documents later where he would scrawl, "Get him!" "Why haven't you gotten him?"

While I was underground, my play, The Trial of the Catonsville Nine, premiered in Los Angeles. At the premiere, the FBI was in the audience. Before the play began, the producer played a recorded message from me. The agents all stood up, thinking I was somewhere in the auditorium, but I wasn't.

During this time, Phil was in Lewisberg prison, and there was an informer with him. Phil entrusted letters to him, and it turned out he was handing them over to the FBI. In one of those letters, Phil mentioned that I was living on Block Island.

One day shortly afterward, there was a terrific storm, and I was coming into the house. The other guy in the house saw someone in the bushes with binoculars. My friend said, "I think we're in trouble."

Then two cars came racing up the driveway. I wasn't going to let them break down the door. I just went to the door and stood there and let them take me off.

They couldn't fly me out because the storm was too bad, so we went out by Coast Guard boat. The sea was pretty rough. I hadn't had any breakfast, so I was fine, but both of the FBI guys were sick. That's why if you see the picture of them taking me in, they look so glum. They were green from whopping up their breakfast. [Laughs.]

I ended up serving two years. It was hard. I nearly died at one point when I had to have some dental work done. He was going to extract a wisdom tooth. He went into an artery that went to my heart, and my heart stopped.

I was never in very good health in jail, but I did a lot of work. I smuggled out a lot of writing. We had Quaker friends visit, and the rule was you could embrace someone coming in and leaving, so I would slip this stuff into their pocket while we were embracing. The authorities were always hyped about stuff being smuggled in. They didn't realize we were smuggling stuff out.

When I got out, I began teaching here in New York at Union Seminary. I taught for three years. After the war ended, I continued to take my leads from Phil, and we got very deep into the antinuclear movement. That resulted in the first Plowshares case in the spring of '80.

We had been to all these nuclear sites, air shows, airports, submarine bases to protest, but we had never gone to a factory where these things were being made. Then we found out that a certain nuclear weapon was being made at this secret plant in King of Prussia, Pennsylvania. We decided we would need a name for our action, and we took it from Isaiah II, "Thou shall beat your swords into plowshares." That's how the Plowshares movement was born.

It was ridiculously easy to get inside the plant. There was one rather aged guard who reached for the phone. It was a huge place, the size of several football fields, and we didn't know where these things were. We just knew they were there. Then we suddenly came upon a whole group of them ready for shipment. We also came across a lot of blueprints of weapons, and we threw our blood on them, made a circle around them and said the Lord's Prayer. Then the eight of us were arrested. We were tried in the winter of '81. By this time, the church was in our corner, so it was a very different atmosphere from Catonsville, but the judge was so awful that in the middle of the trial we decided to stand and turn our backs to him. We just didn't see any sense of continuing. He was denying any kind of expert testimony. He was just

Daniel Berrigan in a recent publicity photo for his latest volume of poetry.
(Courtesy of Daniel Berrigan)

racing to a conviction and treating us with enormous contempt, so we said, "Let's stop the show."

He was confounded because we weren't creating an uproar. We were just showing our contempt for his contempt. He threatened our attorney, Ramsay Clark, with jail, then cleared the court, and at that point it was all over.

We were convicted and served several months in jail. The case was appealed for years. The judge's behavior was so outrageous toward us he was removed from any jurisdiction. Eventually our sentence was reduced to time served.

In the '80s I began working with AIDS patients until I got mysteriously ill myself. There was a lot of to-do about whether I had gotten myself infected. I never really found out what it was, but I never could go among the ill again. That was after about eleven years of it.

When I look back on our work in the '60s, I see us along with a lot of other people as an ingredient in the antiwar pot. All of us made it politically impossible to continue the war and in the course of it made it morally impossible to launch more nuclear weapons. Daniel Ellsberg pointed out that Kissinger threatened to use nuclear weapons some twelve times at the Paris peace talks, and he never did it. It wasn't because he had any virtue.

Also, we helped remove two presidents from office. But from the point of view of nuclear production and nuclear research, things are worse all the time. Just last week, five nuns did a Plowshares in Colorado, so the work continues. It has to.

David Cline
The Vet

When a university professor named Staughton Lynd picketed the Pentagon in 1965, only one other person showed up in support. The first anti-Vietnam demonstration in New York City drew barely a couple of hundred people—including those who showed up to throw rocks and jeer at the protesters. It wasn't until 1967, after the war had been escalated dramatically, that a well-organized protest could be counted on to draw thousands of demonstrators.

The early protesters were mostly politically oriented students and veterans of the older left, many of them pacifists who had demonstrated against nuclear proliferation in the 1950s. Then, in 1967, a Vietnam veteran named Jan Barry formed Vietnam Veterans Against the War. The group provided a major boost to the antiwar movement. Nobody could accuse the members of this antiwar group of being slackers. They had fought in the jungles, and in some cases they had been severely wounded. Now they were saying it wasn't worth it. Like the rest of the country, they had heard the government's side of the story, but unlike most Americans they knew from firsthand experience what the truth was.

While President Lyndon Johnson insisted we were fighting for democracy, soldiers saw a corrupt South Vietnamese government interested only in preserving its own power. While the president insisted that the Vietnamese people welcomed the Americans with open arms, the veterans said the peasants they encountered seemed sympathetic to the enemy. And when napalm and saturation bombs seemed to be destroying the entire country, the soldiers asked, what was being saved?

Many of the dissenting vets had no background in political protest. They considered themselves patriots who had gone off to fight as their grandparents and parents had in previous wars. Because college students could get draft deferments, most of the soldiers came from working-class backgrounds and had only a high school education. Certainly, they couldn't be dismissed as communist rabble rousers.

David Cline was one of the Vietnam veterans who had turned against the war. How did he feel about serving in the armed forces and Vietnam when he was drafted? What was it like to be in battle? How did his combat experiences change his thinking? Did the war affect his political views? I also wanted to know if he had suffered from post-traumatic stress, an all-too-common problem for combat veterans. If so, how bad were the symptoms, and how did he cope with them?

I ring the buzzer in the foyer of a dilapidated Jersey City tenement. In a minute, I hear footsteps and the door is opened by a bearded, craggy-faced man in his mid-fifties. His thin, sandy hair is soaked to his scalp. In a gravelly voice, he apologizes for making me wait, saying he was in the shower when he heard the buzzer. He is wearing jeans but no shirt, revealing a very thin frame. As he turns to walk up the stairs, I notice the white scar that snakes up his back. It's the kind of scar that must have been a good deal angrier forty years ago.

Inside his apartment, the smell of tobacco hangs in the air. It's midwinter, and the apartment is cold. Only a small area of the kitchen is warmed by an open oven. On the kitchen table are stacks of CDs and political leaflets. Unframed posters decorate the walls. He disappears for a moment into another room to get dressed. When he returns, he lights a cigarette, and we start the interview.

There were three brothers in my family during the Civil War who fought in Antietam. One of them died. Another lost his hand. My grandfather was in World War I. My father was in World War II. I was in Vietnam. The general attitude in my family was you were supposed to serve.

My father was a machinist. He joined the Merchant Marine during World War II. He got torpedoed, but never sunk. It was a very risky job. They'd be running supplies through the North Atlantic on ships that were like steel tubs. They had the highest casualty rate of any branch of service, but they got screwed for many years not being recognized as veterans.

Right after they came home from the war, all these guys started getting their wives pregnant. I was born January 8, 1947, in Buffalo, New York. The area was pretty much German and Irish. When black people started moving in there was a white flight, so when I was in fourth grade my family moved to Eaton, which was a small town outside Buffalo.

As a young person, I remember hearing about the civil rights movement and having sympathy for it. I thought that the whole idea of segregation and prejudice was stupid. It denied people their humanity. But at that time, my father reflected a lot of the community. "We got here to get away from the blacks. They're no good. They're lazy." That type of shit.

The area I lived in there was hardly any black people, but it was next to the Seneca reservation, so I had contact with Indians. People had an attitude that Indians were no good. I had Indian girlfriends, and I used to catch flak for it. I had this one girlfriend who was adopted by these white people like their slave. They would have her babysit for the kids so they could go out. Her revenge was to invite me over to her house after she put the kids to sleep, and we would screw on the living room floor.

My brother Bruce got a guitar when he was sixteen, and I got a guitar after that. We would be down in the basement with our little record player, and we'd get these records and try to figure out what kind of music we would play. I remember we got The Freewheelin' Bob Dylan. We didn't like his voice. We said, "This guy sounds like he's dying. His underpants are too tight." But as we're listening to the record, my father opened the door and said, "What kind of shit are you listening to down there? Shut that shit off," so after that we were for Dylan, because it was like part of the generation gap. We might not have used them terms, but we saw there was a struggle between our thing and the adult thing.

Anyway, after listening to Dylan's voice a few times, it begins to grow on you. I also liked that his music was asking questions about war and things like that. It put thoughts in my mind.

My parents wanted me to go to college, but at that point I had lost interest in any academic stuff. I was going to clubs, chasing girls, drinking beer, and getting into fights. After I turned eighteen, I got drafted. People were already raising questions about the wisdom of America being involved in Vietnam. But my father and grandfather had been in the service, and I didn't think I was really capable of judging that. I just thought, "I'm gonna believe the government."

A lot of it was that I was not ready to say, "I'm in charge of my life. I better look into it." As a young person you are not too sure of yourself. I wish somebody told me to be a little more sure of myself then. I was just operating from, "I'm just a kid, what the fuck do I know?"

After we got sworn in, they put us on a train to Fort Dix for basic. When you get to Fort Dix, they give you these long green coats and hats, and you look like a DP, a displaced person from World War II. You feel like a fool. In the military, if you don't say a curse word every third word, something is wrong, and so people are cursing you out and intimidating you. You're a fucking new person, and they're humiliating you. You just try to get through it

They cut your hair. They issue you your fatigues. They assign you to a unit, and they proceed to verbally harass and abuse you and begin to train you. They're shaping you into being part of the machine. They try to brainwash you in a sense.

Meanwhile, you get stronger from it. You're doing exercises. You learn how to use weapons and march and how to function as a unit. They try to bring out in you the spirit of killing and the spirit of the animal that goes back to caveman days, to fight instead of flight.

After basic training, they sent me to Advanced Infantry Training. That was in Tiger Land, in Fort Polk, Louisiana. It was swamplands, and they said it was similar to what Vietnam was like. That's when I knew I was going to Nam. They were training me to be a grunt.

Fort Polk was a pisser. In front of the church, they had a sign that said it was a Christian duty to kill communists. At that time, the town was still segregated. Other guys said they saw signs excluding blacks and Puerto Ricans. Sometimes, blacks would walk into pool halls and start fights with the rednecks. I liked to talk to southern black guys a lot because I liked southern soul music. But among southern white and black guys there was still a big civil war fight thing going on.

They used to have different magazines in the PX. One of them was *Ramparts*, a radical magazine. It ran excerpts from Martin Luther King's speech on Vietnam, and that was when I began to question things. I still remember him saying, "A nation that continues year after year to spend more money on military defense than it does on programs for social uplift is a nation that is approaching spiritual death."

I talked about it with some of my friends, and we'd ask ourselves, "Are we doing the right thing?"

"Yeah, we're doing the right thing."

The official line was we're over here to help the people resist communist aggression. They would indoctrinate you with either that rap or that you're gonna kill communists. The "kill communists" thing didn't have no appeal to me. It did to some guys, who saw them as the godless enemy, but the idea of helping people made sense.

Before we shipped out, we were sent home for a while. My parents were worried, but I said, "Don't worry about it. I'm gonna be all right." I wasn't on their wavelength anymore. I was into my world, the military world, where as a young person you can smoke, you can drink. You're not a kid anymore.

From leave, we were sent to Fort Louis and then to Vietnam on a boat. There were a thousand or two thousand guys on the boat. We were on there for seventeen or eighteen days with nothing to do but watch old John Wayne movies or go up and watch the flying fish.

We landed in Da Nang in July 1967. Once you get off the ship, you get your duffel bag, get divided up, and then two days later they flew us out. There were 500 of us flying to Cu Chi. When we landed there, that's when I really knew we were in Vietnam. It's smelling that humid, sick smell, the very heavy air.

First they issue you your jungle gear and helmet and put you through these orientation courses. They tell you about booby traps and about black syph. If you get that, you can never go back to the States, because they can't cure it, "so wear condoms." You're listening to this shit while you're sitting in these bleachers, and this was when I started to think it was bullshit. They started talking about the gooks and how you can't trust them. You don't know who's with you and who's against you. They told us how they put broken glass in the soda bottles, so don't drink Coca-Cola, and the prostitutes put broken glass in their pussies. If you're captured, they'll cut your dick off and put it in your mouth. "Don't surrender."

In other words, the picture they painted for us was, "You're in a hostile world, don't trust anything. You've got to do a year, and that's what it's about. Don't worry about thinking about leaving, just make it through today. If you make it through today, then you worry about tomorrow when it comes."

I got assigned to a combat unit. The battalion I was assigned to was called the Manchus, fourth battalion, ninth infantry regiment of the 25th infantry division. As a combat infantryman, you would go out on field operations for maybe two weeks, three weeks, sometimes one week, sometimes four weeks. You'd be out in the bush. You're taking salt tablets, so your shirts get all white from the salt coming out of your body, and they get crusty. You can't bathe, so you get funky. We didn't wear underwear because you get jungle rot.

David Cline posing for his "cherry shot" in Vietnam, 1967. (Courtesy of David Cline)

Then you come in from the field and the first thing you do is take a shower. Then you'd put on clean fatigues and sneak out of the camp and go to the village and screw prostitutes. Then you'd come back into the base camp and get fucked up. I started smokin' pot in Nam. I don't think I ever got drunk once in Vietnam, but I got high. We only smoked pot when we came in from the field.

There was a lot of good stuff in the PXs—tape recorders, record players. I got a camera and a little fucking battery-operated record player, but I ended up getting only one record, Fred Neil. I had never heard of him before, but he's still my favorite. We'd get smoked up and listen to that stuff over and over again.

> I'm not the one to tell this world how to get along,
> I only know that peace will come when all hate is gone.
> I've been a-searching for the dolphins in the sea
> and sometimes I wonder do you ever think of me.
> —Fred Neil, "The Dolphins"

In the bush, foot soldiers like me were bait. The United States had all this firepower, artillery, jets. The Viet Cong and North Vietnamese had rifles, mortar and some artillery, no jets. We were out there to make contact with them so they would attack us, and then they would bring all this firepower and try to decimate them.

Sometimes, we'd be working in an area called the Hobo Woods. There area was full of a lot of jungle. In the jungle, leeches would be fallin' on you, and you'd have these big fucking red ants fall down your shirt. Oh, it was really fucking miserable, also because the jungle was really humid. I'd have my gear and my helmet on, and the sun is beating down on you. One of the things I remember most about Vietnam is constantly having a headache.

I never saw anything like My Lai. But it was standard knowledge that when they used to interrogate prisoners, they would take two or three of them up in a helicopter and they'd throw the first guy out before they started asking them questions. Then they ask the second guy, if he won't talk they throw him out, and then they ask the third guy. I saw people pushing people around, but it wasn't like people indiscriminately killing people. A lot of guys weren't really into that. They used to have a program called the Chu Hoy program. Chu hoy means open arms, and they would drop these propaganda leaflets all over in Vietnamese, encouraging them to defect. So every now and then people would surrender, and sometimes guys would say they shot chu hoys, but I didn't see anybody ever shoot a chu hoy.

In the field, sometimes they would fly us out one meal a day. The meal was good, but lining up for chow wasn't always a good deal, because you'd have half the guys out on the perimeter and half the guys lined up, and there was a good chance you'd get mortared when you lined up. The Viet Cong knew a target of opportunity when they saw one.

Mostly we ate C rations, which came in a cardboard box. Your main dish would be in a can, whether it would be ham and lima beans, chipped beef, or spaghetti. There were five or six different things. Then you'd have some crackers, and some kind of dessert or fruit, a little packet of toilet paper, a box of four cigarettes, salt and pepper, instant coffee, instant creamer. You'd drink the coffee from the cup on your canteen. The fruit cocktail, the peaches, or the pound cake were considered luxuries. The worst were the ham and lima beans. They used to call them ham and motherfuckers. Them are nasty to the point that people wouldn't even eat them.

In the evening, we stay out in the bush. They'd just tell us, "OK, we're gonna stay here for the night. Dig foxholes."

We'd sleep three to a hole. We'd usually dig 'em three or four feet deep if we could. It depended on the time, the hardness of the ground, and how long you were gonna stay. They were around six feet by four feet, big enough for two guys to lay down and one guy to stand up and watch. You'd put sticks over the top, fill sandbags, and put the sandbags over the sticks to protect you from mortar rounds. You'd build up the front so you can shoot out. Then we'd take claymore mines and place them out in front of us. You'd set those in the ground twenty-five to fifty feet out, and you'd attach a detonator that you can squeeze, so if someone was attacking you you could detonate 'em. Sometimes you'd put out trip flares, or if we were gonna be there a while, they'd fly out concertina wire and we'd string that around, and we'd put tin cans on the wires so if someone was sneakin' through it would rattle.

I would be on guard duty the first hour, and you and the other guy would sleep. Then, after one hour, I'd wake him up, and I'd go to sleep for two hours, so you'd sleep two hours and be awake one hour, which makes you be a crabby motherfucker, because you're not getting no good sleep.

You're pretty much scared shitless all the time you're out there, but eventually you just live with it. I remember the first time I got shot I ate dirt. I didn't want to get up. Then everyone else started getting up, so I did. You can't just stay there. To survive you've got to move. You just have to learn to live with the fear. Some people react to it by overcompensating. They're so afraid they become totally wild. Some people just emotionally collapse.

When you were on movement, there was always a guy shooting at you, just an individual sniper. We also hit a lot of booby traps. It was always this unexpected thing. Boom, something happens.

At night they'd mortar you, and during the day they'd shoot at you. Mortars are pretty scary because you hear the tubes drop. They go "phoop" when they fire them, and you don't know where they are going to hit. When it comes in, you stay down, cover your head, and pray. That's all you can do. You don't want to get up and run because then you are more susceptible to shrapnel.

On the sweeps, they would always want me to carry the machine gun, because I was a little taller. If you were the little guy they would make you the tunnel rat. I did refuse to carry the machine gun. If you opened up with a machine gun, they would shoot everything at you, so your casualty chances on a machine gun was worse.

I never walked point [in front]. The point man was also the one who would usually catch a wire [which would explode a mine], because he was the first man. Sometimes, they would be at eye level or at foot level. One time there was this sergeant who thought he was like John Wayne. He wore sunglasses in the field and all that shit. He used to be [a] real gung-ho motherfucker. We told him, "Man, you have to get rid of them sunglasses because you can't see them wires."

One time he walked into a booby trap with them aviator glasses around his ears. It blew his whole fucking face off. The glasses were hanging off of his ears, but his whole jaw was missing. He died. He was so fucking cool, you know?

At first, it freaked me out seeing dead bodies. The first ones I saw were a couple of Viet Cong, and I remember how mangled they were, and after a while they smell nasty.

You'd see friends of yours get killed. There was a guy named Grant, who was from over here in Jersey. He was this goofy guy. He was missing his front teeth. We would have these discussions, and he would say, "I don't care if I die."

Then he went home on leave, he met this girl and fell in love and got engaged, and his whole attitude changed. He wanted to live. He got killed two months after we got there. He walked right up on a Viet Cong, and the guy shot him, like, eight times. When he died, it really got to me.

You have to numb your emotions so that it don't mean nothing. Sin loi, which means sorry about that in Vietnamese. You feel bad about it, but you couldn't afford to let yourself mourn or reflect. You just had to forget all that shit. I've had problems all my life since I came home with that, because when you learn to suppress or numb your emotions, when you come back here and if you have a family, you can't afford to do that. Your wife and your children want you to be there. If you shut it all out, that's one form of what they call post-traumatic stress.

I was wounded three times in Vietnam. I got three Purple Hearts. The first time was on August 30, 1967, less than a month after I got there. That was the first big battle I was in—the Battle of the Horseshoe. It was called that because the Saigon River went around in a horseshoe shape. The Viet Cong built concrete bunkers all along the edge of the river. We landed in the middle of them, and they shot the shit out of us. I was on the third wave coming in on the landing, and when we came in you could see the tracer bullets flying through the gunship as we were coming in.

In the middle of that horseshoe was all rice paddies, which are flooded with water. Around the edges are the dikes, where the farmer can walk around. We were running along the dikes and getting fired at from all sides. This little kid from Chicago slipped over the dike into the paddy. He was loaded down with his bandoliers and machine gun bullets, and he started sinking. He started crying. I turned around and got on my knees on the edge to pull him out, and I took a round in the upper back. It went through a flak jacket, hit my rib, and exited my lower right back. My lung collapsed. I fell into the rice paddy and went into shock.

Somebody later told me after the fight broke up they were able to medevac me out. I was reported dead at that time. My left lung filled up with blood, and they had to put a tube in it.

I was hospitalized for forty-five days from that wound. They had new medical techniques where wounds healed faster. They reinflated my lungs, and instead of sewing the wounds shut on top, they would sew the inside and leave the top open, so it would heal up. Later on, they would sew the top. Forty-five days after I was reported dead, I was released from the hospital.

They kept me in the base camp pulling preliminary duty for two weeks. Then they sent me back into the field. So two months after I received that wound, I was back in combat.

I was always scared, but I never thought I would refuse to fight. This kid that was crying when I got shot, he would freak out every time he got into some kind of situation. I saw him one time take his weapon and smash it against a tree. They refused to take him out of the field. They said, "Oh, that's an act. We're gonna make a man out of this kid." We thought they should get rid of him because he might cost you your life. I don't know if the kid lived or died, but if he's still alive, he is emotionally totally destroyed today.

When I went back in the field, they moved us to Tay Ninh. We did a lot of night ambushes over there. They're scary, because they send you out with ten to fifteen guys. We used to wear them soft bush hats and you'd have a mosquito net because the bugs are eating you up. You can't smoke. You have to stay awake because you're laying there behind some tree line waiting for someone to come along. You set up a position along a site where you think they might come. If someone does, you shoot 'em. If no one comes, they make you move the ambush. You're up all night, and you have to rest for part of the day. You're filthy. You're walking at night, so you're scared and just trying to make it through each minute.

The second time I was wounded was on December 11. I think we were in Cambodia, but I can't confirm that. We were in an area that the ground was real hard. We couldn't dig the holes very deep. All in the jungle they were yelling, "Fuck you, you die tonight, GI." They weren't more than thirty yards away. We knew we were gonna get some shit.

They were trying to get us to shoot at 'em, because when you shoot back at 'em, they can tell where you are. They would mortar you, wait a few minutes to get you to come out of the hole, and then they would mortar you again. There was this new lieutenant in the field who didn't know that. He wanted to go check the positions, so him and this sergeant and the radio man and another guy got out of their hole and we got mortared. I got hit in the shoulder. The sergeant was killed; the lieutenant's shoulder was slit with shrapnel. He lived. Davis, the sergeant, was a good man. He was a black guy from Georgia. He was thirty-two, an old guy who loved soul music and was always trying to get us to sing.

After it happened, we ran to the center of the perimeter to call the medevac, and they started mortaring us again, so we had to dive behind these anthills. They had these big black ants, big suckers, and they were biting us as the mortars were coming in. I was laying there debating whether to run from the anthill because the mortars were killing me and the ants were bitin' me.

Finally they stopped. I had just one little piece of shrapnel in my shoulder, and I told 'em, "I ain't goin' in [to the base for treatment]. We're gonna be hit tonight, and I wanna stay around." I was mad. I wanted to just get those motherfuckers. But they ordered me on the helicopter, and I went in. They pulled the shrapnel out of my shoulder and discharged me in the morning.

Eight days later, I was at Bo Tuk. That was the last battle I was in. It was an old French fort. There was live American ordnance laying all over. When we saw that, we knew we were in deep shit, because that meant they had enough of their own shit and didn't need ours. Usually they would mortar you at night, but when we started digging holes that day, they started mortaring us during the day.

At one point, I dove over this tree that was falling down, and I landed right next to a butterfly bomb, a little yellow bomb with a flat head and fins on it. They are an antipersonnel weapon. I was shitting in my pants because I thought, here is this mortar coming at me, and it's gonna detonate this fucker. Luckily, they stopped about twenty feet away.

That night I was in a foxhole with two black guys, Jamison and Walker. I had just gotten a letter from home. My father said these black kids had broken into my aunt's house and robbed them and beat them up. My father didn't write about the "fucking nigger animals," but it was saying that, and he got that idea planted in my head.

At two in the morning, we got hit with a human-wave attack of North Vietnamese soldiers. They just came charging at us. They overran the position next to ours. We see this figure coming from the next position over, and we don't know if it's one of our guys or one of them. It's one of them. He comes up and sticks his rifle in the hole. I see the front side of an AK-47. He shoots me through the knee. Before I black out, I aim my rifle straight up at him and shoot him through the chest.

I blacked out and came to a minute or two later. The North Vietnamese are running up on holes and shooting people and setting the artillery on fire. My knee was shattered and my gun was jammed. So Jamison and Walker said, "Let's get the hell out of here."

Remember, I got this idea from my father, "You can't trust the blacks," and I'm saying, "Don't leave me here, guys." And they said, "We're not leaving you here."

Jamison threw me on his back, while Walker laid down fire, and they carried me into another hole and left me there. I had to lay there eating Darvons all night, because they couldn't bring a helicopter in to get me out. It was a battle.

I wouldn't be alive if it wasn't for them two guys. In the morning, they pulled me out of the hole and sent me to the hospital. They also carried me over to the guy I had shot. He was sitting up against a tree stump, and he had a gun across his lap, and he had a couple of bullet holes in his chest, and he was dead.

I looked at this guy. He was about my age, eighteen, twenty, twenty-two. I thought, he's just a young guy. I wondered if he had a girlfriend and if his mother was going to find out how he died. What I was doing was seeing him as a person, not as a gook. "Gook" is a term to dehumanize someone. When you kill a gook, you're not killing a human, you're killing something else.

Now my mind was refusing to dehumanize that person. And I was thinking, "What's the fucking point of all this?"

Then I got sent back to the hospital at Cu Chi. Eventually, I was medevacked out to Japan and then back to the United States. If your wound was going to take longer to heal than your tour of duty, they sent you out, and the bullet had busted my whole joint up.

I never got a chance to thank Jamison and Walker. I'm still searching for them on the Internet.

In the hospital library, I found a book called The New Legions by Donald Duncan. Duncan had been a Green Beret, and then became antiwar. That book was what made me become politically conscious. Basically what he said was, "We're fighting on the wrong side," and a lot of what he said made sense to me.

I came to the conclusion that what the people were being told was not what we were doing. We were supposedly helping the people, but the people who liked us were the crooks and the corrupt landowners that were running the government, so what we were doing was fighting against the people.

The majority of the people were living in misery and poverty and just wanted to live. Some of them were fighting to get the foreigners out of their country, and they were fighting the French and the Japanese before us. We blow up the firecrackers every Fourth of July to remember how we wanted to get the British out, yet we wanted to fight them when they are trying to get their independence. You can say what you want about communism and all that shit, but you don't fight for no fucking theory, you fight for your country.

David Cline (rear) at a rally in support of his brother (second from right) Bruce's refusal to enter the draft, Buffalo, 1969. (Courtesy of David Cline)

The war went on from '65 to '73. I also thought, I just went through this shit, and now they're trying to draft the next bunch. Every year another graduating class got sent off to fight. If you were in fucking fourth grade in '65, you had a chance of going to Nam. You're talking about everyone you knew and their younger brothers, so my brother is gonna go, and my buddies are gonna go. I felt that instead of trying to forget it, I had a responsibility to try and tell people what it was about and try and stop the war.

While I was home on convalescent leave, my brother got his draft notice. He decided to hook up with this draft resistance group and take a stand against the war. He and another fellow took sanctuary in a Unitarian church. He was eventually convicted of draft resistance. He got a three-year sentence, working in a hospital in Rochester.

My father was really opposed to what my brother did. But he ended up in a lot of fights with the so-called patriots in my hometown who badmouthed my brother, and he came around to recognize what we did.

But breaking with tradition was not easy. The Vietnam War caused a lot of the conditions that were accepted generation after generation to become no longer what they were in the past. The veteran of the last war has historically been used to convince young people to fight in the next war. Well, Vietnam began to change that when the veterans came home and said, "Whoa, they're lyin' to you people."

That played a major role in getting America to change its opinion against the war. It's easy to dismiss college students or intellectuals. For middle America, if the blacks or the hippies or the Chicanos don't like it, who cares, but when the guy came home was like your own son and daughter, it had an impact.

I was still in the Army, so I went back to Fort Hood, where I hooked up with these people that had a project called GI coffeehouses. These were some old civil rights activists that set up these coffeehouses at a few bases. The purpose was to encourage the GIs to express their minds. They could chill out and listen to records or talk politics. It was really a free space in a military atmosphere. They had underground papers and different literature and stuff there. The coffeehouse staff lived on a commune.

This guy named Bruce Peterson, who we used to call the Gypsy, started an underground paper at Fort Hood called The Fatigue Press. We would write articles against the war and for servicemen's rights. In the military, you are under the Universal Code of Military Justice, you're not under the Constitution. Even though you are defending your country, you don't have the rights of a citizen. They arrested him in his car, saying they found a few seeds of marijuana inside. He went to prison for five years just for that.

We'd clandestinely distribute the papers on base. In the military you could have any literature you wanted—one copy. If you had more than one copy, you could be charged with intent to distribute and be court-martialed, so what we would do was go on the base at night and distribute them in the barracks and around different areas.

After I got discharged, I hung out and organized and smoked a lot of pot. I stayed in Texas at the coffeehouse until the end of '71, beginning '72. I was burned out from living there. It was rough organizing. You're under a lot of surveillance from the police. One time we had a shoot-out with the Klan while we were going to Houston on a convoy. We used to fight with the cowboys. In those days, if you had long hair, they all used to think you were "a goddamned hippie."

We had a lot of musicians come to our club. Phil Ochs, Barbara Dane, and Pete Seeger came down. We asked Johnny Winter to come, but he said, "Can't help you, it won't help my career."

Jane Fonda came through once. I spoke one time with her. I thought she was an idiot for posing for that picture with the anti-aircraft weapon, but I think a lot of the things said about her weren't true. There's one story that she spoke to the prisoners, and they passed her little notes, and she went up to the camp commander and gave them to him. That was totally fabricated. She was an easy target because she was a woman. I believe a lot of it has to do with sexism.

We had three or four bedrooms at our commune, and then we had a whole stack of mattresses, and on weekends we used to allow GIs to sleep on the floor. She stayed there one night, so that night we had fifteen guys sleeping on mattresses in the room next to hers, and she comes out the next morning in this gauze nightgown. You could see her naked right through the thing. She knew what she was doing. Those fifteen GIs liked her.

After Carter came in, he gave amnesty to draft resisters, but it didn't include veteran soldiers who got bad discharges. A lot of guys got less-than-desirable discharges. Sometimes they were drug related. Sometimes you refused to play the game no more. A lot of black guys got 'em. It came from the unrest and the turmoil. We tried to get universal discharges for all veterans, but we were unsuccessful.

This is not against draft resisters, but some people could buy their way out of the military. The lower classes were stuck, yet they were the ones who got fucked in the deal. It was almost as if Carter was protecting his friends' kids, but fuck the other people.

After '72, I moved up here with the woman I was with. We had a daughter, Ellen. Then we got divorced. I was working at the Postal Service. I became involved with the union there. In '78, there was a work stoppage, and they fired 200 people. I was identified as one of the leaders, so I was fired.

I was also involved with the Vietnam Veterans Against the War. One time we seized the Statue of Liberty to protest veterans' benefits cuts. I was the ground coordinator at Battery Park. We seized it twice. The other time was against the bombings.

We started a program of talking to high school kids about the war and military service. By the early '80s we started working against the war in El Salvador and Nicaragua, because we saw that as not really learning from the Vietnam experience. We sent trucks down to Nicaragua loaded with wheelchairs.

We also began to promote reconciliation between America and Vietnam.

We not only wanted to promote reconciliation, but we also wanted to investigate issues that were still outstanding from the war. We identified those as Agent Orange, Amerasian kids, and the MIA/POW issue.

I went back in 1988. That was pretty heavy. I went back to Tai Nin and Cu Chi. Right where we used to pull ambushes they had a big monument to the war. We burned incense there and met with some former Viet Cong from that area. Even though I'm not a warmonger, I was looking at these guys and saying, "These were the motherfuckers that were trying to kill us, and we were trying to kill them." But we ate lunch together, and in the end it was a liberating experience because you could put that feeling behind you. Here's these guys in NVA uniforms and shit. But they were actually very friendly. I think the Viet Cong probably had similar feelings to ours, checking us out.

In 1980, I started working for the Port Authority, first as a toll collector and then in field-side operations at all the airports. Then in 1985 or '86, I got elected to union office. I moved up to vice-president of the local, working full time representing employees in disciplinary hearings.

I also ran into a lot of problems. I suffered from post-traumatic stress, and I had a problem dealing with people, and I used to drink and get high. But when Reagan came in and declared a war on drugs, I couldn't afford to buy pot no more, and it wasn't too long that I got involved with cocaine on weekends.

I also drank to deal with bad feelings and being unable to cope with them. Even though I was dealing with it on a political basis, there was a whole part of it on an emotional level that I wasn't dealing with. The drinking started with war problems, but if you drink long enough, you drink because you have problems with drinking.

Eventually the cocaine and the alcohol caused me to become really fucked up, especially in the early '90s. It came to the point that I thought the end was coming. I thought, I stayed alive all through Vietnam and I'm gonna die like this in the streets of America. I hit bottom, and I was disgusted, so I started going to meetings. I didn't like them at first. I'm not a religious person. One of the things I lost in Vietnam was spiritual beliefs. I used to pray to God to protect me from being shot, and I kept getting shot. I came to the point where I thought, that's all bullshit. What matters is you and you, the guys on my left and right.

I'd go to meetings for a couple of weeks, and then this compulsion to drink would just take over. Then once I'd get drunk I'd start with the drugs. Then my money would be gone, and I'd get pissed off again.

The last time I got drunk was March 7 to 9, '97. I went back to a meeting on March 10. The following week I walked by a liquor store, and I could hear the bottles calling my name. They knew me personally. "Dave, come here." I didn't know what to do. I just started chanting to myself, "Don't drink, don't drink," and I started walking to that cadence, and I walked home, and I made it.

After that, that compulsion disappeared. Now I'm involved with Alcoholics Anonymous and things like that. That's been good for me. Today I don't use. Cigarettes is the one habit I can't get rid of.

Recently, I been working on a lot of stuff. In 1996–97 I started the Jersey City Vietnam Veteran Memorial Committee. In this city, sixty-one guys were killed in the war. They had a memorial, but nobody really knew it was there, so we started a campaign to renovate and rededicate it. Last year we had a second memorial commemoration. We located a lot of families of the dead guys.

We put out a newsletter, and we have a pretty good program. It's not prowar or antiwar, it's about remembering the dead. It's really helped build a community around the people in this area, among veterans, family members, and other folks. I've also been working on the homeless problem. About a third of all homeless are veterans, and we've been trying to get some federal money to open up some transitional housing in this area.

I still have metal from the bullet lodged around my spine. I had pieces of the bullet coming out of my back for about ten years. I would get little black spots on my back, and they turned out to be tiny little pieces of metal that would come up to the surface. I'm 60 percent disabled from gunshot wounds. I also get Social Security because in the early '90s I found out I was HIV positive and Hepatitis C positive. I take medication, and the virus is undetectable.

Still, the medicine lowers my energy levels, so it's hard to work full time. When I stopped drinking, I almost changed my mind because I started feeling the pain from these wounds. I have muscles missing from my lower back. One leg is shorter than the other, so my whole body is twisted.

I used to get a lot of bad dreams. I would relive that scene where we were overrun. I would wake up all sweaty and get freaked out. But I didn't want to deal with too much emotion. In war, that's a survival mechanism. In normal life it doesn't work. I had problems with my marriages because of that.

I talk in schools to kids. I like to let them know the misery we went through. Kids get inoculated with a lot of this Rambo and Chuck Norris bullshit. Video games today emphasize destruction. I don't like any of that stuff, even action movies, because it reduces killing people to just an act.

David Cline in 2002, awarded for his efforts to halt the U.S. military's use of Vieques for bombing exercises. (Courtesy of David Cline)

People say, "It's just a fantasy," but it's a shitty fantasy, so I try to talk about what the reality was like, and I talk about some of the politics. When they ask what this has to do with them, I say, "Well, if we go into something like this again, it's not going to be me they're after."

I tell 'em they have to stand for what's right, and part of that is to find out what they are being asked to do, and to do that they have to know what's going on. Kids don't like history. Now I read a lot of history. You'd be surprised how many veterans want to learn history—not war stories, but what happened, and what really went down.

I tell them they are the ones who have to walk in their shoes, that other people may try to tell them what to do with their lives, including Uncle Sam, and it may not be the right thing. That's what Vietnam showed us: don't trust the government. That don't mean you walk around like some militiaman, hating the world, but if you don't know what you're being asked to do it could end up causing you a lot of pain, just like it did for me.

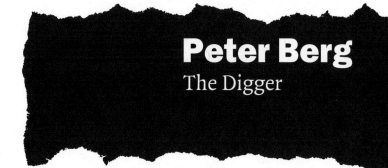

Peter Berg
The Digger

In 1858, a San Francisco merchant named Joshua Abraham Norton declared himself emperor of the United States. For the next twenty-one years, wearing a military uniform and plumed hat and carrying a sword, he was a common sight greeting his loyal subjects on the city's streets. When he died in 1889, some 30,000 people attended his funeral.

The acceptance that Norton found in San Francisco says a lot about the city's long tradition of tolerating—even encouraging—eccentricity and free thinking. When the hippies took over Haight-Ashbury and the neighborhood became the seedbed of the 1960s counterculture, they were just continuing a San Francisco tradition, like Rice-A-Roni.

The term *hippies* stems from the word *hipsters*, whose ultracool ways were chronicled by the beat writers in the 1950s. The anti-authoritarian beats were pretty cool themselves, and a whole population of nonconformists coalesced around them in San Francisco's North Beach section.

As a literary movement, the beats had their coming-out party in October 1955 with a group poetry reading at a converted auto repair shop called the Six Gallery. That night, Allen Ginsberg, a twenty-nine-year-old New Yorker who had never read publicly before, sent the crowd into a frenzy with a breathless reading of his partially completed epic poem, "Howl."

Ginsberg, along with Gary Snyder, another poet who read that night, provided a direct line from the beats to the hippies when they appeared onstage at the hippies' coming-out party, the Human Be-In, in Golden Gate Park in 1967. Snyder's eloquent writing about the earth's beauty helped give rise to the environmental movement, which remains one of the 1960s' most important legacies.

Another link between the beats and the hippies was Ken Kesey, the author of the classic antiestablishment novel *One Flew Over the Cuckoo's Nest*. In the '60s, Kesey and a group of people he named the Merry Pranksters toured the country in a psychedelic bus they called *Further*. The Merry Pranksters were not unlike the beats, except they preferred LSD to alcohol and the Grateful Dead to bebop. Completing the circle was their mad driver, Neal Cassady, a legendary country-crossing nomad who, as the fictional Dean Moriarty, was the central figure in Jack Kerouac's *On the Road*.

But even the way-out activities of the beats paled in comparison to the revolutionary antics of the Diggers, who combined street theater and anarchistic politics with daring, humor, and mischief. The Diggers saw themselves as "life actors," and their stage was the Haight. Their panache made them the dashing pirates of the counterculture. Their thinking was always original; their goal, to expose the hypocrisy of a bankrupt society that was concerned more with money than the freedom and welfare of its people.

Peter Berg was a Floridian who came of age at the time of James Dean and juvenile delinquents and went on to become one of the Diggers' most visible and creative members. I wondered what led him down that path. I also wanted to hear about the legendary Digger creations, such as the Free Store, where everything was free. In his post-Digger years, Berg became an environmental activist, which remains his life's work to this day. How did he use his Digger ideas to raise concerns about the environment?

The October leaves seem to be aflame on this gorgeous October day as I drive through Amherst, Massachusetts, on my way to meet Peter at the Sirius community, an ecovillage outside town. In this idyllic setting, the Sirius residents eat organic foods, practice recycling, and generally strive to live a less polluting lifestyle, a cause that Peter promotes around the world.

When I pull up to the community center, he is waiting at the front door and comes out to greet me. His gray hair is pulled back to a short ponytail. He makes it clear he is doing this interview only because I have agreed to be his chauffeur. He says he doesn't enjoy looking back. Indeed, he speaks passionately and convincingly for the work of his Planet Drum organization, which is leading a vital ecological movement around the world. His life as a San Francisco Digger may be in the distant past, but his maverick thinking and his willingness to challenge established power has not diminished with age.

My father was an alcoholic who kept getting fired from job after job, allegedly for drinking, but I don't think that was the only reason. He was sort of a barroom socialist. He was a dropout from medical school who liked to hang out with working-class people. He had a photographic memory, and I'm told he could regale people by reeling off whole pages of H.G. Wells's *Outline of History*. For a while he collected rents. He sold hot dogs. Before he died, he had finally gotten a job that was near his capability—as a lens grinder. Sometime before I was six, he tried to kill our family—literally—by pumping carbon monoxide from the car's exhaust pipe through the window. One of my brothers hit him over the head with a liquor bottle to stop him.

After he tried to kill us, my mother bided her time until she could build up the train fare, which she did with the help of the neighborhood butcher. Then she took my sister and me down to Florida to get a divorce. Florida was one of only two states in the '40s where you could get a divorce within ninety days. Also, my mother had no means of support, and my older brother, a fighter pilot and a veteran of the Pacific war, was stationed down there.

We lived with my brother and his wife in a town named Interlachen, just below the Georgia border. Florida crackers, very rural. I wanted to relate to the kids, but we never got past our accents and our strangeness. I remember being called something like "nigger-loving Jew Yankee motherfucker." I had to ask my mother what they meant. My family wasn't Jewish. I didn't know what a Yankee was. Motherfucker was really remote, way-out-there language. And the only black people that we saw were a couple of kids that we tried to be friendly with. I would love to imagine us walking to school along that two-lane blacktop, smilingly accompanying the Negroes, as they were called at that time, but that wasn't what happened. We encountered people a couple of times and said hello, and they responded with terror.

I don't remember all of this as a bad time. I learned to fish. I spent weeks in the water. I was told I was the man of the family before I became an adolescent. I got exposed to my mother's side of things, much more so than most boys. I think that made me sympathize with the underdog in general.

I was not a very big person. I had asthma, and it was difficult being the man in the family and such a twerp that anybody in the school could knock me over, and in that school they did knock me over. But it also made me feel hip, that I knew things that the supersociety didn't talk about; that I knew the inside of it: the woman's point of view or—in the South, certainly—the northerner's point of view.

Race was an overwhelming issue. In the early days of the civil rights movement, there was a lot of white people talking to each other about "uppity niggers." For me, it was either accept what they were saying as true or look at it skeptically. I was a skeptic. I wasn't an outspoken ally, but I wasn't an enemy either. Here's how it worked down South. If you were white, and you were talking to another white person who was interested in reinforcing racial separation, before they make a racial statement or say something, or before they tell a racial joke, there will be a slight pause. It goes something like this: "There was this big fat nigger woman once . . ." Pause. If you say something then, other than, "Oh yeah?" the whole thing goes in a different direction. If you say, "Oh yeah?" then you get to hear how she got her nipple caught in a mechanical clothes dryer or hear about some other sexual violence or made-up unintelligent behavior.

In a situation like that, I've not responded, in which case the story wasn't told. I've also been asked why I didn't want to hear the story or whether I was "too good a Christian" to hear the story.

There was also "You disapprove of this kind of joke? You think you're better than I am?" "Are you a nigger lover?" "Don't you know how close we are to Armageddon?" Or "Now I know who you are. You're not one of us."

So you see, that little pause could get you killed.

We stayed in Interlachen for two or three years. Then we moved to southern Florida when I was nine or ten. In south Florida, I was still an outsider. I expected trouble and it always came. Sometimes I fought back and succeeded. Once when a kid hit me, I waited until he walked away. Then I pulled his hair from behind, banged his head on the sidewalk and kept banging it. When I stopped, I reached over for a handful of sand and filled his mouth with it.

I remember thinking to myself, this is what it feels like to not take this shit anymore. That kid had hassled me all the time, but he never got near me again.

Around that time, I started listening to "race music" in defiance of what we called "hillbilly music" or country and western music. I remember when I first heard "Sixty-Minute Man" over the radio, my friends and I looked at each other and said, "Whoa, they're playing that on the radio?" This was generation-making stuff. White kids listening to black music, wow! And then Elvis Presley came across the radio. Before I went to college, Elvis was the most impressive popular culture phenomenon that I remember. I brought a girl to an Elvis Presley concert in my car. I didn't go to the concert, because it was a girl's thing, a hysterical teenage girl's thing to do. And when I picked her up, she got in the car and told me, "I peed in my pants." It was outrageous to hear a girl say that.

It was something like the way my mother described girls feeling about Frank Sinatra when they heard him, but it was also different. This was when girls were wearing short shorts and boys were wearing white T-shirts with a pack of cigarettes rolled up in the sleeves. We were the '50s people that James Dean tried to capture. We were the Levis, wide leather belt, white T-shirt, slicked-back hair, gang-fighting type.

I did get involved with a local gang. I was called "Professor." I was the little guy with the glasses. The strategist was the meanest, toughest guy in the gang, a rangy, scrawny, boney-knuckled, hard-core, father-beat-the-living-shit-out-of-him, tough kid. We were called juvenile delinquents. Mostly we shoplifted or stole hubcaps off cars, but at the time I was also a member of the Latin Club. I was on the radio three times as a Quiz Kid. I was a prize student. Teachers loved having me in their classes. I got into a scholarship dorm at the University of Florida. I was only sixteen at the time.

It was another place where I didn't fit in, though, and I got voted out after the middle part of my second year. After that I began living off campus. That's where I found all the students who didn't fit in. Being with that group was the awakening of my life. We were a dozen people of a student population of over 10,000. We were the members of the French Club and the French Film Club. Imagine a French Film Club at the University of Florida in the middle of the '50s!

A Korean War veteran named Marvin Longton was the center of our group. He founded the Florida Review literary journal, read British novels, and was a jazz fanatic. He read Auden and got the first copy of Allen Ginsberg's "Howl." I owe so many interests to him. He turned me on to Norman Mailer and John Clellon Holmes and Italian writers.

The others in our group included a guy who was an English-Egyptian expatriate. His father had been in the diplomatic service, but he was a total outcast at the University of Florida. There was a girl whose name was Carol Bizarre, who was of mixed racial background at this all-white university. There was a Hungarian-American who was early into the development of information systems; a girl from Texas named Denzel, who smoked cigarettes out of a cigarette holder and wore a beret; an artist who had grown up in an orphanage and who was an excellent draftsperson and metals artist. We saw ourselves as being different from the student body, but to them we were total geek material.

We were hipsters, but we weren't really political activists, except after the first civil rights act was passed in 1957. The question then came up whether the University of Florida would be integrated. We put up signs which said, "Integrate in '58." For just that, people were disciplined and questioned, and some were suspended.

Mostly I read novels and poetry. I just read through authors straight— Hemingway, Mailer, Remarque, Camus. Because I had read Steinbeck, I wanted to see the great American phenomena, so I hitchhiked to the Midwest. I spent a summer working in a Chicago factory after I read Nelson Algren because I wanted to see his America, too.

After I read the beat writers, I dropped out of college to go to San Francisco, thinking I could meet them on the street. Gary Snyder has a line, "In those days you would hitchhike a thousand miles to have a conversation with a friend." I was like that.

I went to North Beach, which was a place where people actually sat out on the sidewalk and played bongo drums. But I didn't know anybody. I didn't meet the people I thought I would meet. Still, I listened to people talk about peace, about Caryl Chessman, who was being put to death in California, and McCarthy. These weren't subjects people were talking about in Florida, but I also felt terribly lonely with no one to talk to.

Because I wasn't in school, I was draft eligible, but I enlisted to avoid National Guard requirements afterward. While I was in the Army, a friend told me about a sit-in at a department store not far from where we were stationed in Virginia. There was a lot of excitement on the street, a lot of police and a lot of citizens with Confederate flags eager to get these people crunched. The police had dogs on leashes biting the young students, terrified young black college girls in chiffon dresses.

Inside, the white people were standing around the counter, yelling insults. Maybe there were three or four people sitting in, while the crowd behind them were six or eight deep. The people sitting in were stoic, as though they were bracing themselves. There was no conversation, no reacting between them. The police finally grabbed them and took them off. Then the action moved outside, where there were more dogs on leashes and water cannons.

I wanted to somehow exhibit my solidarity, but I felt there was no way to do it while I was in uniform. Still, I felt guilty about it, and after that I considered myself to be a hard-core integrationist.

When I got out of the Army, I went to the Lower East Side of New York and eventually got an apartment with a black woman I had met while I was in the Army. Those years I spent in New York in the early '60s were terrific. I'd go to jazz clubs and art galleries. I listened to Sonny Rollins, Coltrane, Mingus, Monk, Wayne Shorter, Billy Higgins. I wrote poetry. I was cast in a play.

The group I ran with was generally far to the left of Martin Luther King in terms of civil rights. We thought of Kennedy as a warmongerer. There was an early rally against the war in Vietnam. Hardly anybody was protesting the war at that point, which was in 1963. I remember marching from the Lower East Side to Times Square and from Times Square to the UN, with a group of somewhere between one hundred and five hundred people.

You could see the whole pre-hippie transformation taking place in the Village. One day the doorman at the Village Gate was a guy in a coat and tie, complaining about a bunch of weirdos showing up. A couple of weeks later, it's a new guy, only he's wearing a beard, lots of jewelry, and a leather vest, and a leather pouch hanging on his side. I saw women wearing short skirts, peasant blouses, and sandals. I had no idea where they came from, but I fell in love with a number of them, and it broke everything apart with the woman I was living with.

It really felt like we were in the forefront of a massive social transformation. American society of the 1950s was being left behind. There was a lot of cracking of walls, and there was going to be a flood. But was it going to be up to the ankles, the knees, or the neck? It was a very exciting time, and I believed I had a role to play in the new society, so I left my job and I abandoned the idea that I would be a productive employee and a salaried member of mainstream society. I was just going to give myself to the world of experience and see what came out of it.

I decided to move out to the West Coast and ended up in San Francisco. One day I walked into the office of the San Francisco Mime Troupe and told them I was a writer, a director, and a performer. The Mime Troupe was trying to set up a freer, public-access-oriented theater with this new art. The city of San Francisco had a permit requirement for anything that was done in the park. We advertised that we were going to do a performance in Golden Gate Park without a permit. We put out the word among the entire alternative community. The police said they would prevent it, so a very, very large crowd of prominent alternative culture people showed up to see what would happen at this performance in the park.

For many people that was the seminal moment in the San Francisco '60s revolution. It created an affinity between beat culture, artists, New Left, drug exploration, students, rock and roll.

After the crowd and the police had gathered, the theater director got up to address the audience and said, "Ladies and gentlemen, we are presenting an arrest" and was, by the police.

That gave me the idea of guerrilla theater as a weapon in a guerrilla war, which is an underground war against repression. It wasn't about putting a play on. The idea was that people who saw the play would actually take part in it. They wouldn't just be an audience, and this production would be a social action to cause or aid the revolution.

I wanted to wrench people out from where they were and put them here with us. There would be no before, no after, no applause, no tickets, no line, no idea. There was just a performance.

I wrote a piece about a prisoner of war who is beaten to death. It was titled "Centerman." This prisoner is in the center of a group of three prisoners, who are marched around an exercise yard by a guard. When this one prisoner reaches out to grab a flower, he is fatally beaten by the guard.

For this to be guerrilla theater, I had to bring it someplace where people weren't expecting a play and where they would look at the guard as if he was really in the Army. We went to great pains to costume him exactly that way and to make sure the prisoners looked like prisoners.

We wanted to have the guard march the prisoners through an unsuspecting crowd to someplace where they would put on the play, and while he was marching them to be abusive to them and get people yelling, "Don't treat them like that!" or "What are you doing?" or "What is this?" "What's going on?" "Who are these people?"

We did this at a Free Speech Movement rally at UC Berkeley during speeches by people like Mario Savio and others, and it was just electric. While the guard was beating the prisoner to death, the crowd couldn't believe it. They were screaming, "Don't do that!" When we were done, we didn't stay around long enough to get credit, we just got in our VW bus and drove off.

We did another one titled "Search and Seizure," in which several people who have been arrested for drugs are interrogated by cops. We sat that down in the middle of rock and roll shows. People couldn't bear to watch it. It really got them screaming. We weren't asking them to take a political position, we were simply outraging them with the reality of this situation and making them make a choice right then: act to prevent it, or at least say to somebody beside them, "I can't stand it. I can't stand it."

These plays were done at the beginning of the time that a psychedelic revolution was happening in America and dropouts from all over the country were coming to San Francisco. I never agreed with the image of the hippies as kids with mindless grins on their faces, covered with peace symbol pins. That was the media's image. They came to San Francisco because they were disenchanted with American society. They thought society was materialistic, war mongering, and bigoted. They thought the jobs that were being offered were dull and robotlike, and they didn't want to waste their lives. They wanted to do something else.

But even among the rebels who were attracted to the city, there were differences. There was the hard left (or the Old Left), the New Left, who were war resisters, civil rights activists, et cetera. There were the social-cultural transformation people, who included the psychedelic revolution, the arts revolutionaries, and then there were the Diggers.

I left the Mime Troupe to help form the Diggers, who were a natural extension of guerrilla theater. Billy Murcott named the Diggers. He had been reading about social revolutionary groups in history. The Diggers were a movement in England during the seventeenth century that essentially said, "Everything is free. Do your own thing," but with a very strong Christian overlay. The Diggers then dug up the lawn in the middle of the city to plant crops for people without land. Billy thought this could apply in some ways to living together without money in Haight Ashbury. We also took the word *digger* to mean to *dig*, as in "I dig it."

To the Diggers, "Everything is free. Do your own thing" was a statement that society is oppressive in more ways than just segregation and war, but also in terms of work, social relationships, men and women, love, and human identity.

If we say everything is free, then society isn't free. I said, "Put 'free' in front of anything you think of and then do it."

The first Digger action was giving away free food in Golden Gate Park. We called it Digger Stew. I opened a free store named Trip Without a Ticket. There was no manager or cash register. When we got there in the morning, there

Peter Berg (right) in Aspen, Colorado, 1970. On the left is his wife, Judy, holding Ocean, their daughter. At center is Destiny Gould with her daughter, Solange. (Courtesy of Chuck Gould)

would be heaps of things on the sidewalk that people had given us. We would just put them on the shelves, and people would come in, find something they liked, and leave with it. We saw it as inducting the customers into the Digger group. People from the Army would come in and take off their uniforms and walk out in clothes they took from the rack.

The tie-dyes that everybody knows from the '60s started in the Free Store. A woman who became a Digger named Luna Moth had been studying indigenous methods of dyeing clothes. People were dropping out of straight jobs where they wore white shirts to work but began taking drugs and not going to work anymore. They wanted to sit in the park, listen to rock and roll, have sex, and watch balloons and light shows. So we had all of these white shirts because nobody wanted them. Luna found this way to make them usable to the psychedelic generation by dyeing them. She brought pots of dyes into the Free Store, and people tied up clothes and made their own tie-dyes.

We didn't have any leadership. When reporters or authorities came to the Free Store and asked, "Who are your leaders?" We'd say, "There are no leaders. You're either a Digger or you're not, and if you're a Digger everyone is the leader. It doesn't matter."

We did events in the streets that we knew would cause riots. One day we passed out flyers on Haight Street, asking people to play the Intersection Game. The idea was you walked from one side of the intersection to the other, and you just kept walking in all the possible directions, a square, an X, and you had to complete them all. We had so many people doing this with crowds watching and laughing that pretty soon traffic was piled up for twenty blocks.

The Death of Money came next. At that time, we would just sit around and say, "What is the most outrageous thing you can think of?"

"Let's have a funeral procession led by animals. Ecology is being killed because of money and industrial society. Let's have the animals sing a death march and bury money."

So these large puppet animal characters carried a coffin that was full of large imitation pieces of gold. There were people dressed in black animal costumes, singing the Supremes song, "Get out my life, why don't you, babe." But instead of singing it as a rock song, they were singing it as a death march.

That was a terrific event. We handed out pennywhistles and flutes and flowers. There were people on rooftops. The crowd completely filled the streets and sidewalks and stopped traffic until the police came with paddy wagons to carry people away. This time we were accused of violating the public nuisance law, so the Diggers made use of that by changing the spelling to "newsense."

The last Digger activity was an event called Free City. At that point, the police had come into the Haight Ashbury so heavily that they had made it an undesirable place to be. At the same time, people were experimenting with amphetamines or heroin, drugs which were fundamentally different from marijuana and LSD; they made people start stealing and sleeping in doorways, generally being antisocial. The ten-people-wide sidewalks became ten people slumped into a doorway.

The police had also made the streets one-way traffic and installed orange vapor lights. With the cops patrolling up and down the street, it looked like the Berlin Wall. Our idea was if they were going to try and take our neighborhood away from us, we'll take what we do and put it in the rest of the city, so we took over City Hall steps.

Every day we handed out free food, read poetry, played music, and conducted demonstrations on City Hall steps. The mayor was a Democrat, and he couldn't just come down on us. There would have been too much popular protest. Then one day, he left the city to make a speech somewhere. The police took advantage of his absence to move in on us. One person was arrested for wearing a shirt in the form of an American flag.

We kept it up, though. We didn't let them stop us, but we had our own end date—the summer solstice. And on the summer solstice we did an event in five different neighborhoods in San Francisco and then said the Diggers were over. We had done it for two years, and when it was over it had accomplished what it was supposed to accomplish.

What has flowed forward from it? I would say American society has been changed tremendously. Take the guy who was arrested for wearing an American flag shirt. Nobody would look twice at that today.

So many more things are acceptable today: the language that you hear, even on television, or read; sexuality. A lot of things we put "free" in front of have changed. They are free to be sexually active if they want to. They feel free to make their own lives. A high school student today is almost like an adult in the 1950s in terms of exposure to information, creativity, language, and sexual freedom.

I think that everyone growing up today has a period when they have a hippie moment, and they do what they think hippies did. The Diggers had something to do with that: feeling free to be expressive at a younger age.

When we were giving out free food, I would sometimes lead people out into the country to pick up onions that had been left behind because they were the wrong size for the machines. An industrial machine was forcing that decision. Those onions make the same soup. It doesn't matter what size they are, so we began to see how the sources of food were being mismanaged by the people running industrial agribusiness. Clearly, society needed to be reconstructed to take nature into account.

One of the earlier things I wrote for the Diggers was that industrialization was a battle with nineteenth-century ecology for breakfast, and that wars against ecology are suicidal. Many people had never seen the word *ecology* when that was written in 1966.

There was a lot of logging around the Black Bear commune in northern California where I lived for a while. It was just ridiculous. If you were in an airplane you would see these huge squares cut out of the vegetation on the mountainsides. We walked through those areas, which had been clear-cut. There was nothing alive in them. They were just stumps and torn-up ground where they dragged logs out.

It was shocking. No way in the world would this ever regenerate properly, and there was nothing we could do about it. The Black Bear commune was a branch of the Diggers. They extended the Digger ideology in a rural context, but it was changing. We were going from "Everything is free. Do your own thing" to "Everything is interdependent. Act responsibly with nature." I was hopeful that it could spread to other groups, so I got one of the very first portable videotape recorders, put it in the back of a truck, and with my family took a cross-country house-trucking trip as part of a caravan. We went to communes where people wanted to put the practical aspects of their lives— food, child rearing, education, health—into their own hands, and we would interview them and also show them the interviews we had made along the way.

While we were on the trip through the back country of North America, we witnessed the extraordinary ecological destruction that was happening everywhere. For example, in the Ozarks, we drove through miles of forests that had been killed by an Agent Orange–derived chemical. It was provided free by the government to kill hardwood, and most of it was used on hickory trees. Imagine wanting to kill a hickory forest. Why? It's such a valuable wood, but they did it to plant fast-growing pines for an agroforestry industry of pulpwood. They could plant that over and over again, supposedly.

We would come into areas like the Tock's Island Dam Project, where the government was going to flood an entire fertile valley with topsoil that was hundreds of feet deep. It was going to drown scores of ancient wonderful farm buildings to create a water coolant lake for a nuclear power plant.

In the Diné country, the Navajo country in New Mexico and Arizona, we saw uranium mine tailings. What was left over from mining uranium ore was scattered along the road on the way to a dump of standing gravel. We're talking fifty-sixty-foot-high mounds of rocks that were radioactive, with kids playing on and around them.

If you brought any of these things up today it would be a national scandal, but back then no one knew any of this. We were outraged. I asked myself if we were all to go back to the land, what issues would we be confronting. More and more it occurred to me that the most important question to consider was the position of human beings in natural systems. The direct involvement that a human being has with natural systems, the bounty and harmony of it, became the central issue to me.

We put together the Planet Drum organization to make people aware of what was going on and get them to do something about it. I also began

Peter Berg discussing environmental politics at the Third North American Bioregional
Congress outside Vancouver, Canada, 1988. (Photo by Judy Goldhaft)

writing articles about bioregions, which is now an accepted term, and there
are bioregional groups across the country.

Everyone lives in a bioregion. Every place has its own unique set of natural
characteristics, such as climate, land forms, watersheds, nature, plants and
animals, and so forth. People can fit into their bioregion by learning to adapt
to these features.

We decided that Planet Drum should start a publication to serve the movement. We're still publishing it. In 1989, we began the Green City Project to
give cities a thrust toward bioregional thinking and to encourage them to restore and maintain natural systems. For example, we encourage cities to
restore wild corridors within city boundaries. Urban parks can be connected
with wildlife corridors. This would literally tie cities in with nature. If you

connect the parks together with wild corridors, animals could move freely between them.

With the help of environmentalists, peregrine falcons are returning to cities and using the tops of office buildings as hunting platforms for diving down and taking pigeons as food. Almost everybody who lives in a major American city will soon be able to see peregrine falcons hunting downtown.

We show cities how they can bring back urban creeks, like the Gowanus Canal in Brooklyn or the Los Angeles River or Strawberry Creek, which runs through the University of California campus at Berkeley.

Planet Drum has forty publications on a variety of topics. We provide information on how to create renewable energy systems and replace automobiles with point-to-point transportation systems, like calling up a van to go to the airport. Cities can set up large-scale recycling for every household and business. Also, shower or bath water can be reused to flush the toilet. There's no reason why we should be putting pure water down the toilet every time we flush it. This would probably reduce water use in the U.S. by 50 percent.

We are also expanding internationally. Now there are bioregional groups and activities in Japan, Italy, Spain, Ecuador, Mexico, and Canada. We're helping rebuild the Ecuadorian city of Bahia de Caraquez, which was destroyed by an earthquake, as an ecocity. The city passed a law that it will be an ecocity. There are reports about it on our Web site.

I was asked recently to summarize in talk what I had done for more than the last thirty years, and I said that it could all be seen as trying to liberate people fully in whatever space they held. Plays free of a stage, hippies as free people, Haight-Ashbury as a free neighborhood, and bioregions as self-governing countries of the planetary biosphere. It has been a continuous process of liberating myself and fitting into wherever I happen to be.

Elsa Marley Skylark
The Artist

In his memoir of the 1960s, *Sleeping Where I Fall*, actor and ex-Digger Peter Coyote writes that during her life, his friend Elsa Marley has embraced enough movements, events, and friendships "to fill a small library."

It's true. Elsa has been involved in nearly every major cultural movement since the end of World War II. In the early 1950s, she was with the jazz musicians, the beat writers, and the abstract expressionist artists of New York City. In the '60s, she was in London when the Beatles and the Rolling Stones were taking the city by storm. Later in the decade, she was in San Francisco, where with her artist friends she began the rock and roll revolution. When the hippie dream soured, she joined the growing movement to the country, cofounding Black Bear Ranch, a commune hidden in the mountains of northern California. In the '80s, her own artistic interests took her to China, where she found herself in Peking literally around the corner from Tiananmen Square when it was occupied by thousands of students demanding democratic reforms.

When we meet, she says she has just returned from the Philippines and is planning another extended trip to China, where she will film a documentary. Elsa, who prefers to be called Elsa Marley Skylark, works in a studio in Oakland, California. The walls are filled with her art, which is heavily influenced by her years spent in China. I wanted to know, as she is a living bridge between the beats of the '50s and the hippies of the '60s, how does she remember both generations? Also, what is it like to live and work on the cutting edge?

She takes a break on this warm Sunday afternoon, pours herself a gin and tonic (and me a special tea from Honshu, China), puts her feet up on the couch and, with her eyes sparkling, begins to reminisce. In the richness and variety of her experiences, she is the embodiment of the '60s ideal that all should be able to live their lives to their fullest potential. And while she understands her children's occasional exasperation with her dedication to her art, she wouldn't have it any other way. To Elsa, an artist's life is lived on the edge. It's a life of risk, experimentation, and discovery. If she hasn't reaped great financial rewards, the richness and variety of her experiences are evident in her work and have given her a life that has truly been well lived.

"And there's still so much more to come," she says.

O ur commune started rock and roll in San Francisco. We were this group of crazy artists, just trying to make money to go to Europe. We were spending the summer with our babies and dogs in Virginia City with a rock group called the Charlatans that had a little gig in a bar up there. We smoked a lot of dope and talked about different ways of making money. One way was, somebody would get married. We'd invite all these CEOs from all over the country to come to the wedding. Of course, they wouldn't come because they wouldn't know who it was, but they would be too busy to find out. Instead, they'd have their secretaries send some silver or something, and we'd cash it in.

That plan was rejected because no one wanted to get married.

Then someone said, "Listen to that stupid band downstairs. They can't play worth a damn." They were like the Grateful Dead in the beginning, just clunking around while they figured out how to do it.

We said, "We can get them and put on a party in San Francisco," and so one of the dope dealers who was with us said, "We can rent Longshoreman's Hall." We would use his dope money to pay the rental fee. So we put on this party. We thought we'd get maybe a couple of hundred people. Four thousand people showed up, and so we decided to do another one, although to get the money to pay for that, somebody else had to make a dope run to Mexico. It got to be a regular thing, and it was enormously successful. Within six months, the whole San Francisco scene became popular. Think about it. We changed the world because we wanted to go to Europe. We never did get there, though. We created a phenomenon, so who needed Europe?

I was not a San Francisco native. I'm a Canadian. My Dad was an express agent with the Canadian National Railroads. He and my mom met in Canada, and that's where I was born in 1937.

I announced to everyone when I was six years old that I was going to be an artist. My mother said, "That's very nice, dear, now do your piano lessons."

When I was sixteen, I ran away to go to the Vancouver Art School. I supported myself by waitressing. Eventually my grandmother came to live with me in this dumpy two-room apartment with no kitchen. She modeled at the art school. She was a socialist and a suffragette and a very free spirit. She was also a golf champion. She ran away from my mom, too.

In my third year of art school, I went to New York for winter break. A friend gave me somebody's address, saying, "It's kind of a crash pad. You can go and stay there."

There were just mattresses on the floor and not much else. The apartment was in Greenwich Village, which was a great place to be for an artist in the mid-1950s. The Cedar Bar was hip and happening. You would be sitting next to Miles Davis on one side and Wilhelm de Kooning on the other. De Kooning wound up being a good friend.

There were lots of intense conversations, maybe a little dope. They were called reefers at that time. People dressed in black and wore shades. The conversations were about art, and we'd go to readings by beat poets. I remember one poet standing up and reading, "The city, the city, the city . . ."—that type of stuff.

In those days, you could be Debbie Reynolds or you could be a beat. Debbie Reynolds was not very appealing to me, nor were the beehive hairdos and very restrictive behavior. Fortunately, there was all this underground stuff that was going on, which was fascinating, and I'm a poet. I love poetry. I married a poet. He burned his first novel because it was too much like Kerouac's *On the Road*. I met Mike on that first trip. Two kids, Yoni and Aaron, came out of that. As a little kid in Yugoslavia, Mike had Nazis shot dead on top of him, and he was strafed on the way to school, so there was no way in the 1950s that he was going to join the American army. In San Francisco, he wrote "Ban the H Bomb" in spray paint all over the city. This was during the time of McCarthyism when people in coffeehouses hushed me up for talking about my granny the socialist.

New York was a nighttime place for me. It was too noisy during the day. I walked the streets at all hours of the night. The library was open all night, so you could do research. You could go to the jazz clubs in Harlem. It was really a fun time. Poetry, abstract expressionism, and jazz, they all run together.

In those days, we were always in and out of each other's apartments.

I miss that. One day, I got to talking with this red-headed person who was my neighbor. She turned out to be Diane di Prima [a popular beat poet]. In the course of conversation, Mike came up. I was heartbroken then. He was away, and I was pregnant, and what should I do. She said, "Well, you should have the baby, just like I had Jeannie. We don't need a husband to have a baby."

Right after I conceived my second child, Mike began cracking up. By then I was living in London, working on a commission. Part of the reason for the split was that I had started to get recognition. It was very chauvinistic in those days. He was supposed to be the major artist, which I didn't understand. I just assumed I had equal rights.

Mike got so bad that he nearly killed me and the baby, and I left. That was one of the big low points of my life, and I was pregnant on top of it with my second child. Not long after, he committed suicide.

We came down to stay with Diane in San Francisco. The first place I lived was on Oak Street. I took a job, taking care of three dope-ridden guys. One of them was a musician who worked with Janis Joplin. We formed the Family Dog commune that started the rock shows. For a long time, I had no idea what was going on in the bathroom, but I was pregnant and had a little kid and needed someplace to stay. We lived in the back. Then, we moved into what turned out to be the Family Dog house on Pine Street. The reason why we called it the Family Dog house was because there were a lot of dogs. There was this sea of dog tails in the kitchen all the time.

We started a psychedelic shop called Magic Theatre for Madmen Only. There were all these beautiful Victorian homes, and there was a lot of junk being thrown out on the streets from these old mansions as the people who lived in them were dying off. We'd go in and raid an empty mansion and come away with silk stockings and sell that stuff in the store.

Our house on Pine Street was the nucleus for the rock people who were coming in and out of the city. People were always coming in and out. In the early days, everybody was on the road. Kerouac's On the Road was not just fantasy—everybody was doing it. So there was this constant New York–Mexico City–San Francisco–New York again–back to San Francisco.

Janis Joplin was in and out of there. She was the best musician of all of those guys. They were kids who just didn't have experience, but Janis came to it with a natural given talent. I liked her. She was fun, but I thought she was kind of foolish. I had already been to Europe and back and had all these other adventures. I couldn't stay up that late with her. I had to be up early in the morning with two kids.

At thirty, I was kind of an elder in the community. It frustrated me that the flower children who came to San Francisco in 1965 didn't know their lineage, and they certainly weren't very intellectual. I remember talking about Kerouac with one young person, and she said, "Who's Kerouac?" I couldn't believe it, because all through the '50s, Kerouac was this big figurehead for the movement that I was involved in, and she had no idea who he was. She didn't read books. She was just into the music, making beads, and having babies.

I met my husband Richard at this time. He was a longshoreman who came out of that Jack London–socialist tradition. There was a history of literary longshoremen and artist types in San Francisco. His mom was a communist in London, and quite a leading one.

We moved in together, and there were all these characters who were our everyday neighbors. Our house was open. People would come in and out during the daytime. The Hell's Angels were around. They weren't bad guys; and there were the Diggers.

There were a lot of geniuses around, having deep conversations about creating a future through poetry and art and about the universe. My son is working with DNA protein connectors. He is a neurobiologist. It was that deep.

I also made money by modeling for the art school. Someone was interested in having a kinetic model, and he arranged to have all these swings and tires to swing around on, and he gave me this whole room to play in, and so I developed this slow-motion dance. I had some friends who were doing improvisational theater, and we got to talking one day, and I told one of them I would like to combine the strobe lights with the dance thing. He said, "I would like to do it with a reading from Revelations in the Bible about the horrors of Babylon," which made it into a piece that was critical of society.

Three of us got together and we did this nude dance, although we were covered in light. The dance was photographed, and we sent the pictures in to *Playboy* magazine. They published them.

Every Thursday night, we would put on this dance, called Revelations, in this huge attic. Revelations was by invitation only, because you couldn't dance nude publicly. Musicians would come by and play. At some point we suggested that the audience take off their clothes, and people did.

I met the Diggers through Revelations. Peter Berg saw it, and he brought his friends. I was tired of the rock and roll scene anyway. Even in its early days, I felt like it was getting stifled by success. You've got to really watch out for success.

I helped out with the Free Store, helping to stock it and mind it and making sure people didn't steal free things. We used to stop the kids from stealing the stuff. We'd scare the shit out of them and then give it all back to them.

That was around the time that the world discovered the Haight. Suddenly there were all these poor old kids that had run away from home and needed to be taken care of. The Free Store and the Digger House, the free clinic, the free this, the free that were all in response to what was happening to our community.

And then the tour buses started happening. "And there's an authentic hippie." "There's a child, and a baby carriage, and another child behind her." "My goodness, we don't see that back home in Ohio," or wherever they were from.

Lynn Brown, who was this gorgeous actress, got into carrying around a little mirror. Anytime someone wanted to take her picture she would put this little mirror in front of her so they would take their own picture.

You had the kids, then the tourists, and the entrepreneurs trying to get the kids stoned. Then the heavy dope started coming in from the gangsters. The same thing was happening in New York, and it just was not a safe place to raise your kids anymore.

When Indira was born in December 1967, we left for the country because a friend had a beautiful place on the Klamath River in Witchapec. We had been studying at the birth center with some friends who had given us a birth kit. In the case was a hypodermic needle to stop bleeding.

We were up there, planning to have the baby at home, when in the middle of the night the police came in, saw the needle, and took us to jail. I was in labor, so they placed me under guard at the hospital for three days. It turned out to be false labor. Finally the DA came down and said, "Well, you haven't really done anything wrong, and we don't have much proof, so you're free to go."

I asked them where my husband and friends were, and they said they had been released, but they hadn't told them where I was.

These dumb country cops, all they knew was there were these long-haired people who had recently moved in. They had found raspberry-leaf tea and said it was marijuana. They found vitamin C pills, which they said was acid. They had made sure our arrest was on TV: "Pregnant Woman Leader of Drug Gang." So everybody thought we had all this stuff, but there was nothing. The irony was, we had plenty of dope back in San Francisco and never got busted.

Still, our two kids had been taken away from us and placed in foster homes, and they wouldn't give them back. That was the worst. It was almost Christmas, no kids. I was so devastated about losing them, I didn't even care about the baby anymore. Eventually we got the kids back. We went to trial nine months later. Richard gave this speech about Thoreau, how we had gone to the country to live this pure life. He is an actor, so he gave a really good speech.

The judge said, "This is ridiculous. Send these people home."

By then we had decided to permanently move out of the city. I went with a couple of people looking for places in the Marble Mountains, and we passed by a company called Big Sky Real Estate. It was this dinky little place in the middle of a field. I told them we were looking for someplace that was remote, where we could raise children and be free and relate to nature.

He pulled out a file folder on Black Bear and handed it to me. I read it over, and I said, "Terrific, that sounds perfect."

It was an abandoned gold mine about 350 miles north of San Francisco that had a town site with a store and post office. There was still lots of gold in the creek, although it was not profitable to mine.

We could buy it for $22,000. We didn't have that kind of money, so to raise it we drove to LA in a Coors truck. While we were in LA, we lived in the back of the truck.

People gave us money all over the place. One of our friends, who had been an LA Digger and saw himself as a Sicilian hood, had his little black book. He knew the actor James Coburn, and he went to Coburn's house and set his American flag on fire. That convinced Coburn to give us a check.

A famous filmmaker gave us money. He was going to come and make a film of us, but he never did. The Doors gave us money. Poor Peter Tork of the Monkees, he was so sweet. We stayed with him part of the time, and the Digger boys just about emptied his house. I really regret their doing that. Richard approached the Grateful Dead, and one of their managers gave him money to go and score dope and bring it back. Then they would give us a cut of the cash. The problem was they didn't trust Richard, so to make sure he came back he had to leave me and the baby with them as collateral. It was quite pleasant. I just sat there and listened to music.

We got to Black Bear in time for the most severe winter they had in forty years. We were snowed in under six feet of snow for six weeks, and we ran out of food. Here we brought thirty-five of these city people to the country. Only one of us had grown up in the country and knew how to chop wood and haul water. One guy came down in his bathrobe in the morning, expecting to read the reviews in the paper. Was he in for a surprise.

We had to walk out on snowshoes twenty miles to get food. It was almost like the Donner party. I was pregnant with my last child. Just before I gave birth, I weighed less than I did before I got pregnant. When the dog had puppies, we cooked them up. We were that hungry.

When the baby was born, we fried up the afterbirth with onions and ate it, not because we were hungry, because it was spiritual. Someone read that that was what primitive people did, so we did it. We ate a lot of things, mountain lions . . . but the most difficult was the puppies.

Even if someone wanted to give up, there was nowhere to go. You had to go over two mountains to get out of there. Richard drove the truck into town and disappeared for a week or ten days. I was frantic. Then he showed up, finally. "Hi, we've got a whole truckload of food." They just took advantage of a break in the weather and went down to the city. We greeted them like heroes. When I saw the first crocus in the spring, I got down and kissed the ground and gave thanks that nobody was dead.

In the spring, we got a couple of goats for milk. We also had a donkey named Happy. It must have thought it died and went to heaven, because it never did a lick of work. Also after that first winter, the Indians brought us mountain lions and a lot of salmon. They were good neighbors. They came down the road to see the naked women and stayed to arm wrestle and have dinner, and then they came back with 100 salmon. We would stay up all night with what we called "night kitchen" to can the salmon. We did it in shifts, and we had enough salmon to last the whole year.

I had devised this slogan, "Free land for free people," and they took me up on it. When we first got to the ranch, there was no place for Richard and I to live, because everybody had filled up the main house. So we built a dome out of plywood and bolts that was fifteen feet in diameter. Six of us lived in the dome the first winter. I had a little stove and a kitchen in there and a little studio where I learned how to do watercolors. We found a bearskin, which I used as our door.

We didn't know what to do with all the people who had showed up. We weren't going to call the police and evict them, so Richard said, "We'll just

Elsa Marley Skylark and her daughter, Yoni, in Yreka, California, in the early 1970s.
(Courtesy of Elsa Marley Skylark)

organize them." In the loft of the main house he found all these old clothes. There was a marching band uniform there. He put that on, and he got a blackboard and a pointer stick, and he made a list. "OK, this crew is going to be crew A, and they're gonna do this," just like he would have done on the docks. Everybody politely listened to him, amazingly enough, but the next morning when he went back to start on the work shifts, the blackboard had vanished. That was it. It was an anarchistic ranch, but he and the others, one of whom did carpentry work, got together. They were going to start a new political party called the Get With It Party. Their idea was to get with it and not just proselytize, and they did. The first thing they did was build a shitter, and it's there to this day, a six-hole communal shitter. The first winter, there were the single people and the married people. Were the married couples staying faithful? More or less. I sort of started the orgies there, because I decided to have an art class, and I decided to have a male and female model, and I wanted them to face each other in classic Indian pose. They got very interested in each other, and it started an orgy, so until my son Orion was born, we weren't sure whose baby it was.

In the second winter, we all lived together in the main house, because Richard and Efrem felt people were having their private stashes and it was getting cliquey. This group got packages from home with cheese in it, and they didn't share with everybody else, and they'd have special dinners and others weren't invited, and so this elitism developed. We really wanted to be equal, and we felt that in order to be unified we would all live together. The kids all slept in the kids' room, and we all slept in the big main room. There was a sea of mattresses all over the room, and there was no privacy. We were in this spot. Peter Berg and Judy were next to us, and then on and on down the line. There would be all this lovemaking going on. Richard would be sitting there reading his pornography. I'd be reading my poetry book, and Judy and Peter would be reading God knows what. We were sort of the older adults. Once somebody said to Richard, "What's an old man like you doing in a place like this?" He was thirty-three at the time.

Anyway, all around us was this sea of grunting and groaning and oohing and aahing. Every once in a while, Richard would look up and say, "Elsa, Elsa, who's that?"

I'd tell him, "Oh, it's Don and Carol." Carol by then had left Efrem, and Don had left Harriet, so it became Harriet and Efrem and Don and Carol, and they're still together twenty-five years later.

Especially when there were sixty people in the main house, just surviving the day took a lot of energy. In the winter when it was snowing outside, everybody was housebound. We'd go out to get wood and milk the goats, but that was about it. One winter we set a timer, so that every hour it would go "bing" and everybody would go out and run around the house three times and back in again until the next hour, just to get a little exercise.

Everything was communalized, even the diapers. Some of the men complained about doing them because we didn't have a washing machine, so they had to be done by hand. Diane di Prima went out and got everybody Pampers and was severely criticized for doing it. Of course the women loved it. It was the men who complained.

When spring came, everybody went back to their old space. People just needed to get away. People left and new people arrived. The newcomers were pretty much welcomed. We didn't get that many drifters, because we were eight hours away from the city and you had to go over those two mountain summits. That was one of the reasons why I wanted a place that would be difficult to enter. I didn't want it to turn into a dope scene. In fact, because of our bust, we had put down this rule that they were not supposed to have dope, except for specific occasions where everybody took acid.

We were busted that first spring, though. I had been in the city and was coming back and followed something like ten cop cars down the mountain road. All they found was a little bit of grass with one of the couples, but they pulled up all our tomato plants, thinking they were marijuana plants, and they took pictures of themselves doing it. That turned out to be the best thing that happened to us because the DA would never give them a warrant to come in again after they made such fools of themselves. They published the pictures in the local paper, and everybody wrote in, saying, "Those are all tomato plants." They totally embarrassed themselves.

Any money we made went into a pot. There was a lot of fund-raising going on to keep it self-sufficient. We had a five-acre garden and thirty goats, so we made a lot of Parmesan cheese. We worked with the forest service fighting fires in the summer. I was on the first female firefighting team. We had a doctor and a nurse. Richard is a really good doctor. He never finished high school, but he's got all the skills of a doctor.

I had problems with other members of the group because I wanted to work on my art. We had a meeting about what everybody was going to do in the spring. When I said I wanted to work on my watercolors, I was really ostracized. At the end of the meeting, I went into the woods and vomited, it was that bad, having sixty people attacking me.

But over time, nobody built the sawmill. Nobody had finished the chicken coop. Nobody had repaired the barn, but I learned how to do watercolors. And now they have become doctors and lawyers and Indian chiefs, and they all collect my work.

Every time some new thing came to the ranch, everybody just embraced it. At one point, Maoism came to Black Bear, so everybody was put on the hot seat of self-criticism for hours at a time. I thought it was absolutely ridiculous. The idea was to undo the psyche of the individual. The person would have to admit to being selfish or wrong, and it could end up being hours of emotional torture.

We called the garden Li Ling Meadow after the Li Ling commune in China. When I got to China and found out what really happened in the revolution, I was absolutely horrified that we had played revolution. The man who taught me how to do calligraphy had learned to do it with his left hand because they had completely busted his arm. There were a lot of suicides. It wasn't about those apple-cheeked people that you saw in the posters.

The women's movement had a bigger impact on us than Mao's Little Red Book. One winter, for some reason, the guys had left. For about six weeks it was all women, and we found out all kinds of things. The ranch became amazingly efficient. There were women who were mechanically minded, and there were women who became carpenters. There were the artists, and they continued to be the artists. I gave art lessons. We fixed the barn and figured out what the guys had done to the power wagon and why it wouldn't work.

Gail and I killed a goat because we needed the meat. That was quite an experience. First we talked to it. Then I sat on its back while she slit its throat. Another time we had this whole thing about killing a pig. First Morningstar wrote a poem [sings]: "Oh, pig, we come in on honor of thy spirit . . . " We were ringing bells and all of that stuff, and the pig got all freaked out. They shot it in the head, but the pig had a very hard head and ran all over while they were chanting, "Oh, pig, we ask for your spirit." [Laughs.]

We were almost totally isolated. You had to go to town to get the mail. We didn't have a phone. We didn't have a radio, no newspapers, no TV. We did get a CB after a few years. We heard about things from the people who came up and down from the city, so there was kind of a human telegraph line.

Sometimes we would lose track of the day, even years. I loved history, and I said at one point, "Let's get rid of history. We'll start from the time we moved to Black Bear, and that will be year zero, and we're gonna name every year a different name." Year one was going to be Apple Blossom. Year two was Year of the Babies, whatever event that took place. It didn't really take, fortunately. It was another one of my crazy ideas.

To amuse ourselves, we told stories. We did plays. We got rid of Christmas, because there were so many Jewish people who didn't want to celebrate a Christian holiday. We had Kids' Day instead. Everybody made presents for the kids. Eventually Christmas sort of snuck in. Kids would come to my studio and we'd celebrate.

One problem was we could never keep a schoolteacher. Every one that came dropped out, so after a few years Richard and I moved off the ranch to a town on the river. By that time we had five or six school-aged kids on the commune. They needed to go to school, and the school bus wouldn't come all the way up to Black Bear. On the weekends and holidays, we'd go back to the ranch.

Before he went, my son Orion objected strenuously. I remember him saying, "I may take my body to school, but I'm not going to take my spirit." But he forgot about it the next day, and he was fine.

We ended up staying in the mountains fourteen years. I left in 1980 when Richard and I split up. He was having an ongoing affair with a woman in the city, and I was devastated. I had a nervous breakdown and had to leave. I moved out and ran a gallery in a town near Sacramento. Then I came to San Francisco and ran an arts organization. After that, I decided I wanted to go back and get my master's degree because I couldn't teach in colleges any more with a BA. Eventually I got a house in San Francisco, and the kids all came to live with me.

In 1987, the same year I went to China, we gave the land away. We had a big party, and anybody and their children who had been at the ranch for a year could ask for title. We just signed everybody on, had a big powwow.

Having that sense of community, that's what I learned in the mountains. What I learned in China was how important family is. When I came back in the early '90s I saw that our family needed patches and repairs. Your father is off here. Your mother was off in China, and Sharon, Richard's significant other, is holding things together, so Sharon and I organized Sunday dinners, and all the adult kids came. It was mandatory for a while, but they got to like it and it did bring the family back. Now I look at other families, and we didn't do so bad.

Elsa Marley Skylark today. (Courtesy of Elsa Marley Skylark)

When Richard came back from Czechoslovakia, he joined us. After twenty years, we finally got divorced. Now he makes an excellent brother, a much better brother than a husband.

I think it's very important to stay fluid but also remain connected with your underlying spirit. I could have been a businesswoman, but to me it's more important to make art, and I have to remain a free spirit to do that. I've been criticized by the communards, by my mother, by my children, by my husbands, but eventually they come around. The kids are proud of me now.

The main dream I have for my kids is that they remember who they are. I didn't want them to be so close-minded that they wouldn't be able to venture forth and find themselves. And they certainly have done that. I also think it's important to take risks.

I still love to go back to Black Bear. I do two or three times a year. It's still free land for free people. There is a whole group of younger people there now, who are making the same mistakes that we made. They chop wood and carry water. It's a great school for learning how to survive in the wilderness and become an adult in.

Mine has been a life well lived, and is. It gets more and more exciting as I go on. I've had so many different experiences. I wouldn't have lived my life any other way. I've had to get over my feelings of guilt that maybe I wasn't a good enough mom because I was an artist. In their teenage years, the kids used to say, "You're an artist, you should never have had kids," but the grandkids love it. They may never be artists, but they have great experiences with Granny.

Marilyn Salzman Webb The Feminist

One evening when I was in my mid-teens, as I was doing my homework with the radio on, a news report made me laugh out loud. It seemed that traffic had come to a standstill at a corner in Manhattan because a group of women had stationed themselves on the sidewalk and were whistling and making rude comments at the men on a construction site. I could imagine what they were saying. "Hey, Daddy, shake those buns!" "Is that a hammer in your pocket, or are you just glad to see me?"

That creative, classic 1960s protest served as my—and many others'—introduction to women's liberation.

Across America, women were demanding an end to being treated like second-class citizens at home and on the job. The few college graduates of the '50s and early '60s who sought a career instead of marriage were generally shoehorned into the "women's professions": teaching, nursing, and social work (although if a woman was pretty and had nice legs, she might be given the opportunity to push trays down the aisle of an airplane as a stewardess). As late as 1971, there were fewer than 10,000 women lawyers out of nearly 325,000 law school graduates. In 1961, less than 6 percent of medical students were women.

Women who did venture into the workplace found it rough sledding. Most were routinely paid less than men for the same job. They had few chances for promotion and faced routine sexual harassment with little or no recourse.

It's difficult to pinpoint the exact genesis of the women's movement, but a strong case can be made for July 13, 1848, when Elizabeth Cady Stanton sat down for tea with four friends in upstate New York. The group wondered why, in this democratic country, women had almost no rights to speak of. To redress the issue, they decided to hold a conference six days later, which they called the Women's Rights Convention.

At the convention, the seventy women in attendance voted unanimously to adopt a "Declaration of Sentiments," which enumerated their complaints. These included the fact that women could not enter medicine or law; that married women had no property rights; that married women could be beaten or imprisoned by their husbands with no recourse; that women could not vote; and that women were forced to submit to laws while having no voice in their formation.

They also voted to accept a twelve-point resolution, which included the demands for women's suffrage and expansion of other rights. The women also expressed the hope that similar conventions would be held around the country. They were; and in 1920, after nearly seventy-five years of lobbying, the Nineteenth Amendment to the Constitution was passed, giving women the right to vote.

By then, the movement for women's suffrage had spurred a parallel effort by a nurse named Margaret Sanger to legalize birth control. Sanger was arrested repeatedly for her actions. In 1916, she founded the nation's first birth control clinic in Brooklyn, New York. It was barely open a week when police shut it down. Sanger was convicted on obscenity charges and imprisoned for thirty days. Until a 1936 Supreme Court ruling, even information about birth control was legally considered obscene, and as late as 1965, several states still banned married couples from legally obtaining birth control.

The most controversial issue tackled by the women's movement was abortion rights. Until the last third of the nineteenth century, abortion was legal across the country. Toward the end of the century, however, largely at the urging of the American Medical Association, it was criminalized, state by state. Still, the practice continued relatively uninhibited. One estimate is that in the late nineteenth century, there were some two million abortions performed annually.

By the beginning of the twentieth century, medical professionals commonly denied medical care to a woman who was dying from complications related to an abortion unless she told authorities the name of her abortionist. This led to an increase in abortion-related deaths. By the late 1920s, some 15,000 women died annually as a result of botched back-alley abortions, often performed without anesthetic and in unsanitary conditions. Some women even aborted their own babies with knitting needles. Only in 1972, in the U.S. Supreme Court case of *Roe v. Wade*, was abortion made legal nationally.

Early on in my research, I had read that a woman named Marilyn Webb addressed a major liberal rally in 1969 about women's issues and was booed off the stage. How did that happen? What impact did that have on her? I was also curious about how Webb came to the movement and how it made her later career as an author possible. What were her parents' views of women's roles? Did her mother influence her in any way? How much opposition did she have to overcome, not only from men, but from other women as well? And how has her work changed the lives of the next generation?

As I sit and talk with Marilyn Webb in her book-lined office, it's apparent that the Little League's open-door policy toward girls came thirty years too late: I can hear the anger in her voice as she remembers being sent home from Little League tryouts.

I was a very good athlete, and it never occurred to me that I couldn't play in the Little League, but when I got there the coach said, "You can't try out. You're a girl."

My mouth dropped open. All I could say was, "Well, everybody knows I'm the best first baseman here."

When I told my mother, she thought it was time to enlighten me that this was the way of the world. "Well, that's how it is. You'll have your own games."

I was a little bit of a tomboy, which didn't always sit well with them. I wore a cowboy outfit almost every single day when I was around nine, and my parents were embarrassed because people in the neighborhood used to ask if I was a boy or a girl. My mother used to ask me, "Couldn't you do something more girlish?"

At home, she was a very traditional housewife, but she was always doing something political. She was a union organizer for the International Ladies Garment Workers Union. She was also very involved in civil rights and brotherhood projects. Largely because of her, I came out of my childhood knowing that there were human issues that needed to be addressed in this world, but because I grew up in the McCarthy era, there was also a fear that was attached to political action.

There weren't really sports for girls, so I was a cheerleader in high school. I was also the prom queen and an honor student, but my high school years were

Marilyn Webb in her Hopalong Cassidy days. (Courtesy of Marilyn Webb)

not happy. My sister died of kidney failure when she was thirteen. Then my father died four years later of a heart attack, but it was really from a broken heart.

After my sister died, I decided I wanted to be a doctor. My mother was against it. I remember her saying, "I should tell you this right from the start, girls are not doctors. We're not paying for you to go to medical school. If you went, you couldn't have a family."

She was being protective, but even if I wasn't going to become a doctor, I knew I wouldn't be a stay-at-home mom. I knew I would support myself in some profession.

My grandfather also had old-fashioned ideas when it came to women. When I was in high school, he told my parents, "Don't let her go away, because then she won't be marriage material. She'll get ideas of her own."

I did go to college. I went to Brandeis University, which had a wonderful intellectual atmosphere with an aura of sophisticated students from the city, kids who had gone to private schools and wore black and had long hair.

I just loved learning. I got an A+ in physics. My mother and father were actually astounded that a girl actually could get that kind of grade, and they gave me a subscription to *Scientific American*. I cherished that for years and years. Still, I learned to take a girls' major—psychology—because I couldn't go to medical school.

Brandeis had an incredible faculty. They even had Eleanor Roosevelt teaching a course there on the UN. All the professors were so expansive in their intellect that they influenced me not just in what they were teaching but in what could be possible for the human mind. They would force you to really think through what you were saying and thinking. They didn't criticize your argument unless it was a poorly crafted one. They were more interested in the learning process and the thinking than they were in the result. I found that to be wonderful. It wasn't like in high school where you were learning facts. You were having your mind shaped by the greatest thinkers of the time.

On the other hand, there were no discussions about women's issues. We still had locked dorms and curfews, and if you had sex your roommates told on you. I almost got thrown out of school for sex. I was bad, and my girlfriends decided they were protecting me by telling on me when I didn't come home or made them sign in for me. I didn't think there was anything wrong with it. My boyfriend would throw pebbles against the window, and I would sneak out through the door. He could be out because the boys didn't have a curfew, but we did.

My friends were all virgins who were saving themselves for marriage. They had already picked out their silver patterns, and they weren't even dating anybody that they had planned on marrying. They didn't see themselves as sexual beings. They saw themselves as flirts, but you didn't give, because then you didn't get married. "Why buy the cow if you could get the milk for free."

I didn't buy any of it. I wasn't sure that I wanted to get married, but why did that mean I couldn't have a relationship? If they weren't going to buy the cow, it didn't matter to me. I thought, I'm getting just as much out of it, too. Why is this a problem?

In terms of sex, my biggest worry was getting pregnant. My friend Karen got pregnant and instead of having an abortion, she ended up marrying this Argentinean guy. She moved there and had this child. She was an extraordinarily talented pianist, but her piano career was gone.

All of these conversations about sex pushed me into thinking more about what it meant to be a woman. I started reading more women's books, although there weren't that many. I also made new friends. These were more sophisticated women who took themselves seriously. Their center of gravity was in what they were doing rather than in what they had to protect. Their minds were thinking about themselves as doing people in the world rather than receiving the love of a man—not to say we didn't have boyfriends, but that the self-defining thought was "What are we as human beings?"

They were different from my earlier friends, who went into safe women's professions, like teaching or social work. Then they got married and had children, moved to the suburbs, and got big diamonds and drove nice cars. Years later when I'd see them at reunions, that's how they defined themselves in life: by their good works for charity. They weren't stupid or unsophisticated either.

I didn't know what I would be, although I knew I wouldn't be deliberating over my silver pattern by the time I graduated. At first I thought I wanted to be a psychiatrist, but there was still that medical school issue, so I decided to get my Ph.D. in psychology at the University of Chicago.

In school, I came up with this idea based on the Mississippi Freedom Summer, to start a preschool run by welfare mothers where we would teach them to teach the kids. It was extraordinarily successful. It was helping them learn, and at the same time it was helping them get involved with their kids.

We got a big grant to open more schools. This was all a part of the beginning of the northern civil rights movement, where there was some effort to give welfare mothers a voice.

Right around that period in the fall of '65 there was this SDS [Students for a Democratic Society] national council meeting at the University of Illinois. We went. By this time, we had heard about a letter that Mary King and Casey Hayden had sent to the women in SDS. They had been involved in the southern civil rights movement and were unhappy about the way women in the movement were treated. A group of us gathered in the cafeteria while someone read the letter, which basically said, "Here we are fighting for other people's issues, but in the process of doing this we are being put in very much a second-class position within our own organization." The letter also asked us to look at our own position in SDS and the role of women in the organization.

When we started reading this letter, we were a very small group, but then it kept growing. Soon, almost all of the women who had come for the national council meeting were sitting in our group. People were saying, "Oh, yeah. That's true."

While we were out there talking, a few men came by to stand there and listen. They were very threatened. They decided that we hated men and that we were talking about them. Then they started taking over the conversation until we finally told them, "You know what? We'd like it if you left."

We went around the room and each of us talked about where we were, what we did, our role, our politics, and our vision for the future. After listening to everybody, we realized there was a shared experience, that the problem they had down south in SNCC, we had in SDS.

This was the first time I remember ever asking questions like "Who is doing the shitwork and who is in leadership positions?" We realized that the people who were doing the shit work around the office, the day-to-day licking of stamps, were women, and they were also doing the cooking and the cleaning and the door knocking. The men were becoming the spokespeople, and doing the writing, and were in the leadership positions, and how come this happened? We asked ourselves, what was it in us that made us fulfill those roles? We would go around the room and talk about growing up. How come these things happened?

When it was over, many of us were inspired to start gathering small groups of women where we lived to look into these questions. This was really the beginning of the women's movement.

Around that time, I had to put together a committee to work with me on my doctoral dissertation. I contacted one professor whose specialty was the moral development of children. He told me to come to his office and bring all my papers that had to do with this preschool I was running. When I got there, he proceeded to leap across his desk, pull off his tie and pin me against the wall, kissing me and slobbering all over me.

I was mortified, because I thought there was something I had done to precipitate this. Then he informed me that the only way he would be on the committee would be if I allowed him to do this to me. When I pushed him away, he told me to get my papers and leave.

Around the same time, another professor called me up and asked me if he could come over to my apartment. I thought he was going to talk about my work. When he got there, he said he wanted me to sit on his lap, and he wanted to give me a bath.

There was no such word as sexual harassment at the time, but the message was clear that unless I slept with these people I could not have a committee. These were my closest teachers. I had no one to turn to. After three years of coursework and prelims, I didn't have a committee, and I thought it was my fault. Also, these were important professors. If I had said something, nobody would have believed it.

Since I was interested in being a therapist, I had to go into therapy as part

Marilyn Webb, 1966. (Courtesy of Marilyn Webb)

of the training. So I was in therapy, and the guy kept saying to me, "Why do you want your Ph.D., anyway? Why do you want to be like a man?"

Eventually, I realized I was screwed at the University of Chicago anyway, so I took a job as the Washington Bureau Chief of *The Guardian*, which was a progressive newspaper. I never did finish my dissertation. Years later I wrote an article on feminist therapy, and I called up that therapist and reminded him what he told me, and he said, "Yeah, I was wrong. Sorry."

I never mentioned what happened to me to my women's group. Then, years later, I found out that the same thing happened to my friend Joanie at the University of Chicago. She had never mentioned it either, and she was my best friend. It not only tells you how secret this was at the time, but also how pervasive.

In Washington, I started a consciousness-raising group for women, and that summer I joined a massive teach-in around the country about Vietnam. My job was to create curricula for teaching Vietnam in the schools. I spent the summer talking and traveling and meeting other women about this curriculum we had developed. We also discussed issues they were faced with in their own communities. These were the same issues we had talked about at the SDS conference, shit work and priorities. Teachers, for instance, were at the lowest level on the totem pole. We asked, "Why is that?" The answer was that most of them were women.

That fall I went to Cuba, and I was very impressed with the work being done there in health clinics and in education and with women becoming voices in their communities.

That helped me realize this was an international issue of real importance. When I got back, we started talking about organizing other women around the women's issues. I wrote a series of articles about this. Then we started a group of programs which were a precursor to women's liberation.

One of the first things we started to do was abortion counseling. Remember, it was still illegal at this time. We lined up doctors to work with women who needed abortions. We weren't secretive about it, but this was underground work. Most of the women who came were middle-class women, college women, young mothers. They knew they wanted to get abortions, but they were afraid of dying. We're talking about back-alley abortions where women were bleeding to death, being hacked to death, people using knitting needles for abortions where you run the risk of perforated uteruses, huge infections, and maimed babies that you gave birth to anyway. They wanted abortions for all kinds of reasons: because they wanted to finish college or they had health problems. It was all very moving, and we felt strongly that there was no reason why women had to suffer like this.

We also taught a course on the roles that women play. It dealt with work, love, marriage, children. We talked about child care and equal pay, and roles and stereotyping. A lot of it was about pride—women's pride. In this day and age, women don't like to think of themselves as feminists. It's kind of old-fashioned. But then it was kind of like black pride. I don't think it's old-fashioned. I think it's important.

Younger women today don't realize how far the culture has come and why and who is responsible. My daughter today is the beneficiary of all of this stuff. She grew up thinking she could do everything. She could have a job, a house, a career. She didn't have the obstacles we grew up with. But she says, "I'm not a feminist." The term is hard edged, so she and her friends don't like the word, but while they might not realize it, they are feminists.

There came a point in 1968 when a widespread notion developed that it was time to try and build a national movement. We gathered a group of thirty or so women in Sandy Springs, Maryland, for a conference. We tried to get delegates from each of the cities where we knew these issues were being discussed, but some people refused to come. They said we were being divisive and taking away from major issues, like the antiwar movement.

Even among those who came, there were real differences of opinion in terms of priorities and points of view about what it meant to talk about women's liberation. The biggest differences came up when Roxanne Dunbar read something from the SCUM [Society for Cutting Up Men] Manifesto, which was written by Valerie Solanas. Solanas had shot the artist Andy Warhol. Roxanne argued that that was a legitimate act for a sexist man. I was appalled. I didn't think guns were legitimate ever. I couldn't believe she was arguing that it was OK to shoot a guy. There was also the idea of separating from men, which I didn't agree with either.

Out of that conference came an idea for a larger meeting, which we held in a YMCA camp in Chicago around Thanksgiving. Again, I was surprised about how divided we were, but I was also amazed at the brilliance of the women. The meeting gave me a sense of respect for what I was doing in a way that I had never had before, because the power of several hundred who were smart like this was overwhelming.

Even with the divisions, we came out of the meeting all charged up, and that group really provided the basis for having the movement grow across America. One of the first media actions was at the Miss America contest in 1968. Imagine thinking that being Miss America is the pinnacle of women's success. It was like being crowned the ultimate prom queen or cheerleader. When you think of that versus something like Madame Curie, how low can you aspire to?

We were calling attention to the problem with that image, and we had fun doing it. There were people with mops on their heads and brooms, saying a woman's role is to mop and broom. Someone was leading a pig around. Women were burning their bras. People were cheering and laughing, and for the most part the people got it right away.

After Nixon was elected in '68, a number of antiwar groups organized a counter-inauguration in Washington. We wanted to be a part of it as a coalition with men. We thought that women's liberation could be another arm of the left or of the antiwar movement and that men would get it right away. We also thought they would help us nationally to organize a women's movement. You could have an SDS chapter, and you could also have a women's chapter. People would connect, depending on where their hearts were.

The feminist group in Washington wanted to do this, and I was asked to speak for them. Thousands of people came down to the demonstration. I was terrified at the prospect of speaking to such a large group, and I spent hours writing my speech. I was very careful, trying to think about who I was addressing and what issues should be on the agenda. I decided I would talk about equality, abortion, child care, and treating women with respect. It was a pretty mild speech. I wasn't attacking men. I didn't see them as the enemy, so I had no reason to think that the men in the audience, especially this one, would be hostile.

But when it got to be our turn to speak, Dave Dellinger got up and said, "The girls from women's liberation are now gonna speak, and they have asked us to clear the stage of all men, including the wounded GI."

There was a wounded GI in a wheelchair, and I was horrified, because I never said that. It immediately created hostility. Then, when I started to speak, I hadn't gotten three sentences out when fistfights broke out. People were yelling, "Take her off the stage and fuck her." "Fuck her down a dark alley."

These were supposed to be my brothers and sisters! Dave Dellinger tried to get me off the stage, because he decided I was starting a riot.

Over thirty years later, I can still feel the shock. I'm still shaking. Here I was saying we want to have control over own bodies, and we are being told to fuck ourselves.

Afterward we had a little meeting back at my house to try and figure out what to do, and I got this phone call from a woman who sounded to me like someone I knew from the SDS. They thought it was counterrevolutionary to talk about something as bourgeois and conventional as women's rights when we should be fighting against imperialism. She said to me, "If you or anybody like you ever gives a speech like that anywhere in this country, we'll beat the shit out of you wherever you are," and then she hung up.

That was the moment I suddenly knew that we couldn't build a coalition with the left. Woman's liberation was going to be an independent movement. Clearly we had to organize separately, so I decided to focus my energies on women only.

In Washington, we formed a group called the Magic Quilt, based on the notion that it would be a series of small groups that together would make up a whole blanket. We were constantly getting new constituencies, suburban women, church women, nurses, clerical workers. It didn't grow because of our organizing. The time was right, and there were huge numbers of women whose time had come. Housewives didn't want to be home doing only what they were doing. In the churches, they had problems with the religious teachings that wouldn't recognize their equality. Nurses were low paid and being treated terribly by doctors. We talked to them, and as a result a nurses union was formed.

When the Senate held hearings on birth control pills, three or four of us went down there to see what they would say. They had no women testifying. It was all men. I could not contain myself. I got up and I said, "Excuse me, you haven't asked any women how we feel about these birth control pills, and I would like to say on the part of women that I've been talking to that we fear their safety."

They sent the cops after us and threw us out.

We did a series of things like that all over the city. We were the first generation of women doing this, so we got a lot of bruises. One of them, of course, was that marriages were difficult. Also, we didn't earn the money it was possible for women to earn now, so we were often poor, single mothers, if we had kids at all. Some couldn't afford kids, and that was the sacrifice they made. We had to make a lot of those kinds of choices that people don't have to make today.

I got a lot of criticism for being married. The problem with marriage wasn't so much about sexual freedom as it was about the role of women within the nuclear family. Some women wanted to smash the nuclear family, because to them the role of the wife is as the indentured slave. For me, the issue was how easy it is to fall into that because it's how you are brought up as a woman and a man in America. Eggs had to be broken before the omelets could be made. I got divorced. Lee is a really good person. If it had been today we would have stayed married, but the strains of the culture put a lot of strain on our relationship.

In the radical women's movement, they were also against having children. They said that having a child made a woman into a biological indentured servant, so when I had a child the pressures against me were also hard on my marriage. It was a crazy time. Some people even believed if you did have a child and you had a son, you should give him up.

They were also against having leaders and media stars. When I ended up getting visibility on television and in the press, people in Magic Quilt got angry, and I was asked to leave. I was devastated, but in another way it was a relief, because I was tired of doing administrative work.

I decided to start a newspaper on women's issues. I called up a bunch of people and we got it going. We called it *off our backs*. It would be a monthly that would cover women's news for women. It also had a humor column, a cartoon called "Chicken Little" about the fears women had, and even a centerfold of men.

The first issue came out in 1970. It was really the first such magazine for women in the movement, and it was good. It also got the women in Washington really pissed off, because they had kicked me out, and here I was doing this other thing that was becoming very popular.

Then some very strange things started happening. Suddenly the arguments in our group were getting very divisive. One person who joined our group had a Chicago police identification tag fall out of her pocket. I suspect now that we were infiltrated by the FBI to create trouble. They were afraid of the movement, so they tried to destroy it. So many books I read about the movement in the '60s and '70s leave the impression that the movement was overwhelmed by women squabbling. Now I think that that tension was deliberately created.

Then the same thing that started happening with the Magic Quilt happened with *off our backs*. I was getting a lot of media attention. Also, I could write very easily and edit very quickly, and they asked me not to do that, to train other people instead, because they didn't think anybody should have more skills than anybody else. Everybody should be equal.

Well, everybody isn't. They have different skills, but I agreed to this. Then that fall, I was asked to be the keynote speaker at a conference on women. When I came back, I was asked to leave.

Again I was devastated, but again I landed on my feet. I must have been so annoying to those people in Washington. They kept trying to get rid of me, and I kept popping back up. I moved to Vermont and started a women's studies department at Goddard College. The program I set up ended up being the first women's studies program in the country.

Setting up the program was a fabulous opportunity. We didn't have the history books that they have now. Women's history did not exist. I had to basically devise undergraduate programs for women to study, so I was making it up as we went along. We read a lot of Doris Lessing and Virginia Woolf. I created courses that had guest lecturers in history, politics, and literature. We did a lot of oral histories of people in the area. There were art classes and literature classes, economics. We also had courses in auto mechanics for women, counterculture courses, women's music, cartooning, and martial arts training.

I was there five years. After I left, I moved to Colorado and I wrote my first book. I've written two since. The most recent is called, The Good Death: The New American Search to Reshape the End of Life. I worked on it for six years. It's about how we die in America and how the American health-care system can be changed to make it better for everyone to have a proper ending to a life well lived.

I think it fits in very intimately with my feminist work, and I didn't even realize it except instinctually when I first started. Years ago, with the natural childbirth movement, we changed birthing and improving the beginning of life. Now we're trying to change health care to improve the end of life.

It also fits in with the women's health movement in terms of information and assertiveness regarding safety, from everything including how we treat breast cancer to the impact of all kinds of birth control pills. Also, the people who are major caregivers are the women in America. And while we've been doing all this caregiving we've changed our environment drastically. A lot of us are working, and that's left a huge hole in the American health-care system, which doesn't address long-term care. Dying is no longer a quick event from

Author and journalism professor Marilyn Webb today. (Courtesy of Knox College)

infectious disease. It's a long-term process of maybe dealing with cancer or heart disease. Who is going to care for them while we're out there in the workforce?

Not to mention the fact that women generally live years longer than men, so a lot of times these years are spent alone, and it's scary for these people not to know who is going to care for them. I speak to a lot of community groups about this, and I'm helping to organize a movement to change end-of-life care. That's where my heart is these days.

The battles are still ongoing. You would think they would stop trying to get rid of *Roe v. Wade* after all these years, but they are, and now people are killing abortion doctors. In order to say that abortion should be illegal, it seems to me that they should be campaigning out there for guaranteed child care. If you're going to support a woman's right to have that child, you should support that child.

I'm proud of being part of the women's movement in America because it has changed American culture for the better. Even with the backlash and the squabbling, it has given my daughter the potential for a life as a woman that I never dreamed I could have.

If the next generation takes it for granted, it's OK in a sense because it's an indication that the women's movement has been a huge success. You never get a girl who thinks she can't play sports. If a woman wants to go into medicine, she can be a doctor.

There isn't equal pay for equal work, but it's a hell of a lot better than it used to be. We still don't have guaranteed child care, but people are conscious of it. There is still inequality in terms of wealth, but there's a larger sense of self-worth and self-respect of terms of what we can be. It's a totally changed world.

Frank Kameny
The Pioneer

Shortly after midnight on June 28, 1969, eight policeman raided a gay bar called the Stonewall Inn in New York City's Greenwich Village. There was no particular reason for the bust. Cops simply liked to hassle gays. But this time it was different, because the 200 or so people inside the bar decided not to be victims anymore, and for the first time they fought back.

It was a warm summer night, and the commotion around the bar attracted a crowd, which grew into an angry mob as word spread about what was happening. The crowd began throwing coins at the cops, mocking their well-known demands for payoffs from gay establishments. The police retreated into the bar and trashed it while waiting for reinforcements. The department's elite antiriot squad appeared within minutes and attempted to disperse the mob, but it grew even larger and now was upping the ante. Instead of throwing coins, people were tossing rocks and bottles, burning trash cans, and shouting, "Gay power!"

Eventually the police gained control of the street, but an even larger group reappeared outside the bar the next night and four more consecutive nights. By the time the protests had ended, the number of people demonstrating outside Stonewall were in the thousands, and a new mass movement was born.

Alfred Kinsey's studies indicated that about 10 percent of the world's population is homosexual. Yet homosexuality has been treated as a crime throughout nearly the entire history of western civilization. In America, homosexuality was punishable by death until 1873.

The first homosexual rights group in the United States, the Mattachine

Society (named after a group of masked actors who were said to have done so to hide their homosexuality), was founded in 1950 by Henry Hay. The need was strong. Gays were forced to live in an underground subculture, because any public disclosure of their sexuality could cost them their livelihood or their lives. The message was driven home in 1953 with an executive order in which President Dwight D. Eisenhower barred all gay men and lesbians from federal jobs. Like alleged communists, they were purged from government and university jobs.

One victim of the purge was a Washington, D.C., astronomer named Frank Kameny. A World War II combat veteran, Kameny decided to fight back. In 1961, he organized a branch of the Mattachine Society, but he refused to operate in secret, and he took a more activist stance. In 1967, he challenged the negative stereotypes of homosexuals when he coined the slogan "Gay is good." He organized pickets against the police and other government agencies that were harassing gays. Before long, his efforts began to pay off. By the time of the Stonewall riots, there were some fifty gay rights groups around the country. In 1971, Kameny would be the first openly gay person to run for Congress, and in 1975 was the first ever to receive a mayoral appointment.

It's one thing to speak up when everyone around you is doing the same, but Kameny's was truly a lone voice in the wilderness. Here was a rare example of pure courage. I ask him about that, and how he decided to step forward when hardly anyone else would.

I learned to read when I was about four. An uncle gave me a large book called The Knowledge Book. I read through that avidly, and I decided very quickly at the age of four or five that I wanted to become a scientist. A year or so later I narrowed that down to astronomy.

I went to the Army in 1943, where I became an 81-millimeter mortar crewman. I went overseas in 1944 and fought in Holland. I saw some very intense combat in Germany until the end of the war.

At that point, I was very much a shy, introverted person. Still, I was in my teens, and male teens have hormones flowing, and mine certainly did. I knew what I was looking at and what was attracting me. I had a few isolated homosexual episodes in school and when I was in the Army. In retrospect, I can look back and bemoan not picking up on all the opportunities that came my way in the Army. There were any number of incidents where people made

Frank Kameny, a decorated infantry officer during World War II.
(Courtesy of Frank Kameny)

what I now know were passes at me, but all of that went totally over my head at that time. Remember, this was a totally different era. While I was aware of my feelings, I bought into the prevailing philosophy, which was that it was a phase I was going through.

In 1948 I finished my undergraduate degree at Queens College. Then I got accepted to Harvard to get my graduate degree in astronomy. After Harvard, I ended up working at Georgetown University in Washington.

In 1954 I was spending some time in Arizona when I ran into someone who turned out to be gay. After talking to him, I realized that wherever I was, I was not disapproving of the idea. Through him I got to know a small group of other gay people. Then, through them, I met a young man who had a lot more experience than I had, and we hit it off. I had what I've referred to since then as a golden summer.

In every city in those days there was an active underground of gay people who knew each other. My friend knew where the gay bars were, and I became part of a small, closeted gay community. That was the first time I had ever heard the word "gay" before.

The term "coming out" then meant coming to terms with yourself and becoming involved with the gay community wherever you were. Nobody ever came out publicly then unless they were backed into an awkward corner.

It was a very, very nasty time. This was after the Kinsey report on human sexuality came out, and it reported that there was a much higher percentage of gays in America than was previously thought. There was an intense, visceral counterreaction to that.

In 1950, there were congressional hearings on the subject of employment of "perverts" in the civil service. As a consequence to that, President Eisenhower issued Executive Order 10450, which stated that "sexual perversion" was a basis of denial both for civil service employment and security clearances.

There were a huge number of awful professional tragedies through the '50s, where if people were found to be gay, out they went, and nobody fought back. I would be the first person to do so.

In Washington, D.C., the police department set up their so-called morals division, which had a so-called perversion section, whose purpose was to, on any excuse, arrest gay people and extract from them names of other gay people. All these names were sent in to the Civil Service Commission, and every one of them was called in and intensely interrogated. The whole purpose of the interrogation was names, names, names of the other people, to make lists.

I was at Georgetown for a year when I got an offer from a government agency called the Army Map Service. I took the job in July 1957. In November I was called in for an interview, and I was told, "We have information that leads us to believe that you are a homosexual. Do you have any comments?"

"What is the information?"

"We can't tell you."

"Well, I can't answer, and in any case this is none of your business."

They moved ahead. At the end of December, I was informed that I was terminated for homosexuality.

That would be only the beginning of my eighteen-year battle with the civil service. When I was fired, everything changed for me. I had a burning sense of injustice. This simply wasn't right, and something needed to be done.

I appealed as far as I could go within the Civil Service Commission. I got nowhere. I went to the House and Senate Civil Service committees. I got nowhere. I went to the ACLU. They assigned me an attorney, and we went to court. We appealed it up to the Supreme Court. Then my attorney saw that we weren't going to get anywhere, and he said, "If you want to go ahead, do it on your own."

He gave me a copy of the Supreme Court rules, and I proceeded to file my own petition to the court in 1961. It forced me to sit and formulate my own philosophy, and ultimately I wrote what was really the first gay rights brief ever filed in any court anywhere. I rebutted the entire philosophy that said homosexuality was immoral. Forty years later it still reads well, but predictably it got turned down by the Supreme Court.

Times were difficult for me after I was fired. I hadn't been in the field long enough to achieve any kind of reputation or status. My possibilities for employment were nil. Toward the end of 1959, I was living on 20 cents' worth of food a day. Eventually I got a job with a local company in physics and optics, but I could no longer work in my chosen profession.

One problem was I couldn't get security clearance, which was then routinely denied to gay people. This was the cold war period. There was a mythology that had grown up, with no facts to support it, that all gay people were cringing, submissive victims of endless blackmail attempts. They were also emotionally unstable, and therefore they were unreliable and untrustworthy in all ways. In point of fact, the only instance of homosexual-based blackmail in the entire history of western espionage was Colonel Alfred Roedl in the Austro-Hungarian army in 1912. Gays have been suffering from Colonel Roedl for practically a century.

By then I had heard about the early "homophile" groups. I visited the Mattachine Society headquarters in San Francisco. There were only five or six such groups in the country in those days. When I began fighting, the San Francisco group sent me a $50 donation, which was a lot of money back then.

The movement then was bland, apologetic, unassertive, unwilling to view ourselves as the authorities on ourselves. They deferred to the "experts." It sounds harshly critical, but it's not intended to be. They were as the era was, but none of that suited my personality, and so I took a very different approach once I started going on things in 1961.

After I filed my petition with the Supreme Court, I formed a branch of the Mattachine Society in Washington, D.C. There were a couple of people I met by sheer chance who were equally enthusiastic. We called ourselves into existence on November 15, 1961. With that, I founded the gay movement locally here in Washington, and with that gay activism and militancy nationally, at a time when those two words were dirty words inside the gay movement.

We had no compunctions about saying what we were exactly about, that there were rights for homosexuals that we were fighting for. The other groups couldn't believe that we were actually saying that we were homosexuals. They used to speak about "sexual variants" and things like that.

We took a strong, positive, affirmative position. We had no compunctions saying that we were fighting for rights for homosexuals. We didn't say, "Well, we have to listen to both sides. This week, we call in a psychiatrist who says we aren't sick, and next week we call in one who says we are. This week we get a clergyman who says God loves us, and next week we get one who says God hates us."

No, we knew where we stood, and we got the people who supported us.

We were concerned about various forms of discrimination and abuse, civil service employment, gays in the military, security clearances, police harassment. We had meetings with the head of the vice squad. We participated in the famous Martin Luther King march on Washington in 1963. I was out there on the mall with a Mattachine sign.

While everybody speaks of the '60s, for gays things didn't really get going until the second half of '69 to the '70s. For us, things heated up around 1965 when we did our first open picketing. Nowadays people picket at the drop of a hat. Open picketing for us, though, was a very radical step in those days, but after a while, we felt we were not getting very far with the government, which was digging in its heels against us.

This is what started it: we learned that Congress had passed the D.C. Charitable Solicitations Act, which required nonprofit organizations raising funds to file and get a permit from the D.C. government. We got one, and that came to the attention of a Texas congressman who became outraged that the government would issue a permit to a group of perverts. He introduced a bill in the house, denying our permit.

The bill never got anywhere, but we demanded a public hearing, and the bill—and the congressman, unwisely for him—granted it, because it turned the whole thing into a media event. We got more publicity out of that than we could have gotten if we had the money to go out and buy it. In fact, the following year we issued a citation to the congressman, engraved on parchment, as the person who had done the most in 1963 to advance the cause of the homophile movement.

Ultimately, he was sent to jail for five years for embezzlement.

In the course of that, I took the opportunity to suggest that the D.C. sodomy law be appealed. That kicked off an effort that was ultimately successful, but it took thirty years, one month, five days, and eleven hours before we got it repealed, and I ended up writing the repealer bill.

In April 1965 we saw a newspaper item about Castro putting gays into concentration camps. Our feeling was while that was bad, the U.S. wasn't much better. We thought that would be a good issue to picket around, and so we assembled ten people and picketed the White House. That was the first organized gay picket in the country.

I think we got coverage from one newspaper, the *Washington Afro-American*. But it went off so beautifully we decided to do it again, and this time we would publicize it. Now we were reported on the wires. One of the scandal magazines showed a picture of us, saying, "These are not real homosexuals picketing, these are actors playing the roles of homosexuals."

All that was the beginning of a lot of things. We picketed the Civil Service Commission building, the Pentagon, the State Department. Our final demonstration was in front of the White House. We had sixty-five picketers, which for us was huge. We were always heckled to some degree, but there were always policemen around, and there was never any real trouble.

Also, on the Fourth of July, we had a demonstration in front of Independence Hall. That was the first of a series on the Fourth every year through 1969. We were joined by a big contingent from New York. They were major events. They created the mind-set which would have been absolutely unthinkable before 1965: gay people themselves taking part in public protest action. That created the mind-set which made Stonewall possible.

Our group also put out a publication called the *Gazette*. We put on the mailing list the president, the vice president, the cabinet, selected judges and congressmen, and J. Edgar Hoover.

One evening I got a call from an FBI agent. He invited me down to the Justice Department, where he informed me that Mr. Hoover was very upset that we had been sending him the *Gazette*. He found it objectionable, and he wanted to be removed from our mailing list.

I pointed out this was a civil rights publication and that we expected Mr.

Hoover to support us, and that anyway we had a First Amendment right to send anything we wanted to anyone, and certainly to anyone in the government.

He said he recognized that, but that Mr. Hoover would really like to be taken off the list.

I said we would have to think about it. I pointed out with some amusement that while many gays were afraid to be put on lists maintained by J. Edgar Hoover, it turned out that he was even more fearful of being placed on a list maintained by Mattachine.

Finally I offered them a deal. I said if Mr. Hoover would give us his assurances that all files maintained on us and our members were destroyed, we would be willing to take Mr. Hoover off our mailing list. However, we wanted the name of someone else in the FBI to whom we could send our publication.

We never heard anything back, and Mr. Hoover remained on our mailing list for a decade, until he died.

I had always been aware of the intense, absolutely unmitigated flow of negativism directed at us. We were sick, we were sinners, we were criminals. You name the negative characterization, and we were it. Of course that has its impact on people.

One day I was watching Stokely Carmichael on TV, and he was exhorting a crowd to chant, "Black is beautiful." I realized they were being faced with exactly the same kind of thing. In our culture, black was universally equated with everything that was bad, dirty, ugly, and negativity in every possible way, so you needed something which turned it around, and that was "Black is beautiful."

We needed something like that. I spent the new few weeks trying to figure out how to do it, and I came up with "Gay is good."

This was at a time when most people still didn't know the term "gay." By then, there were forty or fifty gay organizations, and we had formed a national structure: NACHO, the North American Conference of Homophile Organizations. At their next annual meeting, I introduced a resolution that they adopt "Gay is good" as their official slogan, which they did. I had a friend in the button business. He issued buttons in six different colors of psychedelic printing, and it spread. After a while, it became transmuted into "gay pride" and "gay liberation."

One of our major goals was to get the American Psychiatric Association to change its stance that homosexuality was a mental disorder. That battle started because I and a couple of others realized very early on that in our culture we were never going to get any kind of equality if we were considered to be emotionally disturbed or disordered.

I honestly didn't know where things stood on that issue scientifically. But I was a scientist by training and background. I know good science when I see it, and I know bad science, so I proceeded to see what there was, and I was absolutely appalled. It was shoddy, slipshod, slovenly, sleazy pseudo-science, assumptions pumped in at one end and pumped out at the other end as conclusions—garbage in, garbage out—poor sampling techniques. I could go on and on and on. It was quite clear that what you had was moral, cultural, and theological and sociological value judgments camouflaged in the language of science without any of the substance of science.

We issued a statement, saying, "In the lack of valid scientific evidence to the contrary, homosexuality cannot be properly considered as a sickness or an illness or a disturbance or a disorder. It must be considered an orientation, a preference, or a propensity, not different in kind from heterosexuality and fully on par with it."

That was around 1964. What that did was to shift the burden of proof for homosexuality as a sickness from us over to the psychiatric establishment, and for the next ten years they never could answer it.

We had a lot of things on our platter then, and we didn't push it for most of the remainder of the '60s, but I began to push again on this in the early '70s. We began to work with sympathetic members of the APA. Meanwhile, some of the extreme groups started disrupting psychiatric meetings. Finally one APA member realized unless they took steps to defuse what was going on, they were going to be in a lot of trouble.

They asked me to organize a panel discussion on the subject at their 1971 meeting. Suddenly, during our panel discussion, the doors broke open and in poured one of the extreme groups. On the podium was a group of honored elderly psychiatrists, who had just been given gold medals of honor, and they proceeded to beat the invaders over the head with their gold medals and push them out the door.

The next year, we had a booth at their convention with a sign that said, "Gay, Proud, and Healthy." A famous picture was taken that year at their banquet, in which I and another local gay man were dancing while the psychiatrists were dancing around us.

It took a while after that. The APA has a byzantine, complex internal structure which would do credit to a small country, but things proceeded, and

Frank Kameny, retired astronomer, 2004.
(Courtesy of Frank Kameny)

in December 1973 they altered their official position at a ceremony where they invited us to their headquarters.

All this time we were still trying to get the civil service to amend its rules about gays. We pushed on that with letters, which forced them to respond. We forced meetings on them, insisting we were citizens and taxpayers and if we ask public servants for meetings, we get meetings. I take literally the phrase "public servant," which makes me, as a member of the public, one of their masters. When masters ask for meetings, servants give meetings!

There was also a whole series of cases filed against the civil service by gay people who had been fired. I was involved as a consultant on virtually every one of them all through the '60s and the '70s, and we won nearly all of them.

Finally the courts issued an injunction barring the civil service from firing people for homosexuality. That substantially killed the policy. Through all of this, I was in touch with the general counsel of the Civil Service Commission. He was not homophobic, but he had to operate in that atmosphere. I phoned him after the injunction went into effect. He said they would change the policy, but it would take around eighteen months, which it did. They phoned me at the end of June 1975 to tell me it was going to come out on July 3, and so it did. That ended it.

In 1978 Congress passed a law that said that off-duty conduct could not be considered a factor in employment if it didn't affect the job. It was a great victory that was ultimately nailed down twenty years later when President Clinton issued Executive Order 13087, which extended that as executive policy across the board.

These days, some people call me a father or a grandfather of the gay movement. I have my ego, and I'm very glad to be called that, but I wasn't alone. There were people who preceded me. I guess we saw the trails and blazed them. We pushed against a sometimes willing, and sometimes a very unwilling, larger mass, but I never thought that it was possible that the movement would become as large as it is today. Things have moved so quickly. Even as late as ten years ago, there were few of us who would have expected that we would be where we are now. There has just been massive cultural changes and acceptance since then. Of course, as this has happened, the far right has gotten more shrill, but only because they're fighting a battle they know now they cannot win.

Barry Melton
The Guitarist

Give me an F!

Give me a U!

Give me a C!

You know the rest.

That brief spelling exercise performed during their concerts nearly landed the members of Country Joe and the Fish in jail or in the hospital on several occasions.

But pushing the envelope was something the band lived for. Led by two "red diaper" babies, Joe McDonald and Barry Melton, the Fish was the most experimental and political of the great San Francisco bands of the 1960s. They also made some good music. With the Grateful Dead, the Jefferson Airplane, Quicksilver Messenger Service, Big Brother and the Holding Company, and others, the music they played in such storied concert halls as the Fillmore West and the Winterland helped define the decade, especially in its later years, when the counterculture was in full bloom.

The San Francisco bands took jazz, blues, country, rock, eastern, and classical influences, put them in a pot, and cooked up a stew called "psychedelic" music. The name implied that the music was influenced by drugs, and it was. But more important, the music was a product of players who knew and respected their musical heritage and used it to expand and experiment with the boundaries of rock and roll.

But they didn't forget to have fun. Perhaps the most political song to come out of the Bay area was also the biggest crowd-pleaser. McDonald, a Vietnam veteran, wrote his impassioned "I-Feel-Like-I'm-Fixin'-To-Die

Rag" as a bouncy sing-along tune. With its unforgettable chorus and sarcastic verses, it may have been the most galvanizing antiwar song of the decade:

And it's one, two, three,
What are we fighting for?
Don't ask me, I don't give a damn,
Next stop is Vietnam.
And it's five, six, seven,
Open up the pearly gates.
Well there ain't no time to wonder why,
Whoopee! we're all gonna die!

But when it came to mainstream commercial success, the band's politics were suicidal. Hardly any radio station would play "Fixin'-To-Die," and concert promoters were afraid to book the band, fearing that the Fish cheer would prompt the police to shut down the show for obscenity. It's hard to imagine today, when the likes of Marilyn Manson and even Madonna can freely shock audiences, but in the late 1960s Jim Morrison's relatively tame behavior forced him to flee the country to avoid an extended prison term.

I wanted to talk with Barry Melton, find out about what it was like to be a guitar hero in the 1960s and what his influences were, and hear the inside story of musicians I had read about for years. Having seen Melton countless times while watching the documentary film *Woodstock*, I wanted to know what it was like to be on stage in the greatest concert of the 1960s. I also wanted to hear about the roots of the band's outrageousness and the origin of "Fixin-To-Die" and the Fish cheer.

At his comfortable home in Davis, California, Barry is a generous host and a great talker. If he were to be arrested today, the police might quickly come to regret taking on more than they can handle, as these days he is a public defender. While he works on behalf of the poor, he is very much a part of the system. As we walk around town, he is greeted warmly on the street. One of those who stops for a brief chat turns out to be a judge.

Barry is heftier than he was in his youth, and his gray hair is tucked under a baseball cap. Though he still plays guitar, his rock-star days are long gone. Nowadays he's a suburban Dad, and he looks the part. With his wife and two children, he lives in a corner house on a quiet block in Davis, an

Country Joe McDonald, manager Ed Denson, and Barry "The Fish" Melton in 1965. (Courtesy the Melton family)

agricultural college town. The furniture is mix and match. The room is filled with books and music, and the house is permeated with the warmth of a tight and loving family.

I grew up in Brighton Beach, Brooklyn, New York. In those days, it seemed like half of Brighton's population were remnants of the American Communist Party. Both my parents were members of the Party, so I was what they called a "red diaper baby." I used to deliver *Daily Workers* with my brother every day.

My parents were very sincere, idealistic people. You couldn't just label them as communists. To do that is to give a simple label to a whole constellation of beliefs about civil rights, human rights, fairness, the ability of labor to organize and have a voice. My dad fought hard for these principles. One night when he was organizing down South, he was beaten, then shot and dumped in a river. His friends fished him out in pretty bad shape, but he survived and went back and back and back. You couldn't stop him that way.

Music was an integral part of their progressive politics, so we had a lot of it around us. We listened to Pete Seeger, Paul Robeson, Earl Robinson, and Woody Guthrie. For a while, Woody was our next-door neighbor. He was a celebrity in our neighborhood, but mostly what I remember about him was that he was a little crazy and he played the guitar. I went to his wife Marge's dance school to learn tap dancing. All the little commie kids went to Marge Guthrie's dance school.

In the early 1950s, my father was called before the House Un-American Activities Committee, but he refused to answer questions, and he was expelled from his union. After that, he kept getting fired from every job he got when they found out who he was, so in 1955 my parents decided to move to California because my Uncle John was a shop foreman at the Fisher Body Plant in Van Nuys. As it turned out, the FBI visited the plant and made sure he couldn't work there either.

We put our stuff in my Dad's broken-down old Chevy with a U-Haul trailer behind it and took off for the West Coast. In Pennsylvania the trailer got loose and ran over my dad's legs. We consigned our possessions to a moving company and ended up on a Trailways bus. Dad had to lie in the back of the bus, because it was too painful for him to sit. In Texas, a black woman got on the bus. The driver tried to make her sit in the back, and my mother started screaming at the bus driver. The net result was we were all thrown off the bus.

Imagine how I felt as a kid in this situation. Here's my dad, who can't walk, and we're moving out to California because HUAC is pursuing us, and the FBI won't let my dad hold down a job, and we get thrown off a bus in the middle of the Deep fucking South, man, because my mother is going to do everything but kill the bus driver for mistreating this black woman on the bus. I remember being there by the side of the road and hearing the line my mother and father would use over and over again: "Well, I know it's inconvenient, but it's the right thing to do."

And it was the right thing to do, but it was hard sometimes. On the West Coast, with my dad unable to work, we were falling off the edge. We were living in a one-bedroom apartment that was right out of a migrant camp. It was across the street from the dairy and smelled like it. For a long time, the only thing we had for breakfast, lunch, and dinner was oatmeal.

Eventually, as the McCarthy period passed, Dad was slowly able to reintegrate himself back into daily life, just like all of those people who suffered during that era. But he and my mom never changed their core beliefs. When my mom died in L.A. in 1988, the young minister said he didn't know her well at all. "The only time I met Mrs. Melton was when she came in here as part of our sanctuary protest for El Salvadorian refugees, and I remember we were concerned that the police would kick in the door, and Mrs. Melton insisted on sleeping in front of the door that night."

I don't think my dad ever looked at the exterior of anybody. He always looked at the inside of people. He lived with me in San Francisco in his last years, and he enjoyed wandering around the city. One day I was in my house after he died, and this couple came around. They had spiked hair and everything was pierced. They said, "Hi, we're here to see Jim. Have you seen him? He's our friend."

I'll never forget the hardship and the attempt by the FBI and HUAC to rob my parents of their dignity and their means. I'll remember being dirt poor and having to migrate and being displaced. That was the 1950s to me. They were a lesson about excessive government. I have an absolute and, I submit, healthy distrust of government and government excess and what unchecked government power is. And what I do now as a criminal defense lawyer is just another manifestation of what I've been doing my whole life: defending the minority against the tyranny of the majority, defending people against government excess.

My mother played piano, and she bought me my first guitar when I was five. I became and have become what I was expected to become—a musician. I'd like to take credit for blazing a trail. But in fact I'm really a mama's boy.

I was not an Elvis fan. I didn't get into rock and roll until I played it professionally. I was a bit of a snob and a folk purist. There was a folk music club in Los Angeles called the Ash Grove. Next door was McCabe's Guitar Shop, which was the folk music center of Los Angeles. There were a bunch of kids who hung out and jammed there, like Taj Mahal, Ry Cooder, and the folks who later formed the Byrds: David Crosby and Jim McGuinn.

In high school, my life was a mixture of folk music and the civil rights movement. I used to ride the bus to downtown Los Angeles and work at the CORE office to do Freedom Rider support. I went to rallies that were really the very beginning of the anti–Vietnam War movement. It was so early that only a handful of people would show up.

I sat in at the Los Angeles Board of Education and also at Van de Camp's

Restaurant, which had branches in the South that were discriminating at their lunch counters. Occasionally I'd get taken down to the police station. They'd give me a stern warning and call my mom. You can imagine her response: "Oh, how terrible, officer. He was arrested demonstrating for what? Negroes?" I wasn't going to get punished for that. Still, here they were reconstructing their lives after a very traumatic period, and it was hard on them when they were called to see the school principal because I refused to say the recently inserted "under God" during the Pledge of Allegiance.

The civil rights movement went hand in hand with the blues revival. It began when several record executives traveled to the Deep South to find old blues singers and bring them back North to play at the northern folk festivals and record for the first time in twenty-five years.

As a folk musician, I didn't want to learn the blues music off of records. I wanted to learn from these singers themselves, which is the blues tradition. Muddy Waters supposedly led Blind Lemon Jefferson through the streets with his hand on his shoulder and took him places to play, and that's how Muddy learned.

So here I am, a young kid in high school in Los Angeles, and I want to learn how to play the blues. Bukka White, who is illiterate and can't drive, comes to Los Angeles, and I want to learn everything this man knows, so what do I do? I present myself as his driver. "I will take you everywhere you want to go." All I really wanted to do was play music with him. He said, "Sure." What a small price to pay for a chauffeur and someone to read the menu to him.

We'd sit around, and he'd talk about his home, his songs, what his life was like growing up. Mance Lipscomb was another one. He was old enough that he started playing before the blues came into existence. Mance was just a really generous man and generous spirit. He was a sharecropper in Texas who was amazed at all the attention he was suddenly getting during the 1960s blues revival up North, which gave new life to his career and to a lot of the other old-timers. He was also an amazing player even though his hands were beat to shit from farming.

A little later, I got to know Jesse Fuller toward the end of his life. He was working in a shoeshine parlor in Oakland, playing as a one-man band, when some folk music group took an old song of his, "San Francisco Bay Blues," and made a hit of it. Imagine it. Here's this guy who had spent most of his professional career playing in a one-man band in a shoeshine parlor, and not only does he suddenly get this big check but he's suddenly touring Europe. I remember when he came back, he said to me, "They held me on their shoulders and carried me," and almost started crying.

It was the same thing with Mance. After being a lowly sharecropper at the bottom of every social scale in America, they put him in front of thousands of young white people at folk festivals in the North and were paying him more money for two nights' work than he earned in a year. This was right in the middle of the civil rights movement. Talk about justice, that's justice, because when you hear rock and roll today, when you hear contemporary pop music, these guys are all over it.

After I graduated high school in 1965, I went up to San Francisco. The Bay area was jumping, and although it didn't have a name yet, the growth of the counterculture probably had as much as anything to do with smoking pot and psychedelic drugs. The trouble with psychedelic drugs, though, is people have bad trips. And now that I work for people with drug problems in the criminal justice system, I can tell you that people have been seriously injured by the use of drugs.

Having said that, I don't think marijuana should be illegal. All drugs are dangerous to some extent, including the glass of wine I had tonight. I just don't believe that life is all work and suffering and we shouldn't enjoy ourselves, but if you are an adult and you're doing things with your eyes open and you're moderate, is there anything so intrinsically dangerous about marijuana use that people should go to jail for it? No. Let's be honest here. One of the biggest drug problems in this country is our lack of honesty when dealing with the drug problem.

I also think that people with substance-abuse problems should be treated like people with medical problems, and their illness shouldn't be compounded by giving them legal problems. Substance abusers aren't criminals. Many of them are people with an illness called "addiction." I tell the same thing to my kids, that I don't believe that drugs should be illegal; but drugs are drugs, and drugs are unhealthy and can be a real disaster for young, growing bodies.

When I moved to Berkeley, I shared a place with Bruce Barthol, my friend from high school. Bruce and I and our first bass player, Paul Armstrong, lived in this place next to a club called the Jabberwock. We had this wonderful landlady who lived downstairs. She was stone deaf, thank God, because we were playing loud music upstairs all the time, and she thought we were the most wonderful boys in the world and couldn't imagine why anyone would think anything else.

We had nothing, but we didn't need much. I think we paid $25 each for rent, and our entire food budget was maybe another twenty bucks a month. I survived by playing music or teaching guitar at the Jewish Community Center in San Francisco. I also worked as a carpenter's apprentice.

For a while, just about the only thing we ate was peanut butter—for break-fast, lunch, and dinner. Paul believed that white bread, peanut butter, and powdered milk contained everything that a human being needed to survive, so that's what we ate. Of course, Paul died of a stroke at the age of fifty, but we won't go there.

Because we were next to the club, whenever these itinerant folk musicians came through town, they'd stay with us. Some of the most marvelous musicians wandered through our house: David Bromberg, John Fahey, Robbie Basho, Stefan Grossman, Taj Mahal, Rev. Gary Davis, Mance Lipscomb, Light-ning Hopkins, whoever was out there on the folk circuit at that time. Our house was always open; there was always coffee on the stove, a boxtop with weed floating around in it, an open jug of chianti, good-looking young women, and a place to sleep if you needed it. We'd wake up late, ten or eleven o'clock, and start playing music in the kitchen, play for two or three hours with whoever was at the Jabberwock the night before or whoever happened to be in town.

I went back and forth a lot between Berkeley and San Francisco. I never fell asleep more than two nights in a row on the same side of the bay. I knew many of the other folk-rock musicians. Jerry Garcia had taken guitar lessons from a friend, and I knew most of the guys in the Dead crew. I watched the Byrds come together. Mike Wilhelm, who was with the Charlatans, was a friend of mine down in L.A. And when I came to northern California, one of the first names I was given to look up was Jerry Kaukonen. Later, when he was the Jefferson Airplane, he was known as Jorma Kaukonen.

Most of the people from those early San Francisco bands came from the folk music scene. As I said before, one of the cool things about folk musicians is they played a lot, and in Berkeley, it meant they played in public and jammed with people. That's how I met Joe McDonald.

I met Joe in 1964 when we were both playing music with Malvina Reynolds, who wrote a popular song called "Little Boxes," which was a satire about suburbia. Then we saw each other at a few demonstrations. Joe's father worked for the phone company, lost his job because of HUAC, came out to the West Coast, couldn't find work, and did odd jobs like gardening and stuff, so we had a lot in common, including our political outlook and musical tastes. I told him I had been in anti-Vietnamese government demonstrations in L.A., and he told me about seeing the body bags come in from Vietnam when he was an air traffic controller with the Navy in Japan.

One day in 1965, he called me up and said he and a guy named Ed Denson wanted to make a protest record in connection with the Vietnam Day teach-ins. They needed a guitar player, and I was a hot young guitar player then, so someone said, "You should get Barry."

It probably isn't surprising that we got our first airplay on Radio Moscow. Somebody told us that it was preceded with some announcer saying [in a Russian accent] "American students are very unhappy with their government. Here is song made by typical Americans."

More than likely, that song was "Fixin'-To-Die," an anti–Vietnam War song. Who knew that it would later be listed by the Rock and Roll Hall of Fame among the "most influential" rock and roll songs of all time? It wasn't until around 1967, when the war had escalated, that I realized the song had tremendous power. Around then we'd perform the song, and we were surprised to hear people singing along with it. By '67, it had become an anthem.

As it turned out, that first record ended up creating an identity that could get us booked, and Joe and I went on tour together as Country Joe and the Fish, although at that point it was just the two of us.

Ed Denson came up with the name. "Country Joe" was a nickname for Joe Stalin, and "the Fish" came from a Mao quote: "The revolutionary moves through the peasantry like a fish through water." We were laughing when Ed came up with it, the idea being that people were going to think we were communists anyway, so why don't we call ourselves communists?

Ultimately we realized that we had to put together a rock band if we were going to reach people. The guys we brought in were mostly people I knew, like Bruce Barthol, who became our bass player. The other members were our first drummer, John Francis Gunning, and later, Gary "Chicken" Hirsh, an artist from Oakland. John Francis and Chicken were older than the rest of us. And David Cohen, a New Yorker, whose father was a dentist, played bluegrass guitar and some piano. He became primarily the group's keyboard player.

We made a second EP with the rock band in 1966. After that, we signed with Vanguard, a record company from New York. Before we went with them, Ed met previously with some guy from Columbia records who was supposedly interested in signing us. So that he would know what the guy's vibes were really like, Ed took a bunch of LSD before the meeting. He hallucinated that the guy was the devil, and he decided that we absolutely couldn't sign with Columbia Records.

He had an old friend named Sam Charters at Vanguard, which had Joan Baez on its roster, so we signed with them. Our signing money and our budget for our first album was something like $3,500. It took us about a week to make our first full length LP, *Electric Music for the Mind and Body.*

We were happy to be recorded, but we didn't think we were going to be successful. We weren't trying to be. We were trying to say what we had to say. That's what was important to us. Our music actually had a little bit of everything. It was a mixture of American folk and blues with a little Japanese classical music and eastern music thrown in along with some jazz. That's rock and roll, which is like a giant stew where you can throw anything in there and it will taste OK. The band will probably be remembered as an antiwar vehicle, but most of our repertoire was the same kind of maudlin love songs that other bands were doing. Remember, aside from our political views, we were guys in our twenties who were trying to get laid.

None of us were really interested in being rock stars. Music of the counter-culture wasn't intended to be rock star music. It was anti–rock star, anticommercial. We never expected to end up on top-forty radio and never really did, but a whole bunch of confluent events were happening that turned us into one of the most popular bands of that period.

One of them was the sudden growth of FM and alternative radio, which created a channel where we could be heard widely. FM in those days was truly free form because it was still new and there was so little money in it that no one was watching over it. The early FM stations would play our longer album cuts, which weren't heard on AM radio, and they would play our more controversial songs about the war or about drugs. The kids who wanted to be part of the counterculture were listening to those stations, and they ended up buying our music.

We were actually successful in San Francisco before the Grateful Dead, and in terms of national success we were right up there or maybe slightly behind the Jefferson Airplane. In the mid- to late '60s, being a guitar player was suddenly a hot status item, and I was suddenly a guitar hero. I'd like to tell you

I handled it real well, but in some respects it created a little asshole. I ran rampant and unsupervised into this world of recognition and professional success at an age that you have a hard enough time dealing with picking up your clothes. I handled the money irresponsibly. I bought stupid stuff, clothes, cars, drugs. I went into this wine-tasting period.

My musical ideas had also changed. As a folk purist, I had been opposed to electric music. That was the music of the establishment. Then, before we made *Electric Music for the Mind and Body*, I heard the Paul Butterfield Blues Band in Berkeley. They were the first white guys who played electric music that were any good, or so I thought. I said to myself, "Man, if I could do something like that, I'd play electric," and I did on our second record.

With *Electric Music for the Mind and Body*, we were a rock and roll band, and we were being played on the radio. "Sweet Lorraine" became a hit. *Electric Music* stayed on the album charts for two years, partly because of the music and partly because of what it talked about, which was stuff that other bands only intimated—drugs, sex, and politics, which was pretty shocking.

Our first big event as a band was the Monterey Pop festival in 1967. You can see us in the concert movie. I am wearing an Army shirt that I later gave to Joe. He's wearing it in Woodstock. Monterey was where I saw Otis Redding, Jimi Hendrix, and The Who for the first time. I was sitting next to Brian Jones of the Rolling Stones when Jimi performed. It was the most amazing thing I ever saw. I had no idea anyone could do anything like that. Afterward, me and Janis Joplin got into *Newsweek* magazine. Under our pictures, it said "Featured performers" or something like that. Monterey not only put us on the map, but it put San Francisco and what was going on there on the map.

The other thing that put us on the map, but for different reasons, was our new version of the Fish cheer. We always liked to have fun onstage, and before we'd play "Fixin'-To-Die" we would ask the audience to "Give me an F," and then an "I," and we would spell out the word *Fish*. Then Chicken came up with a different way of doing it.

To understand why it created such a stir, you have to remember the time. To give you a couple of examples: In Newport at the folk festival in 1964, word came down that the cops were going to raid where we were staying because guys and girls were sleeping together. Apparently, it was illegal for nonmarried people to do that in Rhode Island. Another time, we were playing a show on a Sunday in Vancouver, Canada, and we were told there was no dancing on Sundays. During the concert, people got up to dance, and I remember the promoter looking at me desperately. "What are you doing? The RCMP [Royal Canadian Mounted Police] will be all over the place." He was serious. We had to stop them from dancing.

The way we did it was each guy would yell out a different letter, and then the other guy would yell out, "What's that spell?" We were sort of insulating ourselves from arrest by doing it that way. If the cops asked us, we could say, "What did we do? All we said was 'What's that spell?' We didn't say anything." The person who deserves all the credit and the accolades there is Lenny Bruce, not Country Joe and the Fish. Years before we came along, he made it possible for us to do the Fuck cheer. He went to jail, and it cost him his career. It wasn't a joke.

We shouldn't forget that people sacrificed for those rights, which people take for granted today. The fight wasn't about obscenity, it was about freedom of expression, but that one-word obscenity expressed a whole lot about what was going on at the time.

We lost bookings because we did the cheer. We had been booked on the Ed Sullivan show, but after they heard us do the cheer, they paid us not to come on. We were also threatened a lot, but remember, getting threatened in those days wasn't unusual. We were long-haired peace freaks wearing unconventional clothing, touring around the United States at one of the most polarized times in history. I used to dread going to the Atlanta airport, because eventually you would have to go take a leak, and you'd have to walk into a bathroom where the dominant color was olive drab and you risked a pretty good beating.

One night we're playing with Janis Joplin in Cleveland, Ohio. We're having breakfast in this place called the Old Colony Restaurant, which has this Revolutionary War motif to it, with real muskets hanging on the wall, or imitation muskets with real bayonets attached. We're just sitting there when some asshole comes over and starts riding me and pushing me and giving me this shit. Suddenly Janis jumps up, gets this wild look in her eyes, and grabs this musket off the wall with the bayonet on the end of it. She sticks it at the guy's throat, and says, "Listen, you damn motherfucker, I'm gonna run this thing through your goddamned throat if you don't get the fuck out of here." The guy literally turns white. He goes, "OK, lady, OK," and leaves.

I first met Janis in 1966. I knew she had a very powerful voice, but I had no idea she would be such a star. Part of the amazing process was watching friends become stars. You really knew these people on a far funkier level, and then to see them marketed into stars, which may or may not have a lot to do with who they really are, was pretty weird. With Janis, the interesting thing was watching this person, who was basically a very shy, withdrawn, overly self-conscious person, blossom into a star.

The problem was that after a while she began believing her own myth, so as this plain, ordinary person became more and more the center of attention, she became more and more affected. She was wearing all those feathers and drinking Southern Comfort, playing the tough woman. She was in that sort of wine-and-dine-live-it-up-all-the-time,-I'm-rich,-nothing-can touch-me place. It's a little scary when people are too young to be behaving like that, and I'm not saying I was in all that much better control of myself than she was.

Janis messed with heroin, but she wasn't a junkie, and I don't think she meant to kill herself. She was out there having a good time, and she goofed. Nowadays when I think of Janis, I remember her on stage at Monterey Pop, this young woman with her eyes closed singing her heart out. That's the Janis that I prefer to remember.

A lot of people who remember the band today think of our performance at Woodstock, but Woodstock wasn't particularly special when we played there. This was the rock festival era. Country Joe and the Fish had been a headliner at a lot of those festivals, and Woodstock at the time was just another one of them. We were filmed at Woodstock, but we were often filmed at similar festivals. What made Woodstock the big deal it became was that it was one of the few concerts where the film actually came out.

We went on after Joe Cocker, but right after he finished, the sky opened up. We couldn't play because of the lightning, and we wanted to do something to keep the crowd amused, so we all went up there with rhythm instruments to see if we can get some kind of spontaneous rhythm thing going. If you see the movie, I'm the guy who says, "If we all think positively and put our hands together, maybe we can stop the rain" and then starts the "No rain, no rain" chant.

Joe and I were playing with hired musicians by then. The band had already started to die a natural death. We were always breaking up and reforming, even when times were good. It's surprising we lasted as long as it did. We all had different interests and were doing different things. There were tensions over who wanted to be a star, who wanted to go on the road, and who wanted to stay home.

It got to the point where I didn't want to be a professional musician

Barbara and Barry Melton, 1974. (Courtesy the Melton family)

anymore. The road is a great place to be as a young man, but after a while it gets old. More often than not, you find yourself traveling six, seven, ten hours to play for fifty minutes or ninety minutes of the same songs night after night. There's nothing glorious about sitting in a seat and watching the scenery go by out the window, and you start to wonder if you are a professional musician or a professional traveler.

I had always wanted to be a lawyer anyway, so I finally decided that was what I was going to do. And I wanted to be a socially conscious lawyer. As a kid, I'd read this gigantic book about Clarence Darrow, and I sort of wanted to be Clarence Darrow.

You can be a lawyer without going to law school in California. I befriended this guy who owned this bookstore right by the Hastings College of the Law in San Francisco. I asked him for a reading list, and he'd say, "First year, here's what they're reading. Here's the text they're using. Here's the course of study." I'd take those law books out on the road and do the work. I also took a correspondence law course, which I needed to formally qualify to take the bar.

I'm bad at money, so I decided to become a public defender because it's a

Public defender Barry Melton and his wife, Barbara, in France, 2005.
(Courtesy the Melton family)

job working for poor folks and I get a salary, so I don't have to worry about billing. That means I can do what I think is right without regard to the resources of my clients. And I get to fight the government. It's pure. It's about doing what I think is the right thing to do.

Every once in a while, if Joe or I has a cause that we think is important, we'll get together and play. I'm not really in touch with the other guys. We were out there at the left edge of popular music, and of the activist bands of the '60s, we were the most successful and a galvanizing force in the youth movement. These days when I meet kids who are in rock and roll bands, they have aspirations. We were protesting. The success thing just happened.

Before the San Francisco bands came along, rock and roll was primarily this rhythm-and-blues-based, fairly simple medium. We turned it into the garbage can of music. We took sitar music, Japanese music, bluegrass music, country blues, and jazz and threw it all into the pot and experimented with it. That was psychedelic music, and I think the impact is still there today. But ultimately, the importance of San Francisco music in the '60s was not simply the music, it was the whole counterculture scene that helped push the country forward. As musicians, our part was the music.

I've been married to the same woman for over twenty-five years. We have two kids. My youngest son, who is fourteen, is playing the guitar and trying to write songs. We have just begun to play together. The nice thing about playing rock and roll is that you don't have to be culturally distant from your kids. You're doing something they like.

I've never stopped playing. I played with a band called Dinosaurs, which lasted about a dozen years. We never really recorded much because we never had to. We played when we wanted to play, and it was just a great deal of fun.

I don't miss being a rock star. I just like getting together with old friends and playing music. I don't care if it's 200 or 2,000 people if our instruments are all in tune, and me and the guys I'm playing with feel good. I love nothing more than grinding it out for three hours in a crowded club, my clothes soaked in sweat. Even after all these years, there's still something incredibly satisfying about that.

David Meggyesy
The Linebacker

A few blocks from David Meggyesy's home in Berkeley, California, is Bancroft Way on the University of California campus where the historic Free Speech Movement began in 1964. Around the corner is People's Park, the object of a deadly standoff between students and the National Guard in 1969. There's a lot of '60s history here, so it's fitting that Meggyesy, who made history himself in 1969 with a ground-shaking exposé of the National Football League, lives nearby.

Meggyesy was a hard-nosed all-pro with the St. Louis Cardinals (who have since moved to Arizona) when he decided to drop out and write about the inhumanity of the game. The resulting book, *Out of Their League*, published in 1970, wouldn't have been any less shocking if he had shown up at the opening coin toss in a pink tutu and ballet slippers. It was hard to believe that someone would walk away from professional football at the peak of his career—and to write a book, of all things. First of all, who knew jocks could write anything but their autographs? And that a football player had dared to criticize a sacred American institution such as the NFL, and had also taken a thoughtful and outspoken stance against the Vietnam War and was in favor of civil rights, women's liberation, and recreational drug use, was enough to make Knute Rockne roll in his grave.

Consider the context. In the sports world, you could literally count the rebels on one hand and have fingers to spare. There was Muhammad Ali, who had refused draft induction; and Tommie Smith and John Carlos, the track stars who gave the Black Power salute at the 1968 Mexico City Olympics. After that, the most celebrated sports rebel was New York Jets quarterback Joe Namath. But all Namath did was wear his hair long and flaunt the fact that he had lots of sex—which in the 1960s was about as rebellious as having choco-late syrup on an ice cream cone. Namath, however, was loved in a way that the others were not. The fact is, America liked rebels as long as they were cuddly and safe. Meggyesy was neither. And while it's one thing to take a stand when everyone around you is already out of their seats, Meggyesy was all alone.

I was fifteen years old when *Out of Their League* was published. For someone just learning to question the world around him, Meggyesy's book was both thrilling and inspiring. When I decided to write this book, Meggyesy was one of the first people I sought out. I wondered whether he felt the same way now as he did when he wrote *Out of Their League*. I wondered whether he found his calling after leaving professional football. I also wondered how he came to be a dissenter. After all, it's one thing to be a rebel when you come from a family of rebels; it's another when you are taught your whole life that when someone tells you to drop and do push-ups, you don't ask, "Why?"; you ask, "How many, sir?" How did Meggyesy learn to think for himself? And what's he doing now?

It might surprise some people to learn that Meggyesy is back with the game. But as a field rep for the NFL Players Union, Meggyesy says he is putting to practical use the ideas and concerns he raised more than thirty years ago. His wife, Stacy, whom he met and married while in college, died of cancer in 1993. He has since remarried. He has four daughters. A fifth, who was born microcephalic, died at age fifteen. He is a grandfather five times over. His hair is not as long as it was in his post-NFL days, and the beard is gone, but his politics remain firmly progressive, and when he is not working, he is still very much an athlete. That something he wrote more than thirty years ago lives on surprises him and, I think, pleases him as well.

I didn't think I'd write a book when I was growing up. My father wasn't encouraging in that direction. He came from Hungary around the turn of the century when he was nine. He was able to get an eighth-grade educa-tion. Then he went on the road as a hobo, riding the rails all around the country to look for work. Eventually he got to Cleveland, where he put himself through night school and became a tool and die maker. He got married. I have an older sister and an older brother. My mother died four months after I was born. He remarried about a year later, and after that I had three younger brothers.

He was pretty much a communist, although he never was a member of the Party. We didn't have any books in the house, and he wasn't the type to bat around different ideas, except he liked to debate the Christian Scientists who came around.

During World War II, there was a big need for his kind of work, and he made a chunk of money. With that he bought fifty-three acres of land in a little town outside Cleveland called Glen Willow. In a sense, he was one of the first "back to the landers," predating the hippies of the 1960s. He built a concrete block house, and eight of us moved out there into what was basically one large room with a partition for their bedroom. There was no running water, and we used an outhouse with the Montgomery Ward catalogue for toilet paper. I shared a thin mattress with my three younger brothers. We had a single moth-eaten blanket to cover us.

We all worked on the farm. Even when I was very small, my job was to be the cow watcher, which meant my father didn't have to build an expensive fence to keep the cows from wandering away.

We raised most of our own food. It was healthy, but there wasn't always a lot of it, especially when my father was out of work. Occasionally, when I'd get really hungry, I would sneak down to the refrigerator at night and steal hot dogs. If my father found out about it, I got a beating.

My father drank a lot and was a pretty violent man. He didn't like me particularly. When my mother got pregnant with me, she was about to have an abortion, but then she decided against it. About four months after I was born, she died. I've never been clear about what caused her death, but there was a significant amount of resentment against me because of it. Everybody got it from him in our family, but I was the particular target for his frustrations.

He even resented me for being left-handed because all the tool and die maker machinery was right-handed. He'd say, "You'll never make it in this world being left-handed. You'll cut your arm off." He'd beat the shit out of me when I was learning to write. We'd have this ritual at Sunday dinner. He would say, "Did you write?" I wouldn't lie to him, so he'd get out the razor strap and whack, whack, whack in front of the family. I write with my right hand now. I tried to change back in college, but I couldn't.

Part of football is the ability to handle the physical violence, to take blows. You have to have a resilience to that kind of pain, and I've always thought I learned that early on. Football is also about doing what is necessary to get approval by that male father figure, the coach. I wasn't that big, but I was a big hitter. The more I hit, the more approval I got. I was really looking for that because in my father's eyes I was a lowlife who didn't deserve approval.

Ironically, my father didn't like football because he didn't like the violent nature of the game, but when I started to play in high school and was good right from the start, he came around. When I became a star, suddenly he was telling people, "That's my son."

Sophomore year things were getting even rougher at home. My father was drinking more heavily, and he and my stepmother were getting a divorce, so I decided to go live with an uncle in Detroit. My friend Bill Davidson heard about my plans and asked his parents if I could move in with them. They said fine. My father didn't care, so I put everything I owned into a paper bag and moved in with the Davidsons, who lived in the most exclusive section of town. Bill's school, Briar Hill, was a nice suburban set up. As Jesse Jackson said, it was like going "from the outhouse to the penthouse."

It was culture shock for me. Mrs. Davidson took me shopping for nice clothes. For the first time in my life, I was eating three meals a day. We were allowed to go to the refrigerator any time we wanted to. Mrs. Davidson was also a great reader, and she and her husband encouraged us to question things and talk about different ideas.

By my senior year, I was 6-1 and 195 pounds, and I was the best player on the team. Syracuse wooed me and wined and dined me, but I had a couple of cousins who played for LSU. They had a national championship team, and they offered me a scholarship to come down.

It was pretty bizarre when I went there to visit. We took a tour boat on the Mississippi, and there was a long line at one water fountain and no line at another, so I went to drink at the other one. The girl I was with said, shocked, "No, no, no, you can't drink there!" That's when I saw the sign that said, "Colored water fountain."

Then I started looking around, and I saw the colored bathroom, the colored entrance, and I realized all the black people were on one side of the boat and the white people were on the other side. It was just un-fucking-believable. It was the first time I saw real segregation.

Then I went to visit Syracuse. I stayed at a friend's place, and he introduced me to a couple of women. I don't know if they were there to make sure the recruits had a good time, but we did. The coach also wooed me, and I ended up going there. Syracuse also had a great team. We won the national championship my freshman year.

They tried to put me in these Mickey Mouse courses: remedial social studies, remedial English, because the priority was football. I said, "No, I want to take the regular classes that the regular freshmen are taking." They were against it, but they accepted it. If they think you're a good player, they don't fuck with you, and I was a maniac out there. When others would walk, I ran. I threw my body around on the field so much the other players began calling me "Super Psych." But I was also pretty independent, and I wanted to learn.

Many of my teammates didn't even bother going to classes, and no one cared. In fact, they'd have a tutor come around before midterms and basically give you the answers to the test questions. A couple of my teammates told me they were being paid under the table to play football, which was a violation of NCAA rules. During my sophomore year, I started getting paid too.

The other way players got special treatment was when they got into trouble the university would work quietly behind the scenes to keep them out of jail. I saw some players get away with some serious crimes. I got into trouble when I didn't pay a bunch of parking tickets. I could have gone to jail, but the school took care of it.

Everything was designed to keep you playing. If you got hurt, the team doctor would patch you back together and get you back out there. I had several serious injuries while I was in college, and you learned pretty quickly that the doctors weren't interested in healing as much as having you play again.

After my sophomore season in 1960, I was named an honorable All-American, but something began to happen: I started to become ambivalent about hitting. Some days I'd be out there, and I didn't want to touch anyone or be touched. I think that came in part because football started to feel like a job. I wasn't really thinking of playing pro ball. In those days, college was bigger than the NFL.

I was opening up to the world around me. Every school has its little enclave of more progressive, more open human beings, and like everybody else they had their own place to hang out. At Syracuse that place was the Orange. The jocks hung out at the Tecumseh to party. The Orange was more about conversation. There were a lot of different kinds of people who hung out there, undergraduates, graduate students, blacks, and whites. They were the artists, the free-thinker types and were all extremely interesting. It was from them that I learned about politics and civil rights.

The coach called them my "beatnik friends." I met them at the School of Fine Arts, where my girlfriend went. They wore black and smoked cigarettes and were very cynical about the school's commitment to football. They saw the hypocrisy of college football and the militarism that was associated with it. They liked to get drunk and go to the games just to make fun of the fans and the coach. They would call him the "pygmy paratrooper" because he was always talking about his war exploits.

The coach knew about them because he had his inspectors sniffing around the school for any possible threats to the team. He called me in and said it looked bad for the team if I hung out with them. He said, "Some of the people you are hanging out with are disreputable." In his view, they were a threat because they questioned things, while jock culture is authoritarian. If someone above you tells you to do something, you do it because coaches have that ultimate doomsday weapon: if you're sitting on the bench nobody will see you.

The team also had a problem with my girlfriend, Stacy. Stacy wasn't interested in being a little sorority girl. She was interested in ideas. Basically, they didn't like it if you had a relationship with a girl. They preferred if you just got drunk and got laid. If you roughed up the girl a little, that was fine with them, as long as you didn't have a relationship. That was a distraction.

It just seemed to me more and more that college football was clearly a commercial venture, and I was just basically a hired hand. In the off season, I did a lot of reading of some serious books about American society. I also got drunk a lot to deal with my unhappiness and hung out with my beatnik friends. The thing was, there was still a side to me that wanted to play, but by the time spring practices began for my senior season, I had no desire to play anymore. I wanted to go to California. I didn't know what I wanted to do there, it was just California was the land of milk and honey. On the other hand, it had been drummed into me that one of the lowest things you could be was a quitter, and in the end I decided to stick it out.

In the last semester of my senior year, I took a course on issues in American culture. I read a book that had a great deal of impact on me, Michael Harrington's *The Other America: Poverty in the United States*. I remember how struck I was when he posed the question "How is it that in this wealthiest country in the world, 20 percent of our population is in poverty?" For the first time, it got me thinking about the nature of society and what was going on here. The professor also got me to think more deeply about the role of education in society, and for the first time someone told me that to question society wasn't something to feel guilty about.

Although I didn't have much interest in playing ball anymore, I was drafted by the St. Louis Cardinals in the seventeenth round. That laid out a new challenge for me: Could I make it in the NFL? I decided to try and see if I could compete with the best. I did, and I made the team.

Once I got there, I couldn't help but notice that the dining room and the dorms were segregated during training camp. It wasn't something that was really discussed openly, even though this was during the early days of the civil rights movement. On a team there are certain things you don't talk about: politics, religion, or race.

Black players especially had to be careful about this, because they would be cut quickly if they were even thought to be a problem. Any time an example was needed, they knew they would be the example. Blacks were expected to be docile, and they couldn't talk back to white people. To give you an example, there was a great black player named Ed McQuarters. He was a very proud man, not into the bullshit, and he got branded a troublemaker or, in their words, a "militant." Boom, adios. Nobody else in the league would pick him up. He had to go to Canada to play.

Coaches had certain attitudes about blacks, that they were dumb and not particularly tough. That was the reason why you didn't see any black quarterbacks or interior linemen. Then if blacks showed any effort of breaking through the stereotype by saying, "I am smart. I can play that," then the coach's attitude was "Oh, we have a problem here. Here's a guy who is a troublemaker."

There were problems among the players too. We had a big group of white southerners on the Cardinals. If they referred to a black teammate who they thought knew his place, they would call him "a decent nigger." Stacy got invited to a party of the wives of the Cardinal players. After she got there, she noticed none of the wives of the black players were there. She asked about it, and the host told her they weren't invited. This woman's husband had told me during training camp that he thought I would make the team because my competition were "two dumb niggers who are so stupid they have trouble tying their shoes."

In the off-season, I would make speeches to kids about the NFL, about it being the American way. I would tell them that football was a great preparation for life and that those who worked the hardest and were the most dedicated would be the most successful. After a while, I realized that it was bullshit, that decisions about who would succeed and who wouldn't were not

David Meggyesy posing during his rookie year, 1963, with the St. Louis Cardinals.
(Courtesy of David Meggyesy)

necessarily made based on the quality of their play, but also on their politics and the color of their skin.

I wasn't involved in the movement in any real way, but in my rookie year the NAACP asked me to be on a committee about civil rights. That was the first step in a long process of separating myself from the game. I took an off-season job as program director of the National Conference of Christians and Jews in St. Louis. While I was working for them, I met the head of the St. Louis Ethical Society at a program on how to raise unbigoted children. We became friendly, and he encouraged me to read some of the radical literature of the day, such as *Ramparts* and *The Guardian*.

I enrolled in graduate school to study education, and there I met members of the SDS. They were doing a lot of local organizing around Vietnam. I helped out and was surprised to find out how many people were opposed to the war. Many of them were frustrated because they felt their voices weren't being heard in the media.

We set up an antiwar office in our home, and the next year I attended a huge antiwar rally in New York City. It was around that time that a friend came by my house and brought some marijuana. It was the first time I tried it, and I liked it. I also tried LSD and liked that too. Then a friend of mine asked me to speak about the war to a couple of fraternities. It was a conservative group, and they were surprised that a football player could be critical of the war effort, but they listened to what I had to say.

The speech didn't go over well with the Cardinals' management, though. The owner called me in for a meeting and said he had received complaints about the speech. I told him I was speaking as a private citizen, not as a member of the Cardinals team. That wouldn't be the last time I heard from the Cardinals about my activism.

In the fall of 1967, I helped organize a bus trip from St. Louis to Washington, D.C., for the big antiwar rally at the Pentagon. Soon afterward, one of my teammates asked me about it. When I expressed surprise that he knew what I was up to, he told me he had a friend who was an FBI agent, and his friend said I was being watched by the FBI. They even told him they had been keeping a huge dossier on me. That was frightening.

Then Stacy got a call from the wife of our defensive coach. She told Stacy that the FBI had contacted the Cardinals, and the Cardinals management had decided that I couldn't play for them anymore if I continued with my political activities. She also said that my phone was probably tapped, and I should be discreet about what I said and did.

By the spring of '68, I was completely absorbed in movement activities. I seriously thought about leaving football, which was such a contradiction to my growing antiwar activity. But then my third daughter was born microcephalic. We needed the money for her care, and I had little choice but to play another year.

That spring, a series was published in *Sports Illustrated* about racism in sports. It created a huge storm. One of the articles focused on the Cardinals and their problems. The Cardinals, of course, denied there were any problems at all. We had a team meeting, and the coach insisted the story was false. This is how clueless he was: his solution was that the black and white players all go together to a local bar called the Lantern for a beer. It was a pretty idiotic suggestion, considering that blacks were banned from the bar.

I was still playing well, but I was rapidly losing interest in the game. I realized that being identified as a football player was no longer enough. There had to be something more. That summer in training camp, I talked it over with Rick Sortun, another player who was going through a lot of the same things I was. We asked each other, "What are we doing here?" and we shook hands and agreed that this would be our last season.

I was smoking a lot of grass that season to help me relax. A lot of players on the team were getting high. I also continued with my antiwar activities. I became increasingly aware about how the game was being used by the establishment forces to sell the war, with things like patriotic halftime demonstrations and military jets flying over the Super Bowl, that kind of shit. At that time when they played "The Star-Spangled Banner" guys would be milling around. A directive came down from the league that when they played "The Star-Spangled Banner," everybody had to line up over the sidelines with their hands over their hearts. It was like the military again.

I said, "Bullshit. I'm not going to salute this flag," and so I didn't. I just kind of bowed my head. There was a lot of "What is that guy doing? He's not patriotic." People called the team and the local radio stations to complain. Our team was called "The Big Red." The next week somebody carried a banner that said, "The Big Red Thinks Pink."

Management, of course, wasn't thrilled with that, but what really got me into trouble with them was an antiwar petition I gathered in connection with the nationwide moratorium that October. We got thirty-seven signatures out of fifty players. They were supposed to be secret, but when the names were leaked the owner of the Cardinals found out. He called me in and said I had to apologize to the team. The coach also said that anyone who got involved with political activities would be dealt with. Soon afterward, during practice, the coach said to me, "Dave, get out of there." I was finished as a starter, even though I had been All-Pro the year before.

It was absolutely unfair, but what really pissed me off was that I was powerless to change it, so I decided to write a book, exposing football for what it was. I also felt I didn't have a role in this movement for social justice and social change, and I thought it was a way to provoke positive change in society. A writer put me in touch with Jack Scott, who was teaching a college course on the sociology of sport. It was the first of its kind in the country. He had guest lecturers come in, and he asked me to come in and speak to the class.

I told him I was thinking of writing a book, and he put me in touch with someone who was thinking of starting his own press. We signed a contract, and *Out of Their League* was his first book.

I also wanted to be part of the movement. I felt I didn't have a role in this movement for social justice and social change, and here was a way I could. I started writing the book in April. A little while later, I was put in touch with a reporter for the *San Francisco Examiner*. I told him I was retiring and why. The story got a lot of coverage around the country.

I finished the book in four or five months, and it came out a few months after that. It was the first time that somebody had said, "This is what goes on."

The first thing that happened was that the NFL's commissioner, Pete Rozelle, wouldn't let anyone talk publicly about it. Vince Lombardi, the Hall of Fame coach, defied that, saying I was anti-American, that people like me were ruining America's young men. Somebody else used a wonderful phrase that I was "corrupting the young youth." I received a letter from one team's physician. He didn't like my antiwar views. He said, "Sometime you will be under the knife, and it will be somebody like me operating."

I didn't hear much from other players, but I think most of the guys appreciated it. The only player to come out against me was an idiot linebacker, Mike Curtis, who said my daughter was born microcephalic because I had taken LSD.

I did a tour. The first interview was with Howard Cosell, who was wonder-

David Meggyesy with his
daughter Jenny in 1970
after his retirement from
football. (Courtesy of
David Meggyesy)

ful. He understood what I was trying to say. I remember I went on with Frank
Gifford, who was literally shaking. He didn't know what the hell to say,
especially when I talked about the racial issues. I said, "You know it's true,
Frank," but he just sat there vibrating.

By then, I had long hair and a beard and wore tie-dyed jeans and a T-shirt,
looking the part of a radical guy. That's probably why I was doing it. [*Laughs.*] I
did a show with two members of the Rams, who said how great the game was
and what a character builder it was and that I was fortunate to be playing it and
I shouldn't put it down. I said, "Let's talk about the racism or about the bed
checks that treat you like a little boy when you're a grown man with kids. Is
that building character?"

Suddenly I found myself speaking on college campuses around the country. That was fun, because I could talk about how our society encouraged
teaching violence and aggression. Later I helped put together a couple of
conferences about the role of sports in society.

We moved to Colorado. We lived by our wits in an old mining town up in
the mountains. After a while I started working construction, building houses.
I also taught a class at Stanford for athletes, teaching them different ways to
look at their lives and the sports they were playing, their relationships with
their coaches, et cetera.

Around that time, my son Chris was playing high school football, and his
coach quit. The school asked me if I was interested. I told them my ideas about

how I saw the game. I said I saw it as a process of education and growth, that the kids could play and enjoy it without the militarism. They went for it, and I was hired.

I wanted the kids to win, but I also wanted them to have more control over the game. I thought that gave them a better chance to win. I tried to instill a certain respect for the game and a respect for the experience. I didn't jazz it up with a lot of life's lessons. We were kind of the Bad News Bears. We didn't win a game, but we played a couple of strong teams extremely well. I would have liked to have won, but it was really fun. I ran into a couple of guys years afterwards, and they expressed a great deal of appreciation for that experience. That made me feel pretty good.

I came to appreciate how important high school coaches are. It's such a seminal time. The amazing thing was to see this group start out as a ragtag bunch, but by the end of the season they could play, and with a real nice spirit to them.

The next year there was an NFL union meeting out here, and I met with Ed Garvey, who was the union's counsel. I liked what they were doing, so I wrote him a letter, saying, "Hire me as an organizer." I intended to work for the union for six months. I ended up with an office and a secretary as a field rep.

Two years later we had our big strike. We went to war with the owners, and we beat them, pure and simple. We changed the system. I'm still with the union as the West Coast rep. I have eleven teams that I visit. We dealt with the economics. Now we're dealing with other issues that have to do with health and safety. We deal with the helmet issue and head trauma stuff.

I believe that professional football is all about the players and the fans. The owners are just by-products of the whole thing. The players' association should be running the game, and we are slowly doing that. I'm a big proponent of economic democracy—that people who make the stuff should have a lot of say in what is made and how it's made.

My sixteen-year-old daughter is now playing rugby, and she's really into it. When I go to her games, I see them banging around on each other. She says, "Dad, I really love to hit," and I think, why shouldn't girls be able to do that too?

I've refined my thinking about the violence. If nobody is getting hurt, I don't think it's unhealthy. It's only unhealthy when the culture starts believing that everything in the culture is secondary to the violence. That's when violence is institutionalized and we have wars.

David Meggyesy today, the Western Regional Director of the National Football League Players' Association. (Courtesy of David Meggyesy)

If my book has enduring importance, it's that it moved sports into the world. It got people to start thinking about football as an institution in society, that it was part of society and reflected society's values. It also affected how sports writers began looking at the game. After the book came out, they could point to it and the things they wanted to say but couldn't before. Once I opened the door, it allowed them to express their ideas, and that in turn changed how people looked at the game.

Sporting in the best sense is very much a spiritual practice. It has that ability to pull a lot of things together. The old line about sports building character isn't so wrong, but it is important to talk about what kind of character you're building. The kind of good character I see is respect for yourself, respect for your teammates, respect for your opponent, respect for the game.

The nature of sport is to win, and that's an important part of it in that context of respect, but the discipline of the practice of doing it is as important as anything else. You can be a writer, a piano player, or anything, but the basis of it is this notion of practice, refinement, and improvement.

The worst elements of sport are the militarism, racism, and that notion of blind obedience. I still think I was right when I wrote about that, and that's why the book's reputation has survived all these years. The message of that is do what you have to do, and all things follow.

Verandah Porche
The Queen of Poesie

Ten or twelve of them plunked down their life
Savings, Israel bonds, anything they could lay
Their hands on for a hovel and a hundred acres
Of callouses a widow was singing and dancing to
Put behind her.
—Verandah Porche

People have been searching for their piece of heaven on earth ever since God banished Adam and Eve from the Garden of Eden. The search for a better life is what got America settled by Europeans. It's why Thoreau went to Walden Pond; why the West was settled by whites in the 1800s; why young people in the 1950s, inspired by Jack Kerouac, went on the road to find whatever was missing in their lives.

People have also banded together to find happiness. The first spiritual, or utopian, communities in the United States formed soon after the Revolution, when Americans became troubled by the rapid advances of the ongoing industrial revolution. The best known utopian community in America was Brook Farm, which was formed by a group of Massachusetts transcendentalists in the nineteenth century. There were also the Harmony and New Harmony settlements in Indiana. Residents there took vows of celibacy. When New Harmony ended rather unharmoniously after only two years, rumor had it that broken vows may have caused the split.

Celibacy was probably the last thing on the minds of the free spirits who formed Total Loss Farm in 1968; but, like its predecessors, it was rooted in an age of tumult and rebellion. In 1968, the political tone of the country was a screech. Two political assassinations, factional splits in the New Left, governmental harassment, and a continuing escalation of the war in Vietnam were enough to drive anyone to their limit. Many civil rights and antiwar activists had been working for years under the most stressful conditions and were rapidly burning out.

Given all this, it was no surprise that in the midst of the turmoil thousands of young people succumbed to the lure of nature. By 1970, nearly 2,500 communes had been formed around the country. Never mind that few of the back-to-the-landers knew a tiller from a turnip; they were determined to carve a life for themselves in the country.

The transplanted hippies soon discovered that country life presented a host of dangers, the least of which was poison ivy. Gun-toting locals took potshots at them. Sheriffs used the pretext of searching for drugs to harass the new settlers, and then cited unhealthy living conditions as an excuse to take their children away. Hippies were beaten in towns and along roadways. Their homes were firebombed.

Commune dwellers also faced the challenge of using skills not taught in lit class or the front lines of Chicago. Where will the money come from for things like tools or tampons? What do you plant? Who does the cooking? Who does the cleaning? What are the rules? Should there be rules? What happens when couples break up? Who gets to stay? Who has to go? Even if you figured out the answers to all those questions and fifty more, the odds were against your lasting through the first winter.

A few years ago, I came across an account of Total Loss Farm in a used book I had found entitled *Famous Long Ago*, by Ray Mungo, one of the commune's cofounders. Inside the book was a fascinating photo of the fifteen original commune members posing on a hillside. I couldn't help noticing the weariness in their eyes. One of the women in the picture is *Famous Long Ago*'s most fascinating character, Verandah Porche, whom Mungo calls "The Queen of Poesie." The picture of her on the hillside, all big eyes and thick dark hair—a hippie goddess if I ever saw one—certainly made her look beguiling. What was she up to now? Where did she get that name?

I had to find out, so I did what any detective would do—I called directory assistance. After I reassured the operator that there was indeed a person by the name of Verandah Porche, we discovered, much to our surprise, that there was a number listed under that name.

It turned out that Verandah Porche was still living on the farm, the last one

The founding members of Total Loss Farm pose for a group photo in 1968. Verandah
Porche is in the back row, second from the right. (Courtesy of Peter Simon)

of the original group, she says. She gives me driving directions that are a little
more practical than those that are included in Mungo's book ("Turn right at the
old apple tree . . . and straight on till morning"). Actually, it's only a couple of
miles, but because the road twists a bit, Verandah suggests we meet at the tree.

As I drive over a country road in Guilford, Vermont, I spot a large, gnarly
apple tree ahead. As I get closer, I can make out someone standing under it. It
is the old apple tree, of course, and there is a tall, slim, woman—Verandah. She
is obviously older than her photograph of thirty years before, but as I roll
down my car window and say hello I can see the big blue eyes that entranced
so many hippie boys of the '60s.

She gets in her car and signals me to follow. The trip takes five minutes.
Inside the farmhouse, the cozy smell of a wood-burning stove competes for
attention with the aroma of cooling chocolate-chip cookies. The furniture is
old but comfortable. The kitchen, dining area, and living room are in one
large, open space. Verandah puts up a pot of tea, and when it's ready she pads
to the couch, puts her feet up across the cushions, and says, "Let's talk."

I push the button on the tape recorder and finally get to ask the question
I've been dying to ask. About the name . . .

My name was Linda Jacobs. "When I go to sleep, I never count sheep, I count all the charms about Linda," that was the song every child got named by in 1945.

I changed it in college. I was reading Doris Lessing and sitting on my front porch, thinking that I needed a whole new personality. Most eighteen-year-olds need a whole new personality. My friends and I were all giving each other names, because we were playful and kooky and full of ourselves. One friend was Ernest Conversation. Another was Luke Warm.

I wanted to have a name that seemed powerful and funny and distant and unforgettable. V seemed like a wonderful letter, and Doris Lessing had a lot of verandas in her work, so I chose the name Verandah Porche because I was sitting on the porch. The *e* was just a festoon.

What got me started on my alien path was moving to Teaneck, New Jersey, when I was eight years old. Growing up in Teaneck was anesthesia. My mother was obsessed with our appearance. She really did say things like, "What will the neighbors say?"

My parents had really invented the life that they led. It was so completely different from their parents' experience in Russia and Poland. After they came here, my parents became pioneers in this country, and even though we didn't know what they did because they didn't tell us, we knew that they had a tremendous force of perseverance. But by the time my generation came along, there wasn't anything to persevere in except cleaning up your room and taking out the garbage, and there really were no avenues for invention, except to do well in school. Unlike my parents' generation, by the time we came along, children were just sort of unnecessary. We were just supposed to achieve things and be a credit to our family. That was so different from how my parents were raised. They were the mainstays of their parents' existence.

I think this was the typical middle-class rub. They wanted to make it easier for their children, and instead it was anesthesia with a whole lot of expectation, and we didn't know why. It would have been helpful if my father had told me the story of his mother having a nervous breakdown and his being put in an orphanage, or if my mother had told me about having to sacrifice her own college education because some aunt told my grandparents that she would never get married if she were a teacher. We didn't know our parents. We lived among them, and they were certainly upright, valuable people, but it was considered unseemly to reveal yourself, to say why it was you were the way you were. Or maybe they didn't know why they were the way they were.

I tried very hard to follow the rules until ninth grade. I put my hair in curlers. I wore a shirtwaist, nylons, a garter belt [laughs], sensible shoes, and a coat, not a jacket. We hardly ever wore pants. My sisters gave me their pleated skirts of the best wool, and sweater sets.

But they also brought stuff home from college. In ninth grade, they introduced me to the Weavers, Leadbelly, Woody Guthrie, and Odetta. When Bob Dylan came down the pike, I tormented my mother with "The Times They Are A-Changin'." She couldn't believe that was music.

When my mother refused to let me be bat mitzvahed, my brother said, "It doesn't really matter, there's no God," and he gave me these radical novels of Ignazio Silone to read. I also met kids in my ninth-grade class who were red diaper babies. We took buses to Washington for demonstrations to ban the bomb, and I started wearing my uniform: black corduroy skirt and tights. I wore mascara and no other makeup, and I got my ears pierced. I was a little beatnik. It all seems like such penny-ante stuff now, but it was fun to throw my weight around, and now I had my affinity group of people who were rebels like me.

We would take the bus to Manhattan and then the A train to Greenwich Village, pretending we were urban. The Village felt so diverse relative to where we came from. There were people who could pick fast on their guitars and wear denim and be grungy and put their feet in the fountain. There were paperbacks to carry around, coffeehouses to sit in, and people to watch and be watched by. I loved to sit, pretending to read books and having conversations.

When you're a kid and you don't really know who you are, you have that concept that there is an identity you can discover, like a can buried in the backyard, and since I believed that I had an identity and I was trying to find out what it was, these conversations were part of digging toward it and finding my place in the world.

In those days, I learned what a great conversation was, where you didn't know what you thought until you said it, and somebody was going to add that missing piece that was going to be the jigsaw puzzle piece that they found on the floor under your chair, and they just handed it to you, and, whoa, there it is: the Oregon Trail, right before your very eyes.

It wasn't just personal talk. It was scheming and planning. It was, "What are we gonna do about this?" and "What are we gonna do about that?"

"What are we gonna do about integration?" That was the big thing when I was in high school, so we integrated places. My brother got involved with

CORE, and he started what he called Operation Nuisance, which was a whole series of activities aimed at making people hire more Negroes, as they were called then.

My first driving experience was being part of a group of people who were blocking traffic at this swimming pool because they weren't going to allow Negroes to join their swim club. There were banks that wouldn't hire Negroes, so we would start bank accounts and then come back and withdraw all the money in protest.

When I was in tenth grade, I joined the literature club and come under the influence of the most amazing teacher I have ever had—Mrs. Marion Shelby. She was the first adult I knew who could talk to children as if they were on her wavelength. She would take us for picnics at dawn, and she would have the students over to her house, and they would drink tea and be invited to stay all night long for these picnics at dawn. She was completely above suspicion. She was an icon at the school. Every piece of writing we turned in came back with an equal amount of teeny red writing. I never had another teacher like her. We corresponded for years, until she died. She was so effusively supportive and so demanding at the same time. I would open her letters so terrified at how inadequate I felt to meet her standards, and yet I so terribly wanted to.

I went to Boston University in 1963. The thing about BU was you knew who your friends were going to be immediately because the rest of the people were sitting in shorty pajamas with their rollers and playing cards in the basement and waiting for a man to come. At the freshman picnic on the shores of Lake Cochituate outside of Boston, I saw this boy and girl standing on the shore, not far from where I was, and we sort of looked at each other and said, "Oh, look at that phony," because we looked exactly the same. Shortly thereafter, we introduced ourselves and became best friends. That was Richard Wyzansky and Marjorie Cooper.

I moved off campus into a house we called The Hovel. The doors were always open, and there was a lot of good schmoozing. That's where I met Ray Mungo. We took acid together and had a great time tripping around the neighborhood. We had an extremely fake romantic friendship. We were sort of dazzled with each other. We imagined ourselves at the different ages of our lives as friends. We would be at play in the great world and have profound adventures.

People were very politically engaged. We thought that was what people were supposed to do with themselves. I remember occupying the federal building, demanding that they send federal troops to Selma. In Richard's apartment was a baby grand piano. On top of it was a mimeograph machine that Richard's roommate would use to turn out wonderful leaflets quoting Ho Chi Minh that we would hand out on the subways.

I didn't know too many people who were involved in day-to-day grassroots organizing. Most people were involved in drafting statements and delivering statements and not listening to each other's statements. The divisions that would become more pronounced later were already presenting themselves, between the flakes and the hard-liners, and I definitely wanted to be there with the flakes. Because they were so strident, we had a very disparaging attitude toward the Brandeis girls, whom we ran into when we were encamped in the federal building. We called them Fat Girls for Peace.

A few of us banded together and called ourselves The Bay State Poets for Peace. We even had stationery, because we knew if you wanted to have an organization you had to have stationery. It had a beautiful logo of birds made out of hands. It wasn't really an organization, it was just us. In those days, you could be whoever you said you were, and if you said you were the Bay State Poets for Peace then you were. At the Pentagon march, we had our sign that said the Bay State Poets for Peace, and the poet Galway Kinnell came over to us and said, "Who are the Bay State Poets for Peace?"

We said, "We are."

We were so full of ourselves.

When it came to sex, the girls I knew felt that girls should have the same freedom boys did. The boys could sleep with girls if they wanted to, but girls couldn't sleep with boys if they wanted to. We thought girls should be allowed to. Sexuality for me, and I think probably for women my age, was an assertion of will and of right rather than an exploration of sensuality. If you wanted to have a lover you could have a lover, but I wasn't very close to any of my lovers.

I had several young men in different cities whom I could call on when I wanted to, but they never really gave me anything that I wanted. For that reason, I think sexual freedom was an illusion. People would go through the motions and not really understand what their bodies were asking them for or without understanding what it was like to have intimate communication with a partner.

Part of the adventure for men was that finally they could fuck for free. They didn't have to pay to have sex. For women it was allegedly better than the repression their mothers promised for them. The reality was we didn't know any better.

In the late '6os, there was a myth about hippie women and sex. When we moved to Vermont, every once in a while a book publisher or a mechanic would hunker down with one of the guys on the farm, and he would want to know about the hotness of the women, like, "You really have it good up there," or "Is it true that they're better?" It was like the whole alien fantasy of the sexual prowess of African-Americans. Now hippie women had their moment in the limelight as sex bombs. I remember visiting with Kurt Vonnegut and his publisher, and they wanted to know if it was true that we had it better, and my friend Raymond, always puckish, assured them that we did.

In college, some women wanted to get pregnant so they wouldn't have to figure out what to do with their lives. Every so often I would meet some friend of mine who had opted out, gotten under somebody's protection. I did get pregnant when I first moved here, and I had an illegal abortion. It was a very harrowing experience. It was physically painful. It was psychologically painful. I later found out from this sadistic abortionist that it was twins, which made it all the more horrible and more of a relief.

The doctor was recommended by a friend of a friend. He was a mercenary, that's all. He didn't use anesthesia, because that was extra. He charged me $100 more than his secretary had said he was going to.

I left Boston University without graduating. I was more excited by love and adventure and the unexpected. I wanted life to be surprising. I wanted to do something that I hadn't ever thought of before. I was young and the world was gaga and I wanted to participate. I'm sure it broke my parents' hearts, but I wasn't paying attention at the time. I didn't have the attention to pay. There was just too much else going on.

So I went out searching for adventure, and I ended up moving to Washington, D.C., to work for the Liberation News Service, which was part of my adventure. LNS was a radical news service run by two close friends of mine, Marshall Bloom and Ray Mungo. They were very different people. Marshall was a nervous, adenoidal, Jewish freak with big hair, big ideas, and big eyes. He was the kind of person who never let up on things he was passionate about. I really loved him to pieces, but he also drove me up a wall.

Raymond, on the other hand, was a real conflict avoider, even though in his politics he would happily take a stand. He really didn't want to hurt anybody's

Marty Jezer, Verandah Porche, Peter Simon, and Raymond Mungo photographed during a stop in Ogallala, Nebraska, on a cross-country trip in 1968. (Courtesy of Verandah Porche)

feelings or make anybody mad. He was one of the most easy-to-love people.

We covered news from the movement and supplied news stories to college and underground papers all across the country. Some of it was tragic, people immolating themselves. Some of it was ridiculous, like the phenomenon of dried beef falling from the sky.

It was a terribly lively adventure to be able to communicate with people all over the country who were like-minded. It was also playful. When we wanted to, we made up news. We invented a town in Arkansas and a whole bunch of things that went on there, just for the hell of it. So it was playful but also useful. I always had a utilitarian attitude toward the art I wanted to make. I wanted it to be like shoes.

I think Ray and I made $15 a week, but we would always have food. Who thought about eating anyway? We all lived in the same house in the city. Raymond and I shared a room. We would work all night and ride our bicycles home from the office and go to sleep at dawn. Then we'd wake up sometime in the late morning or early afternoon, smoke cigarettes and go to the office and see what next thing was going to come up. That would be anything from draft resistance demonstrations or news from resistance organizations.

Things got ugly in 1968. The night King was killed, we were wandering around the city with our press passes. It was thrilling and horrifying. There was a lot of looting. We saw people pushing whole racks of clothes from department stores down the street; people stealing steaks from the Safeway; people burning down their own homes.

We saw machine guns fanning out from the Capitol building and National Guards on every corner. This was apartheid city. We were thrilled to be at this intersection of history, but it was like somebody else's tragedy. Our news agency got in touch with the militant black organizations, and they said, "Get us guns." Me, Ray, and Marshall were going to get them guns? That was just not going to happen. Around this time, there was also a lot of separatist feeling between blacks and whites. The message from blacks was, "Go home and organize your own community. Stop trying to lend your organizational or even reporting skills to our struggle." I didn't agree with it. People were burning down their houses. I didn't see what good would come of it. I thought that worse was going to come rather than better.

I think that's when the movement stalled—by no longer building bridges. People like me didn't fit in any more. Suddenly we were at loose ends, what were we going to do next?

At the same time, I got sick of the political talk among white radicals that seemed small-minded and fratricidal. There was so much more posturing rather than exchanging and shaping ideas. It was our gang against their gang, and tests of loyalty, and don't try any funny business, which seemed really pathetic.

The Liberation News Service was a perfect example. It was taken over by a shrill group of New York radicals whom Ray called the Vulgar Marxists. They had such crappy manners, these white guys, some of whom looked like grown-up bar mitzvah boys, wearing very leathery gears and chains. They were trying to form alliances with Hispanic or black people, people who were genuinely hard-bitten, who were a lot more comfortable being violent. When they pushed the homophobia card and said that Marshall was nothing but a "fucking faggot," that's when I left. That was the irony of the left in those days—how homophobic it was. Ray and Marshall were both in the closet. They both wanted something else and with somebody else, and that was so sad.

Ray and Marshall came up with a daring plan to steal the LNS printing press and bring it up to a farm in Montague, Massachusetts. There they would move the news service. We pulled off the heist, but the New York group found out where the press was. They came up to Massachusetts, and some of them held us in one room while they tortured Marshall in the other room. They took his pants down and beat him up. They just wanted to humiliate him.

I was just so sick of all the violence. I said to Ray one morning, "I want to go home."

He said, "Don't worry, I know the place," and he went back to sleep.

He had heard that this place was for sale, and we decided—even though most of us had never gone outdoors before—that we were going to move here. I think there were others like us. In that sense, the communal movement was a response to stress.

Ray had found out about this place from our friend Don, who had a little hunting camp down the road. Ray and I went to meet the lady who owned the place and wanted to sell it. I was supposed to be Ray's fiancée.

We never went into the house before we bought it. It was locked. [*Laughs.*] I'm still stunned that nobody said, "This is crazy. We have to see if the sills were rotted." Nobody knew what a sill was.

It was an ugly little house, yellow, like old pee in the snow, but the land was beautiful. There was a peach orchard on top of the hill. The blossoms were all over the trees, and they were irresistibly beautiful, and we just figured, "Well, OK," this was what we decided to do and there were no two ways about it.

After we bought the place, I went back to California with $20, a toothbrush, and a change of clothes, taking Richard Wyzansky's lover, Laurie Dodge, with me. Then I went back to Big Sur, where I had a big crush on a fiddler I had met on my previous trip. Laurie then got in trouble. He took acid and started getting psychotic, so I went back to San Francisco to sort out his situation. Richard came across the country to save his partner. That's the way it was, the country is tilted and you land in California, so we had a glorious reunion in San Francisco.

Somehow, in the midst of some LSD trip, we met Michael, who grew up on a farm in Oregon. He became enamored of our idea. The next thing I knew we were all going to Oregon, and I was with Michael. We went to Oregon to meet his mother, who had the same birthday I had, and Michael's birthday was the day before. These things were very interesting in those days. His mother was suddenly inundated with this whole batch of East Coast hippies, and we all went to work picking strawberries and doing other things to get enough money to get back east.

When we got back to Vermont, we had to sort out who was going to live there. We had ten years of a mortgage to pay, and that sounded like a very big commitment, and we wanted to live with those people we had a commitment to. People came and went pretty quickly at the beginning. Every now and again somebody would come by, and it just so happened that everybody fell in love with that person, and then we broke all of our own rules as far as more people. In general, the only way to come here was to already have been here or to have somebody fall in love with you and then hope that it would last.

When we finally entered the house, I thought, "Oh my God." It was a big joke because the widow who lived here, Rosie Franklin, the day her husband died she moved to an all-electric apartment in Greenfield, and she was singing and dancing about it. The house had small cramped rooms and a rickety staircase. When we started renovating the place, we figured it was built by people who were even more incompetent than we were. I remember one spot that Rosie said was where the kitchen floor collapsed and she fell through to the basement.

There was a little room where the laundry room is now, with ivy wallpaper. We called that the Ivy Room. It was a really undesirable room because it was right off the kitchen, but it did have a heat vent and that was good. Since nobody really wanted to live permanently in the Ivy Room, it got to be a rather transient room, and the expression "Who's sleeping in the Ivy Room?" meant that somebody had taken up with somebody.

Our bathroom was outside. It was part of the whole sense of the life. You would go out to the outhouse and see the stars that you would have missed otherwise.

The townspeople wanted to know what was going on, but after the second winter that we were here it was no news. That's what one of the farmers said: "If you can get through one winter, then you're just like the rest of us."

There were rumors about the women here always being naked, so there was a certain amount of driving by and rubbernecking. We did go skinny dipping in the Beaver Pond. There were little kids from Leyden, just on the other side of the rock wall in the garden, who used to watch us garden without our shirts on. I remember one time when I probably looked a sight, with my shirt wrapped around my head. I walked over to the wall and said, "Don't you have anything better to do than to watch young mothers at work in our garden? Well, take a good look and get out." There was a lot of clatter in the shrubbery, and they all grew up to be juvenile delinquents. We thought it was our tits that did it.

In the beginning, there were other communal groups around the area. When we came to buy the place, we met people from The Brotherhood of the Spirit. At first we invited them to visit here, thinking they would be part of the unfolding of a similar cooperative way of life, but we found that we had so little in common with them. We had these literary and political figures as our mentors. They had this transmedium who helped them get in touch with their Atlantan past. I've never really understood or opened myself up to the value and charm of reincarnation. What the hell does Atlantis have to do with anything here? Was that the good place where everyone had fins and was mellow? And claiming credit for being related to this mythic group seemed like the height of absurdity, so we used to enjoy giving their young people a hard time. I remember sitting in my little house with this very pretty ginger-haired girl and essentially saying to her, "Get a life."

Among our first group there were only a few people who had ever gone outdoors before. There were people who could do carpentry, but the skills that most people had was that they were intelligent and they were interesting to have around.

We didn't make decisions. People did what they wanted to do. There were very few things we had to decide anyway. There were impulses, like "Let's go see our friends in Montague."

We kept track of the world through a radio. We didn't have a TV set. When people went to town, they got newspapers. This place has always fostered great conversations. People really did talk with each other and turn over ideas, and since so many of them were writers, the talk was practice for the writing. In the cupboard, we had a sign that said, "Don't recite it, write it." Another one was, "Not responsible for lost ideas."

Politics was what we did all day, the idea of the personal being political. We believed deeply in the significance of daily life to make it aesthetically meaningful, to make it full of great stuff, whether that was pushing the boulder of humanity up the hill or whether it was flying your head. What we did seemed to count.

It certainly seemed that we were going to live differently from how we were raised to live, and that many people were going to do that. I don't know how that was going to translate in terms of how the country or the planet would change because of our actions. Like many young people, I was so full of my own enthusiasm that I could easily believe that the whole world would be watching my enthusiasm and somehow getting a contact high. We really were young, and every load of apples and peaches that we brought in from the land just seemed so new and exciting, like we were back in Eden.

But that first winter, we were just so new at everything, and it was cold. The wind came through the walls. In some poem I wrote, "What is warm? The fire light barely kindles a memory." Or "itch among the inches of our clothes."

The first winter we went to the Finast and ate hot dogs, potatoes, and onions and tuna casserole. Gradually, we learned how to cook hippie food.

We wanted to live off the land, but we weren't farmers, and this had been an unsuccessful farm for many generations of farmers. It's very easy to understand why people gave up. It's very hilly and stony, with thin soil.

But there were so many of us, and we were young, and we had stamina, and we didn't have the idea that we couldn't. We learned from books and from tapping the wrong trees and from planting things in the wrong soil. We learned from people who were very generous in helping us. Also, plants want to grow. Everything pretty much came up as long as it was weeded. It was wonderful when things started to grow, to see that all the things we saw in the store really did grow like that. You would yank it up and stare at it and think, "Oh, if you just wash it off and put it in cellophane, it will be a carrot."

I read a book and USDA manuals on canning. You don't need to be a rocket scientist to do it, and we had time to learn. There were also these great pamphlets about making cheese. Some of the stuff we made was almost toxic, but other things were delightful.

We got cows and pigs, a single sheep, assorted chickens, occasionally horses. The chickens were a pain in the neck and just loathsome. At one point we set them free and had them fend for themselves, and then we decided that we would kill them. They were shot, and then we cooked them in several changes of water, but they were still too tough even for Chinese food, and so we fed them to the pigs. The pigs liked everything. Pigs are terrific. They are intelligent, clean, courteous, down to earth, and they have the most elegant feet. We also had a goat that sort of wandered around. She thought she was a dog.

The local farmers were helpful. To a certain extent, each of us had our own pet local friend. I had Ralph Rhodes, who was so dashingly handsome he could have been a movie star. He was one of our very first friends. One day, Ellen Snyder and Richard and I had taken LSD, and we were walking down the road and we were cold, and we got the bright idea that if we simply put our feet up in the air, then they would be closer to the sun and would therefore be warmer, so we decided to lie in a snowbank and put our feet up in the air.

We were doing that when Ralph drove up with his son on snowmobiles. We were so afraid we dove into a snowbank. Here was this middle-aged man with silver hair and the most electrifying eyes. He said to us [in a Vermont-like drawl], "Har'yhah. Got any livestock up there?"

"Yup."

"Well, if you're goin' to auction, Friday's better than Tuesday."

We looked at each other and said, "Friday's better than Tuesday." We parted on the most cordial terms. The three of us could barely speak, so we staggered back to the farm, saying to everybody, "Friday's better than Tuesday."

As a result of his association with the hippies, Ralph ended up growing five acres of marijuana. His sister, who was the principal of the elementary school in Leyden, used to talk about finding pink frogs and day-glo salamanders when they were hoeing. They were obviously getting stoned from the crops. She didn't see anything wrong with growing it. She used to say, "If you can take an acre of God's bad land and turn it into a million dollars then you deserve it."

Eventually they were arrested, and we hired an old friend of mine from school to represent them. The cops had already burned the evidence when they got to trial, and I remember him pacing around the courtroom and talking about "the alleged marijuana." He got them off.

Then, in November 1969, Marshall killed himself. He gassed himself in his green Triumph. There was a note that contained a brief apology. Marshall just carried around so much sorrow and guilt, guilt that he wasn't his parents' blue-eyed boy. He was so full of promise, and they just didn't get what he was doing.

It rained and rained and rained after he died. His suicide was a tremendous torment and a challenge to our assumptions. We thought somebody was a pain in the neck, well they would just stay a pain in the neck. A lot of people were dying in those days, though. We would look at one another and say, "Who's next?" People wondered if we could have been more outspoken in accepting him, but he was terrified that people would find out he was gay.

After he died, I wanted very much to continue to feel Marshall's presence. It was a lot of wishful thinking. After a while, I really couldn't remember enough of him to keep it real. That was the saddest part, when looking at the pictures and listening to his words, it just got to be a long time ago. Probably by 1980, I didn't really think about him all day on his birthday.

I think about him every now and again. People who kill themselves do get a different kind of edge in our minds. They die at a certain period, when they still have physical beauty and unfinished promise. I think about all of the people, Stevie Skolnick, our sixteen-year-old LNS photographer, who died in a car accident. He was so pretty and so sweet. Laurie Dodge, who just disappeared, was another. The list continues. We've known so many people who have either died in accidents, killed themselves, or died in some other untimely way. And those people edge into my consciousness differently from the people who just go gray.

After Marshall died, I think we just felt as if we were lost in the universe, and so if we were already lost in the universe, then leaving earth seemed like a completely acceptable thing to do. We took so many psychedelic drugs that winter we called those days the Acid Olympics. I vaguely remember one evening, which was typical, where the topic of discussion was "The Night Pizza Got Introduced to the Russian Court."

One day we saw the movie *Fahrenheit 451*, which was about book burning. From that we got the notion that there might not be more books. I remember convincing everybody that we should memorize books, and since we didn't have anything more important to do other than keeping warm or fed, we started walking around in the snow, memorizing books.

These days, my daughter Emily gets so much drug backlash at school. They have Deputy Dan come to school and the drug-sniffing-dog cartoons. I haven't pretended to her that I didn't take drugs. I tell Emily that people are making a tremendous fuss over something that is a far more complex issue. In the '60s, the chaos of taking drugs was very appealing to people who were brought up in what we considered was a surplus of structure. But my miscalculation was that this would be a positive social force for people who didn't have much of a life structure to begin with. In the end, it was just chaos on chaos. I certainly saw enough examples of burnouts, so that it wasn't hard to see that psychedelic drugs weren't going to be much help.

In the '70s, I got to a point when I decided I didn't want the New Age to come. I became more interested in learning how to root myself here than making pronouncements about the way the planet ought to go. I saw that shooting the breeze wasn't going to keep the house warm, and that there were a lot of people trying to heat their houses with hot air.

There was a political commune in Putney where they made films. They showed one that had people running around during a revolution, and some guy getting emasculated. My main impression was, "Whose world is this that you're talking about? Where is this going to take place?" It wasn't my nine yards of the planet. That's the way I increasingly felt, the more alternative-lifestyle-oriented, the more freaks there were around trying to feel good about one and other, the less I really wanted to be part of it.

What it comes down to on the farm is that ideas didn't count very much. What counts is "Whose grease is on the bathtub?" "Who will shovel out the outhouse when it's time to do it?" That doesn't evolve through any ideas; it evolves through people's good nature and being considerate of one and other and to struggle when it doesn't work.

Right from the start, we had to figure out how to make the $227.10 a month mortgage, and there were plenty of times when it was quite bleak. That plus the rest of the money that it took to get by were hard to come by. They still are.

There were years when we sold our crops at the farmers' market. That certainly was a great passion people had: to try and provide for ourselves and pay our bills and also to feed the people. Others enjoyed having jobs. I was never a great wage earner. I'd work on the farm, and when I got money from my book of poetry, I spent it on the farm.

When women's liberation first became a big topic of conversation, I didn't see how sexism was a major force in my life. It was, but I didn't know it. My first husband was a batterer. Nothing in my experience prepared me for what that was like. If you talk to other people who were here at that time, they knew about it, but they were very conflicted about whose business it was. Ultimately we took our show elsewhere. People just became increasingly hostile toward him, and that isolated me, because I felt caught in between.

I left here with him because I wanted my daughter Oona to have a father. It was a real failure of imagination on my part. It wasn't so long before I too was out of that house and came back to live on the farm. I've lived here ever since.

Over the years, a lot of the people moved on for career opportunities or for love and were replaced gradually by other people. In certain years, there were three or four core couples here, and as the core couples broke up the whole

Verandah Porche, still living at what is now called Packer's Corners Farm, Guilford, Vermont.

dynamic of the place shifted. Now I'm the last of the original group to live here, although many of the others still live nearby.

In the '80s, I was asked to give a poetry workshop in a nursing home, and we had a wonderful time. They all smiled and nodded, and then I said, "Now it's your turn."

They all shook their heads no. They said they couldn't write, their hands were too shaky and their eyes were too dim, but I got them to cooperate, and that has grown into a project where I collect "told poems." I go to nursing homes and visit with people, and I get them to tell me their stories, and together we make poetry out of their recollections. I have whole collections of "told poems" by old rural ladies and retired truck drivers. Most of these people have never written anything in their lives. Because it's therapeutic, the state pays me to visit nursing homes and work with the residents. They write about the minutiae of a life or the great turning points, whether it's making biscuits, getting married, or discovering their husband was cheating.

On the farm, we only have a small garden. We got rid of the last cow in '81 or '82. I was a single parent, and it wasn't feasible to keep them around anymore. Other people were around, but they were all extremely busy.

I didn't think I'd be the last one, but I've never really seen any reason to leave. It's my home, and it's where I raised my children. It's still a place where I can create.

For me, the legacy of the extended family is very durable and very valuable. Our notion was that people could make lighter work by throwing in their lot together, and it still to me makes sense for people to face the challenges of passing through a long, long life with more than just themselves or a nuclear family as a bulwark.

To me, the elements of communal life that counted to me still exist here. It just moved from just this household to the neighborhood. Now there's a large community who live on the hill who are basically alumni of this place, and who are certainly deeply connected to it as we are deeply connected it.

I can walk on this land with my eyes closed, and it still seems like the same place it was in 1968. I guess we've all changed in our looks and our stances, but I feel very much that I came here to do something, to stay home and see the world and have a great sense of adventure, and I've done that. I think I still value most of the same things I valued in 1968. I have never been a particularly acquisitive person, and I've never acquired anything. I am both really rooted and really footloose, and that's not so different from how I imagined I would be. I wanted to make my life into a poem, and I did. Sometimes it is bad poetry, but that's what it is.

Doris Krause & Barry Levine
Allison's Story

This summer I hear the drumming.
Four dead in Ohio.
—Neil Young

In May 1970 college campuses across the country erupted in protest following President Richard Nixon's announcement that America had unilaterally extended the Vietnam War by invading Cambodia, a neutral country.

One of the smallest protests against the invasion of Cambodia occurred at Kent State University, a generally conservative campus in Kent, Ohio. However, Governor James A. Rhodes, who was locked in a tight primary battle for the U.S. Senate, called out the National Guard to occupy the campus on May 2. Two days later, Guardsmen let loose a sixty-one-volley fusillade that killed four unarmed students and injured twelve others. None of the students was closer than 300 feet from the troops. Although the FBI later found no cause for the shooting, no Guardsman was ever prosecuted for the murders.

The four dead students were Allison Krause, Jeffrey Miller, William Schroeder, and Sandy Scheuer. This is the story of Allison Krause, as told by her mother and her boyfriend.

DORIS KRAUSE: Even when she was in the Bluebirds as a little girl, Allison was the leader of the pack. She was very pretty, and people took to her. She was also very headstrong, just like her father, who landed in Normandy during the D-Day invasions and went all through Europe. They were two of a kind that way.

She had a way of charming people. She worked as a volunteer at a home for mentally ill people. She'd talk to the patients there, play volleyball with them. One night, she came home so elated because she had gotten this man to talk to her while they were playing ball, and he hadn't spoken to anyone in something like fifteen years.

BARRY LEVINE: In high school, I was somewhat interested in architecture, and Kent State had a pretty good architectural school. It also had an Honors College, which promised all kinds of academic freedom, so I applied. By the time I was done with high school and had been accepted at Kent, I had lost interest in architecture. Still, there was something intriguing about the school, and the campus was very pretty, so I went ahead and enrolled.

DORIS KRAUSE: It was pretty. When the children were born, we lived in the Cleveland area, and we always enjoyed taking Sunday drives out there. When Allison was applying to colleges, we still had relatives in Cleveland, which meant that at Kent State, Allison would always be close to some family, so she applied and was accepted.

BARRY LEVINE: From the time I got off the bus, I realized I had made a huge mistake. I was bursting with excitement about books I had read, music I was listening to, or different political, social, and cultural ideas I had read about. Hardly anyone I met in the first few days shared that excitement, or even knew what I was talking about.

Socially and politically, it was as if I had stepped through a time warp back to the '50s. I was assigned two roommates, who turned out to be high school buddies from Cleveland. On their side of the room, their wall was plastered with *Playboy* pullouts. On my wall, I put up a poster of a Harvard professor, and these guys were convinced I was a "fag." First of all, I was a long-haired Jew from New York, and they didn't know who Timothy Leary was, so they would tell their friends, "He's got a picture of a man on his wall. There's something really weird about this guy." They liked bubblegum music, and if I was listening to Dylan or Joan Baez, they'd say, "Oh, he's listening to that hippie shit again."

Guys would push me down the stairs, and my books would get knocked out of my hand, which was real high school stuff. Or I'd get my sheets shorted. That kind of thing used to happen in summer camp when I was ten years old.

I also smoked pot once in a while. To them, pot smokers were all communist, hippie radicals. Clearly, Kent State was the wrong school for me. On the other hand, that's where I met Allison.

At that time, you could tell somebody's political leanings by the way they dressed and carried themselves, so if I would see other freshmen who looked like me, I would seek them out. One of the girls I met was constantly talking about her friend Allison. She said her friend was very nice and I should meet her. Then one day I was walking through campus, and I bumped into the two of them, and this girl, Liz, introduced us. Almost immediately, I knew there was something very special about Allison. I made it a point to run into her again, and we started to become friendly.

We discovered very quickly that even before we met, not only had we read the same books and listened to the same music, but we also had thought the same thoughts and felt the very same deep convictions about almost everything. She was also very soft and friendly, very attractive, and had a wonderful sense of humor. She was just a lot of fun to be with.

When everyone else would go out partying, we would go for long walks just to talk endlessly about everything. I have never met anyone who could read my mind the way she could. Sometimes I would be able to convey a complicated and complete train of thought to her without uttering a word. She used to smile at me and say, "I know what you are thinking," and she would get it exactly. When that happens once, you laugh about it. If it happens two or three times you think it's strange or spooky, but when it happens regularly over and over, you know there is something special going on.

A few weeks into the semester, she organized an antiwar parade from the campus to the downtown area in October 1969 to coincide with the national moratorium against the war. It was staged early on a Saturday morning. This was a football school. Most of the students were out drinking Friday night and slept late on Saturday, so not many people showed up. A few weeks later, we visited my friends at SUNY Buffalo in New York and decided to transfer there, so after a couple of months we were just marking time at Kent, waiting to leave. Through the rest of the school year, our relationship deepened and got more intense. By the springtime, we were already making plans to work together and live together during the summer. We even talked about what we'd do after we got out of college, maybe start a bookstore, live on a commune, or go to an art colony. Allison painted, and she drew. She had a real interest in art and art history. Who knows what we would have done. We were only nineteen years old.

DORIS KRAUSE: We went to see her on April 23, and she was as happy as a

Barry Levine and Allison Krause on the commons at Kent State in April 1970, less than a month before the shooting. (Courtesy of the Krause family)

lark. She had no reason not to be. It was her birthday. She had found a boyfriend, Barry, and they were so happy together. We met him for the first time that night, and he seemed like a wonderful man, but that was the last time we ever saw her.

BARRY LEVINE: I don't remember any more antiwar demonstrations until May 1, when there was a rally in response to Nixon's decision to invade Cambodia. Not even a hundred people showed up out of a campus of 20,000 students. At other campuses, there were rallies with thousands of people. It seemed like students across the country were outraged—everywhere but Kent.

We went to the rally because we felt it was important and that finally there was some activity on campus opposing the war. Also, our English professor, Barbara Agte, whom we liked a lot, was speaking at the rally, so we made it a point to be there to hear her speak.

On Friday nights in town after the bars closed, typically, a couple hundred drunk kids would be dumped into the middle of the street. That night, May 1, maybe a few of them yelled antiwar slogans. Someone threw a rock. Soon, a couple of windows got broken. It was more blowing off steam than anything really political, but the local newspaper turned it into "these antiwar radicals, student communists who destroyed our downtown area." The local politicians also jumped on the bandwagon, saying that truckloads of student radicals were being bused in from Columbus, which was another fantasy.

The next day the buzz around campus was that there had been an antiwar riot downtown, even though there had been nothing of the kind. By midday, there was word there would be an antiwar rally on the Commons Saturday night. It started off with maybe fifty students. There were speeches about the war, and then a decision was made to march out to the front of the campus. They went from door to door chanting antiwar slogans, and at each dorm more students would come out, and the crowd got bigger. By then, you had students who couldn't even spell the word Vietnam coming out to watch, just to see what was going on.

On the Commons was the ROTC building, which was actually two old wooden structures. They were empty and were about to be torn down by the university because they were so dilapidated. Before that night, there had been no demonstrations directed against those buildings, while on other campuses around the country that were more politically active, the ROTC buildings were the first things that went. Well, that night, they became a symbol of what the U.S. was doing in Vietnam, and some students started throwing rocks at the buildings.

After a while, someone else ran up to the window and tried to light the curtains with cigarette lighters, but the flame died out. Then another person tried. They were still trying when we left. By the time we came back after a half hour or so, the building was in flames.

That kind of stuff wasn't unusual. Around the country, antiwar demonstrations had moved from protests in the streets to acts of violence against property, and I think Allison and I were of the same mind about it. We both expressed dismay that things were getting to that point, but on the other hand if you balance that against the U.S. government napalming innocent civilians in Vietnam, you come to believe that maybe it's worth destroying a few empty buildings if that helps bring enough attention to the need to stop the slaughter of people in Vietnam.

There have been questions for years about who set the building on fire and why it burned for so long. Some people think that it was set by agent provocateurs among the police. Another theory is that the school let it burn down because it was old and going to be destroyed anyway. Either way, that was the excuse they needed to call in the National Guard.

> These people just move from one campus to the other and terrorize the community. They're worse than the Brown Shirts and communist element and also the night riders and the vigilantes. They're the worst type that we harbor in America.
> —Governor James A. Rhodes, after calling out the National Guard to the Kent State campus

After we got back, word started spreading that the National Guard was on the front campus, and sometime that evening we did see them, marching across campus with their helmets and gas masks on, carrying exposed bayonets. There was almost a script to demonstrations in those days. The police would come, and they'd throw tear gas or march in uniforms with their billy clubs. But it was always police, and it was always batons, and that's what you expected. The worst thing that could happen was you'd get roughed up or hit over the head with a baton. But here was the U.S. Army with rifles. I remember seeing their steel bayonets reflecting off the moonlight. It was surreal. That the National Guard would be called in in response to the destruction of a couple of old wooden buildings was a ridiculous overreaction. We were appalled.

There were jeeps and personnel carriers as big as tanks. The whole thing looked like something out of Czechoslovakia in 1968. By then, the crowd had dissipated anyway, and there were local police surrounding the ROTC building. Police were also driving around the campus in the jeeps, announcing through their bull horns that everybody was to get off the campus and must be in the dorms or be subject to arrest. We went back to the dorm, and I remember people watching out the windows saying the same thing: "What the hell is the National Guard doing here?"

On Sunday morning, the 3rd, we went outside to assess the damage and were greeted with Guard troops positioned around buildings all over the campus. They were standing with their rifles in front of them, but they were relaxed, and it was pretty quiet. Students were approaching the Guardsmen, and there was friendly chatter back and forth.

On the front campus, we saw one particular Guardsman standing at ease, talking to three or four students. He had a lilac in his rifle barrel. We walked over to him and just stood there, listening to their conversation

The friendly National Guardsman with the flower in his rifle barrel whom Barry and Allison encountered on May 3, 1970. (Courtesy of the Krause family)

Allison Krause listens as Myers is reprimanded by his commanding officer for his friendly behavior. (Courtesy of the Krause family) about a mutual friend they had. He was twenty or twenty-one, and his name was Myers.

Off in the distance was an officer watching from the corner of his eye. You could tell he wasn't very happy with the fraternization. Finally he approaches this guy Myers from behind and barks at him right into his ear, "Private Myers."

Myers snaps to attention with fear in his eyes. The officer says, "What division are you in?"

"The Third Division, sir."

You could see the muscles in his neck tightening, and you felt for him, because he was the kind of regular guy you could have been drinking a beer with.

"Don't you have target practice next week?"

"Yes, sir."

"You gonna go to target practice with that silly flower in your rifle?"

"No, sir."

Myers is looking at us, and his eyes are saying: Help me.

"Where'd you get it, Myers?"

"It was a gift, sir."

"Do you always accept gifts, Myers?"

"No, sir."

"Then what are you going to do with it, Myers?"

Myers doesn't answer.

"Why don't you take it out and stop all this peace crap?"

Myers takes the flower out of the barrel, and the officer puts his hand in front of Myers, waiting for him to deposit the flower.

Just as Myers is about to deposit the flower in the officer's hand, Allison, who is standing right in front of Myers and is getting increasingly aggravated at what is going on, grabs the flower from him and looks at the officer sternly and says, "What's the matter with peace? Flowers are better than bullets."

There was a instant there that was frozen in time when she just stared him down, and he stared her down, and then he turned around and walked away, and we walked away.

After the shooting, we got the roster of guards who had fired their weapons, and we looked to see if Myers' name was there, and it wasn't.

On Sunday night, there was another rally on the Commons. This time the rally was not about being against the war, it was that the Guard should get off the campus. There were a few speeches, and then a decision was made to march to the front of the campus at Main Street and have a sit-in in the middle of the street, which is what happened. Maybe a couple of hundred students marched and sat down. It wasn't that organized, and Allison and I stayed on the Commons, but after an hour, we wandered over to Main Street and saw the Guards with their jeeps and their bayonets drawn, surrounding this small contingent of students who were sitting in the middle of the street. Suddenly, some tear gas was being thrown at the students. The students got up and moved out of the street and the Guards started advancing on them with their lowered bayonets. They chased the students off the front campus and back onto the main campus to the Commons.

Then a couple of helicopters came flying overhead with the spotlights dancing all over the campus, and with the jeeps driving around, it was like being in a war zone. And why? Because of a sit-in? We headed toward the dorms, but we ran into a contingent of Guards. They chased us with their bayonets drawn while the helicopters overhead followed us, shining their spotlights on us.

We got to the dorm, but when we tried to get inside, we found that all the doors were locked shut, and there was this big jock inside holding them closed and not letting us in. It wasn't a joke. There were bayonets at our backs. Finally, one of the kids either broke in or got in through an open window and pushed the jock aside. As soon as we got in, Allison lit into this guy, "What the hell are you doing? There are people out there choking on gas. The guards are coming at us with bayonets. Are you crazy?"

She went nose to nose with him. Meanwhile, the Guards surrounded the dormitory, and the helicopters were flying around, broadcasting on their PA systems, *"You are not to go out of the dormitory. You will be subject to arrest. You are under martial law."*

We had a friend, Jeff Gelb, who lived in the dorm, so we spent the night in his room on the floor with about ten other people. At one point, we were all pressed up against the windows, watching what was happening outside. This was a ten-story dorm, and the helicopter was flying real low around the tower, warning us: *"Get away from the windows. If you don't move away you will be subject to arrest."*

DORIS KRAUSE: She called home that Sunday night and told my husband some of the things that were going on on the campus. My husband warned her to be very careful. He never spoke to her again.

BARRY LEVINE: When we woke up the next morning, we heard there would be another rally around noon. I got out there before she did. The crowds were already gathering. Across the field was the burned-down ROTC building, where the Guard was now gathered. It was like two opposing teams on a football field. Maybe we were a hundred yards apart. People were milling around, but there was no tension, really.

Finally Allison came up to me. We talked about what might happen and what we would do. We always had this tendency, instead of going with the flow, to figure out what might happen and what our contingency plan would be. She was real organized that way.

After a while, the chanting started. "One, two, three, four, we don't want your fucking war." "Pigs off campus."

We threw rocks—or, more exactly, I did. Allison would carry them so I could throw them. I had a better arm than she did, but we weren't nearly close enough to reach the Guard. It was more of a symbolic protest.

This was again following the script, except this time we were dealing with National Guardsmen holding rifles. After a while, a jeep came out to announce that our gathering was illegal and that everybody had to disperse.

The students started screaming back, "Fuck you!"

The Guard responded by shooting tear gas at us. As it turned out, the wind was blowing against them, so the canisters would land and the gas would blow back in their faces.

That's when the Guard started to advance, so all the students started retreating back up the hill. We retreated with the crowd of students back up toward the top of the hill as the Guard came towards us. We went over the crest of the hill and down the other side into a parking lot. The Guard followed us over the hill and down, but instead of coming into the parking lot where the students were, they moved into a football field adjacent to the lot. For a while, they stood in this practice field in formation and then, amazingly, several of them kneeled down and pointed their rifles at the crowd of students. Neither Allison or I knew they had live ammunition. We just thought they were empty rifles, but even that was scary to see: ten guys lined up, pointing their rifles at you. We learned later they were equipped with M-1 rifles, the same weapons used in Vietnam. They were very, very powerful rifles. I read somewhere that they could kill up to a mile away.

Forty-five minutes before the shooting, Allison Krause (left of center, facing left) can be seen carrying wet cotton balls in her pocket for use against tear gas. Barry Levine, in the dark coat, is next to her. (Courtesy of the Krause family)

After a while, we could see some activity going on among what appeared to be the officers. It seemed like they were asking each other, "Now what do we do?"

They couldn't come after us because they would have had to get around a fence. We didn't know what they would do next. It occurred to us that maybe we won this round, because it looked like they had to go back to where they started from. For a few minutes there was actually some exhilaration on the part of the students as the Guard started marching back in the direction from which they came. We thought they were retreating. As they climbed the hill, the students started screaming at them, "That's right, go back to where you came from."

When they got to the crest, they stopped for a split second. Then, suddenly, a few of them turned around, pointed their rifles, and this time started shooting. Then the rest of them turned around and started shooting.

We were still very far away, over a hundred yards, and when they stopped marching, we stopped. When I saw one of the Guardsmen turn, I grabbed

Allison's hand and we turned around to run away. It didn't seem like we were in any immediate danger, but I wanted to be as far away as we could. After we took our first couple of steps, the guns began firing. Pop. Pop. Pop. Pop. Pop.

In split seconds you don't know what's going on. I thought they were shooting blanks, but by instinct I pulled Allison behind a car for cover. While we were falling behind the car, the pop, pop, pop continued. We kind of fell down onto the asphalt. As I looked at her to see if she was OK, she didn't respond. Then I heard her whisper to me, "Barry, I'm hit."

I had no idea what she was talking about. What did she mean she's hit? I looked at her, and she whispered it again. "Barry, I'm hit."

I couldn't conceive that they were shooting live ammunition at us, but then I saw a smudge of blood on her face, and in an instant it became clear that this was very, very serious.

What do you do? You're nineteen years old, attending college, and exercising your right to free speech. The next thing you know you are face to face with armed troops shooting at you. What do you do? I gave her mouth-to-mouth. I stroked her cheek. I talked to her, told her the ambulances were coming. From the front there were no wounds. I didn't know if she had a flesh wound or if it was more serious. She was shot in her side near her back. She was on her back with my arms under her. I'm not sure why, but I had gloves on that day. When I pulled my hands out, the gloves were all bloody. She wasn't saying anything. Then she slipped into shock and turned white. Her breathing became labored, and she was drooling. She started to lose consciousness. Something was seriously wrong.

After the shooting stopped, people started coming over and yelling for ambulances. It seemed like hours until they got there, although I read later it was like fifteen minutes. People were screaming, crying. Finally someone showed up with a stretcher. We put her on it and carried her to the ambulance. They said, "Sorry, this ambulance is full."

We carried her to another ambulance down at the other end of the lot. We put her into the back. During the trip, the attendants were just holding her. One of them kept saying, "She'll be OK. She'll be OK."

There was a stretcher above hers, like bunk beds, and there was a student in the top stretcher. As we were driving, I looked up at the attendant and said, "How about him?"

After the shooting, students carrying Allison Krause desperately search for an ambulance. (Courtesy of the Krause family)

He shook his head, indicating that it was a lost cause. He had been shot in the face. I didn't recognize him at that moment, but it turned out to be our friend, Jeff Miller.

Allison was still breathing, but it was labored. Maybe it was a five- or ten-minute ride to the hospital. When we pulled into the driveway, I was saying, "C'mon, Allison, just hang on a little bit longer."

As we took her out, her eyes rolled up and her arms fell off the stretcher, and although I didn't know it at the time, that probably was the moment when we lost her.

We took her inside, and they stopped me. I couldn't go any further, so I sat in the waiting room. It was chaotic. All the wounded and dying students were coming in. Finally, I went to the desk and inquired, and somebody came out to talk to me. I asked how Allison was, and they said, "Oh, she was DOA."

DORIS KRAUSE: I was working at the time, and my younger daughter called to say that some reporters were trying to get me, that something had happened. I drove home as quickly as I could. When I got home, someone from the Westinghouse TV station called to say that Allison was in the hospital in Ravenna, Ohio.

I called the hospital. At first I couldn't get through. Finally, I got hold of an operator and told her who I was and that I wanted to speak to somebody in the hospital. I was put through to the hospital administrator. He came on the phone and said very casually, "Oh, yes, Mrs. Krause, she arrived DOA."

That's how I found out my daughter was dead.

I just couldn't believe it. Who would think that this could happen? Be shot by representatives of your government for speaking your mind? That doesn't happen in the United States. Does it?

BARRY LEVINE: All during the time I was in the waiting room, I was saying to myself, "It's ridiculous to be in a place where they're shooting at us for an antiwar demonstration. As soon as she gets better, we'll pack up. I've got friends in Canada. We'll go there. I hope she's not in the hospital long."

"She'll get better. We'll go here. We'll do this. I'll never take her to another demonstration." And then you're confronted with a nurse who tells you, "Sorry, it's all over."

I tried to see Allison again, but they wouldn't let me. At that point, I was all alone in the world, and all alone in this little redneck town filled with police. Who knew what they were thinking? The immediate report over the wires was that one or two Guardsmen were killed, which turned out to be not true. Even the FBI later said the Guard were never in any danger at all. But here in this little right-wing college town, stories were circulating about these radical communists coming in from other parts of the country who killed some Guardsmen. I was sure they were going to think I was one of them, so I knew I couldn't go back to campus.

As it turned out, after I heard that Allison was dead, one of the nurses came up to me and gave me a slip of paper with her name and phone number on it. She said, "If you need anything, just call me."

I didn't know who she was, but I had nowhere else to go, so I called the nurse. She lived nearby. I went over to her apartment, she let me in, and I just sat in her living room and cried my eyes out for hours. Finally, she and her boyfriend offered to take me to the airport and buy me a ticket home. They said, "When you get there, send us the money back."

When I got home, I was still wearing my bloody clothes. My parents took them and threw them away. The next morning, my mother woke me up, saying, "Doris Krause is on the phone."

You can imagine how difficult that was. "What happened to my daughter?" What do you say to her? Even if I could have explained it to her, I wouldn't have been able to. I didn't know what happened other than we were in a demonstration and for no apparent reason armed troops began firing at us. She told me the funeral would be the next day in Pittsburgh.

I got calls from many friends who knew Allison. Two friends from Buffalo said they would come down to be with me. They started driving down from Buffalo that morning, and as they traveled on the New York State Thruway they were stopped by a state trooper. They had a bottle of prescription medication in the glove compartment. The cop pulls out the bottle and says, "What do we have here?" He takes out the prescription, tears it up, and throws it away. "You've got some illegal drugs here, boys."

That kind of thing happened regularly in this country then. The police hauled them off to jail in some little podunk town in upstate New York. They finally were bailed out and arrived at my house the next morning, just in time to go to Pittsburgh with me and my parents.

DORIS KRAUSE: I don't remember a lot about it, other than there was a tremendous number of people. I can't remember who spoke. That's one of the things I still can't face. I guess I don't want to remember.

BARRY LEVINE: Her coffin was in a curtained area, and before the actual funeral I asked if I could have a few minutes alone with her, and they said yes. I got to speak to her body and say good-bye, which is something that you just naturally feel the need to do. I'm glad I did, but I think I ended up saying good-bye to her in much more meaningful ways by just walking around the campus or in a park where we had been together. The night before the funeral, I went out to the beach with my friends. As we walked along the shore, I began the process of saying good-bye, and I continued to do so for a long time afterwards.

I still had my stuff on campus, but it had been closed down. I called the university about picking it up, and they said I could come on a certain day. I called my former English professor, Barbara Agte, and told her the situation. She said, "Why don't you stay with my husband and me, and we'll help you if we can."

In a sense going back there meant that I could still feel close to Allison, but I was very paranoid—and for good reason, it turned out. Before I left, I told my parents, "I'm going to be in Ohio for a week. If you get any calls from anybody, newspapers, police, FBI, you don't know where I am. You have no idea."

Sure enough, after I left, the FBI came to the door, and my mother told them, "I have no idea where he is, and he's definitely not with his English teacher in Ohio."

So they knocked on Barbara's door. Her husband answered it and told them he hadn't seen me since the shooting. I was upstairs sleeping at the time. They went away, but whenever we would leave Barbara's house in the car, even to go to the grocery store, we'd always see in the rearview mirror a car with two or three guys in short-sleeved white shirts and real short hair. They could have just as easily had a sign on their car that said FBI.

They followed us wherever we went. In every restaurant, a few tables over, there were always three guys in their shortsleeved shirts trying to act real cool. It was frightening, really, because I had already seen what they had done to Allison, and I had no idea what they wanted from me. Then a day or so later the Krauses came out to pack up Allison's room.

DORIS KRAUSE: It was like an armed camp. There were literally tanks there, and they were not going to let us through until my husband said who we were. Finally a professor took us to Allison's dorm.

BARRY LEVINE: She had had a single room at that point. It was just large enough to fit a bed and a dresser. Doris, Arthur Krause, and Allison's sister Laurie came. They were accompanied by a representative from the university, a representative from the dorm, and a highway patrolman. Then there was me and Barbara. Eight of us in this little room the size of a closet.

The room was blocked off with yellow tape. I was the first one in, and as soon as I got inside, I saw immediately that people had already been through the room. There was stuff that had been moved. There were also a few things in there I didn't want anybody to know about, including birth control pills and a small amount of pot that I used to keep in her room.

My heart was in my throat the whole time, because I figured that's all that had to happen. People were already smearing her even though they didn't have anything to smear her with. There were stories in the paper that Allison Krause was riddled with syphilis; Allison Krause was six months pregnant; Allison Krause had met with members of the Communist Party a week before the shooting.

I told Barbara that we absolutely had to get the stuff out of there undetected. There we were with seven other people. How do you do it? What I did was create a diversion, and then managed to sneak it into Barbara's purse and out of the room. She didn't know I had done it.

DORIS KRAUSE: We hadn't heard anything from the university at that point. In fact, we never did, except a short time later we received a check made out to Allison for the return of her spring tuition.

We got a condolence letter from President Nixon. Clearly it was written out of duty and not out of genuine sympathy. Just before the shootings, he had referred to the students as "bums." The day after she was killed, my husband spoke to the press, and one of the first things he said was, "My daughter was not a bum," and he asked if we've come to a place in our country where someone can't speak their mind.

By that time, we were getting so much mail we couldn't believe it. There were hundreds of letters, pro and con. Some said, "Go back to Russia," with Russia misspelled, or "Dirty Jew." Then there were so many people who were so aghast at what had happened and were so kind.

BARRY LEVINE: At some point, I got picked up by the highway patrol to be "interviewed." I said, "I don't know anything. I was there. My friend got killed. That's all I know."

"Who are you kidding?"

They took out a stack of surveillance photographs. They had pictures of people I knew, myself included, and as I was looking through them it felt like somebody had been watching us for many, many months. That was very scary.

The pictures were not only from the four days of demonstrations but also from previous rallies. They put pictures in my face and said, "We're not going to go into your activities, we just want you to help us here. There might be a couple of people in this picture who are politically active. Do you know any of them?"

I wouldn't answer them. Somehow I bullshitted my way out of that situation and got out of there. I did end up talking to a couple of reporters from the *Cleveland Plain Dealer*, though. One day after the interview, one of them called to say that the state of Ohio was going to indict some students. "Some of them are trumped-up charges. We just wanted to let you know that your name is on the list."

"For what?"

"For possession and distribution of LSD."

I said there was no way they could pin that on me because I never had any LSD, and the guy laughed. He said, "If they want to pin it on you, they're gonna pin it on you."

Clearly the state was trying to divert blame from the Guardsmen. I mentioned to Arthur Krause that I was about to be arrested for something I didn't do, and he made a phone call. I found out later that he spoke to one of the attorneys at the White House and told them, "Keep your hands off Barry Levine." He made some threat to them if I was arrested. Later I talked to the same reporter again, and he told me my name was now off the list. Eventually, twenty-five students were indicted, but all the charges against them were dismissed.

In September, I went to school at SUNY Buffalo. I had a support system of friends who got me through the next year, year and a half. I went to see the Krauses a few times. In the beginning, it was very difficult and uncomfortable when I was with them. I didn't know them. I was their daughter's boyfriend. I had met them once before she died, and I'm sure at some level, even though they really were wonderful to me, they must have thought, "Maybe if she wasn't involved with this kid Levine, she wouldn't have been at that rally." It never did come up, and when I did talk to them, they were nothing but comforting and loving, but it was still uncomfortable. It was also upsetting, because I would sit and talk with Doris Krause, and I'd see Allison in her face, which was devastating to me.

As time passed, we drifted apart, but years later, I got back in touch with them, and it felt great. I enjoy Doris's company. I see her twice a year, and it's a healing now for me, and for her too, because it's something that we share. She has since lost her husband, so who else is she going to share the memories of Allison with?

DORIS KRAUSE: There were no criminal charges filed against the Guard. We hoped the government would take these people to court, but it didn't, so we filed a civil suit. We had professors of law from all over the United States come to help, free of charge, but we lost the case. Why? The case was heard in Ohio, where people felt, "How could Governor Rhodes be wrong?" When he testified at the trial, the judge called him "Your eminence." It was just too slanted against us.

My husband had actually received a bribe offer of over a million dollars if he would drop the case. The offer was made by an attorney who had

Barry Levine and Doris Krause remain close today. (Courtesy of the Krause family)

connections to the federal government. The man said to Arthur, "Everyone has his price. What would it take for you not to take this any further? A million and a half?"

Then he named all these people on the board of Westinghouse where my husband worked and said he knew them and that maybe they didn't like what we were doing. My husband, said, "Well, if they don't like it, they'll have to let me know."

He came back home, and he went to see the president of Westinghouse, who said basically, "I don't want you to stop."

But you know we wouldn't have cared if it meant the end of his job. My husband said he wasn't interested in compensation. What he wanted was an apology and an admission of guilt from everybody involved.

In the end they came up with a sum of money, maybe $600,000, of which the bulk went to the boy who was paralyzed. I think we got $10,000. We also got the apology. It was kind of a half-measure apology, but it was an apology nonetheless, and they all had to sign it, including the governor and the entire guard.

It called the shootings unwarranted and unnecessary, and it was. She had every right to be there. How dare they?

BARRY LEVINE: I thought "What if?" a million times. What if we didn't go there? But I have no guilt at all. I wish with every fiber of my being that it was different. But we were running away before they turned. We made it a point to maintain what we thought was a very safe distance.

The first couple of years were very difficult. You're missing somebody, and you can't let go. You don't *want* to let go. You have no interest in doing things. Everything reminds you of her, but life takes care of it. In time, that fades a little bit, but not a day goes by that I don't think about her.

I eventually got married, and I have a son. Even now, when I drop him off at school, I always make it a point to either wave or kiss him or look him in the eye and say good-bye and have him do the same, because I know there's a chance I might not ever see him again. That feeling never goes away.

There isn't a day that goes by that I don't think of Allison. I was able to move on with my life by taking her with me. I have two boxes. One is physical, which I keep with letters, books, notes, and little trinkets. I take it out every once in a while, and I look at it, and I reminisce. It hurts and it's sad, but at the same time it feels good. I also have a little box in my chest, so to speak. Every once in a while I take it out and live with it. If it were just sadness, you'd lock it away, but I've got some great, life-enriching memories that I want to hold on to.

DORIS KRAUSE: We stayed in touch with the other families for a certain length of time. The only family we are still in contact with is the family from New York, the parents of Jeff Miller. There was some tension with the others. There was a feeling from some of them that because their children weren't protesting, as Allison and Jeff were, their children were innocent, which would make our children guilty. We made sure our younger daughter went to school far away from Ohio. She also suffered the slings and arrows from Kent State. She didn't tell us until much later how she was ridiculed in school by her teachers once they found out she was Allison's sister. They thought Allison was a traitor.

For a long time, I wouldn't tell anybody who I was unless I was among friends, because people could be so heartless. We were ordinary people thrust into this. I guess I never got tough enough to let things roll of my back. The university certainly wasn't any help. Several years ago they held a contest for someone to come up with a design for a memorial. They could never get it past the board of directors. Somebody paid for a memorial sculpture by George Segal. He did a statue of Abraham killing his son. It was not accepted by the college. If you go to Princeton University, you can see it on the campus there. The university didn't want any part of it. They even built a gymnasium on part of the site. There was a protest about it, but it was built anyway.

That kind of heartlessness continued until the current administration, which has a different slant on it. After many years I did go back for the thirtieth anniversary. It was nice to see so many caring people. The school participated in the memorials, and they set up scholarships in the names of the four children.

BARRY LEVINE: I went back to Kent a few times over the years. People said to me, "How can you go back there? Wasn't it horrible?" Well, part of it is horrible, but I spent nine months there, and while that one day was the worst day of my life, I also had some of the best days of my life at Kent, because of Allison. So when I've gone back, I've enjoyed it. I sit and visit the places where we played, or where we walked, or flew a kite.

I went back for the twenty-fifth and thirtieth anniversaries. To me these anniversaries are personal, not political. They give speeches. "There can never be another Kent State." "We've got to oppose the government now." I don't see any of that. I see a young girl walking around the campus with a smile on her face, enjoying life.

DORIS KRAUSE: The National Guard were cowards, people hiding behind their masks. When we lived in Washington, we'd go to the FBI building, and they would tell us how from a speck of paint they could tell you the make of a car, the year, and the model. Why couldn't any of them tell me which one of them killed my daughter? We're still waiting to hear from the Guard as to who gave the order to fire. They still won't divulge that. I'd also like to know how a nineteen-year-old girl with no gun could intimidate these big men carrying rifles.

You know, in only two states can the National Guard carry ammunition in their guns and, unluckily, Ohio is one of them. So one lesson is to keep them off campus. The other lesson is how far the government is willing to go to quell protest and then keep people in the dark about it. Our daughter was shot and killed, yet afterward we were treated like the enemy.

BARRY LEVINE: It's very frightening, because it can happen again. Still, I tell my son, you have the absolute right to question authority, but you have to understand that questioning authority can be dangerous, because a government is always going to act to preserve itself.

But do I think it's still vital to question authority? Always, from the beginning to the end of time.

DORIS KRAUSE: There are so many things I still don't want to think about. You know, after Allison was killed, friends compiled a reel of home movies of Allison, and I still haven't been able to look at it because Allison is partially alive in those films. It's just too hard. The anniversaries don't get any easier with time. They just point out what I have missed in my life. I got

Allison Krause's grave site in Pittsburgh, Pennsylvania. (Courtesy of the Krause family)

a letter from someone who said, "There is no greater loss than the loss of a full-grown child." I can vouch for that. I have no idea what she would have done. She was a strong person, like my husband. She could have done anything. But she was just starting out in her life.

BARRY LEVINE: For students and for so many other people around the country, it got to the point that we had to do whatever it took to stop the war, and when the government didn't listen, we threw ourselves on the wheels and the levers to stop the war machinery. Some of us got killed, but in the long run, those who stood up and spoke up helped contribute to stopping the machinery of the war. Who knows how many tens of thousands of lives that saved. That's one way I come to grips with Allison's murder.

Thanks

It never ceases to amaze me how generous complete strangers can be, and once someone sets aside time to see me for no reason other than the fact that I've asked, I'm always troubled when I can't return the favor by including their comments. This happened with a number of people on this project, and although their words don't appear in these pages, their wisdom was a powerful force in the shaping of this book.

Jim Fouratt, Bruce Barthol, Gary "Chicken" Hirsch, Susan and Marty Carey, Happy Traum, Jan Barry, Bill Walton, Jack Weinberg, Bernardine Dohrn, Wolfe Lowenthal, Ben Chaney, Carolyn Goodman, Stew Albert, and Bob Ross, as well as the children of Paul Krassner, Marilyn Webb, Verandah Porche, and Shoshana Rihn, all provided terrific interviews. I hope they'll accept my apologies and my thanks. Jan, in particular, is one of the great unsung heroes of the antiwar movement. His courageous work as the founder of the Vietnam Veterans Against the War saved many lives from being sacrificed needlessly. Bruce Barthol's former bandmate in Country Joe and the Fish, Barry Melton, said admiringly about Bruce, "Out of all of us, he's the one who really stuck with it." I urge anyone in the Bay area to see the San Francisco Mime Troupe and enjoy Bruce's terrific work.

The most difficult chapter of all to cut was Marty Jezer, one of the earliest antiwar activists and a cofounder of the Total Loss Farm commune outside Brattleboro, Vermont. For all his achievements as an activist and a writer (his biography of Abbie Hoffman is must reading for anyone who wants to understand the 1960s), none of it compares with what a universally beloved human being he was. He died of cancer in 2005, and for those who knew him the world will forever be a sadder place.

All of the people who are included are special to me, and several, I'm honored to say, are now good friends, but I would be remiss if I didn't single out Barry Levine and Doris Krause. That they were willing to share such painful memories filled me with respect and awe. To have been so close to two such decent people only confirms that Allison Krause must have been a truly remarkable young woman.

In addition to poverty, my family—that's Sue and Elizabeth, wife and daughter respectively—has had to put up with a lot so I can continue to do projects that are close to my heart. They turn the TV down and tiptoe around the house in the early morning, which is not as much fun as it sounds, and every day I appreciate it.

Everyone should have the good fortune of being taught by great teachers. Here are four of mine:

Edward Taussig taught my junior English class in high school. He was not only the funniest teacher I ever had, he was also the first who showed me that I had some ability as a writer and that I also enjoyed the process.

Gerald Schehr was my social studies teacher in eighth grade, and at a time when not many teachers were cool, he was. He also instilled in me a love of history, which excites and fascinates me every day.

Susanna Heiman was my Sunday school teacher for many years. A Holocaust survivor, she taught me the importance of having a social conscience. Imagine bringing in a Black Panther to chat with a bunch of Sunday school kids. She had that kind of vision and courage.

Josephine Beaudoin tried to teach me algebra for two years in junior high school. That she failed says nothing about her teaching ability, but everything about my inability to absorb numbers. She once told my parents that I would be a major success one day, but that it wouldn't be in math. Nobody had ever said I would succeed at anything up to that point. That boost meant the world to a self-doubting, skinny kid with short, curly hair and ears the size of jug handles. That she also agreed to give me an 85 no matter what my test scores were as long as I worked hard showed a kindness and understanding that still brings tears to my eyes.

Other people who made a real contribution to this book include my parents, Samuel and Muriel Kisseloff; Alan and Nancy Kisseloff; and all the younger Kisseloffs; Jack Fischer, his wife, Joyce, and the entire Fischer family, warm and generous hosts who always make me feel good when I see them; Tony Hiss, Lois Metzger, and the continuing inspiration of Alger Hiss; Agnese Haury; Mark Levine, whose book *Tales of Hoffman*, about the Chicago Eight trial, still makes great reading and whose more recent book, *Negotiating a Book Contract*, should be read by every author. I'd also like to thank Verandah Porche for her frequent acts of generosity and hospitality.

Thanks also to Sharyn November, who originated this project, and Steve Wrinn of the University Press of Kentucky, who enthusiastically saw it to its conclusion. This has been my first venture into the world of academic publishing. Steve, Anne Dean Watkins, Lin Wirkus, Allison Webster, Leila Salisbury, and Donna Bouvier, a terrific copyeditor, have made the transition a pleasure. Susanne Van Cleave and her pink bubbles; Bob Wertz; Rose and Murray Halpern; Peter Gambaccini; Ron Givens; Ann Distelhorst; Ira and Kathryn Miller; Scott and Jodie Greenhouse; Stephanie Von Hirschberg; James Turner; Neil deMause; Jennie Erickson; Ed Kowalachuk; Shoshona Rihn; Joan Barker; Dennis Moore; Nancy Urvant; David Weiss; the McBride family and Fluffy the rabbit; Louis the dog; Douglas Watkins; Michael Rosen; Karen Rose; Elizabeth Zimmer; Country Joe McDonald; Peter Coyote; Edith Tiger; Joanne Grant; Victor Rabinowitz; Fred Powledge; Ben Chitty; Jenny Swinton; Andrew Ross; Alan Canfora; Marie Kearns; Susan Brownmiller; and all the people who said I couldn't and made me try that much harder.

For Further Reading, Viewing, and Listening

General 1960s

Albert, Judith Clavir, and Stewart Edward Albert. *The Sixties Papers: Documents of a Rebellious Decade.* New York: Praeger, 1984.

Daniel, Clifton, ed. *Chronicle of the Twentieth Century.* Mt. Kisco, NY: Chronicle Publications, 1987.

Emery, Fred. *Watergate: The Corruption of American Politics and the Fall of Richard Nixon.* New York: Times Books, 1994.

Gitlin, Todd. *The Sixties: Years of Hope, Days of Rage.* New York: Bantam, 1987.

O'Neil, Doris, ed. *Life: The '60s.* Boston: Little, Brown, 1989.

O'Neill, William L. *Coming Apart: An Informal History of America in the 1960s.* Chicago: Quadrangle Books, 1971.

This Fabulous Century: 1960–1970. New York: Time-Life Books, 1970.

Viorst, Milton. *Fire in the Streets: America in the 1960s.* New York: Simon and Schuster, 1979.

Civil Rights
(Bernard LaFayette, Bob Zellner, Gloria Richardson Dandridge)

Branch, Taylor. *Parting the Waters: America in the King Years, 1954–63.* New York: Simon and Schuster, 1988.

Cagin, Seth, and Philip Dray. *We Are Not Afraid : The Story of Goodman, Schwerner, and Chaney and the Civil Rights Campaign for Mississippi.* New York: Macmillan, 1988.

Cleaver, Eldridge. *Soul on Ice.* New York: Dell, 1968.

Egerton, John. *Speak Now Against the Day: The Generation Before the Civil Rights Movement in the South.* New York: Knopf, 1994.

Halberstam, David. *The Children.* New York: Random House, 1998.

Hampton, Henry, and Steve Fayer. *Voices of Freedom: An Oral History of the Civil Rights Movement from the 1950s Through the 1980s.* New York: Bantam, 1990.

Huie, William Bradford. *Three Lives For Mississippi.* New York: WCC Books, 1965.

Levine, Ellen, ed. *Freedom's Children: Young Civil Rights Activists Tell Their Own Stories.* New York: Putnam, 1993.

Lewis, Anthony, and The New York Times. *Portrait of a Decade: The Second American Revolution.* New York: Random House, 1964.

Lewis, John, with Michael D'Orso. *Walking with the Wind: A Memoir of the Movement.* New York: Harcourt Brace, 1995.

Pearson, Hugh. *The Shadow of the Panther: Huey Newton and the Price of Black Power in America.* Reading, Mass.: Addison-Wesley, 1994.

Powledge, Fred. *Free at Last? The Civil Rights Movement and the People Who Made It.* Boston: Little, Brown, 1991.

Silver, James W. *Mississippi: The Closed Society.* New York: Harcourt, Brace, and World, 1963.

Sutherland, Elizabeth, ed. *Letters from Mississippi.* New York: McGraw-Hill, 1965.

Hayden, Tom. *Reunion: A Memoir.* New York: Random House, 1988.

Williams, Juan. *Eyes on the Prize: America's Civil Rights Years, 1954–1965.* New York: Viking, 1987.

Woodward, C. Vann. *The Strange Career of Jim Crow.* New York: Oxford University Press, 1955.

Eyes on the Prize: America at the Racial Crossroads, 1965–1985. Video series (documentary), dist. PBS Video, 1989.

The First Amendment and the Underground Press (Paul Krassner)

Bruce, Lenny. *How to Talk Dirty and Influence People: An Autobiography.* Chicago: Playboy Press, 1965.

De Grazia, Edward. *Girls Lean Back Everywhere: The Law of Obscenity and the Assault on Genius.* New York: Random House, 1992.

Krassner, Paul. *Confessions of a Raving, Unconfined Nut: Misadventures in the Counter-Culture.* New York: Simon & Schuster, 1993.

——. *Impolite Interviews.* New York: Seven Stories Press, 1999.

Peck, Abe. *Uncovering the Sixties: The Life and Times of the Underground Press.* New York: Pantheon, 1985.

Lenny. Feature film, dir. Bob Fosse, 1974.

Chicago Convention, Chicago Eight (Paul Krassner, Lee Weiner)

Caute, David. *The Year of the Barricades: A Journey through 1968.* New York: Harper & Row, 1988.

Dougan, Clark, and Stephen Weiss. *Nineteen Sixty-Eight.* The Vietnam Experience series. Boston: Boston Publishing Co., 1983.

Hayden, Tom. *Reunion: A Memoir.* New York: Random House, 1988.

Hoffman, Abbie. *The Best of Abbie Hoffman.* New York: Four Walls Eight Windows, 1989.

——. *Soon to Be a Major Motion Picture*. New York: Putnam, 1980.

Levine, Mark L. ed. *The Tales of Hoffman: A Documentary of Courtroom Confrontations from the Most Incredible Trial in American History*. New York: Bantam, 1970.

Rubin, Jerry. *Do It! Scenarios of the Revolution*. New York: Simon and Schuster, 1970.

Seale, Bobby. *Seize the Time: The Story of the Black Panther Party and Huey P. Newton*. New York: Random House, 1970.

Medium Cool. Feature film (documentary), dir. Haskell Wexler, 1969.

Radical Politics (Lee Weiner)

Alpert, Jane. *Growing Up Underground*. New York: Morrow, 1981.

Jacobs, Paul, and Saul Landau. *The New Radicals: A Report with Documents*. New York: Vintage, 1966.

Kunen, James Simon. *The Strawberry Statement: Notes of a College Revolutionary*. New York: Random House, 1969.

Rubin, Jerry. *Do It! Scenarios of the Revolution*. New York: Simon and Schuster, 1970.

Underground. Film (documentary), dir. Mary Lampson and Haskell Wexler, 1976.

Vietnam and the Antiwar Movement (Daniel Berrigan, David Cline)

Baker, Mark. *Nam: The Vietnam War in the Words of the Men and Women Who Fought There*. New York: Morrow, 1981.

Berrigan, Daniel. *And the Risen Bread: Selected Poems, 1957–1997*. New York: Fordham University Press, 1998.

——. *Night Flight to Hanoi: War Diary with Poems*. New York: Macmillan, 1968.

——. *The Trial of the Catonsville Nine*. Boston: Beacon Press, 1970.

Caputo, Philip. *A Rumor of War*. New York: Holt, Rinehart, and Winston, 1977.

Dougan, Clark, and Samuel Lipsman. *A Nation Divided*. The Vietnam Experience series. Boston: Boston Publishing Co., 1984.

Dougan, Clark, and Stephen Weiss. *Nineteen Sixty-Eight*. The Vietnam Experience series. Boston: Boston Publishing Co., 1983.

Hayden, Tom. *Reunion: A Memoir*. New York: Random House, 1988.

Herr, Michael. *Dispatches*. New York: Knopf, 1977.

Hoffman, Abbie. *The Best of Abbie Hoffman*. New York: Four Walls Eight Windows, 1989.

——. *Soon to Be a Major Motion Picture*. New York: Putnam, 1980.

Polner, Murray, and Jim O'Grady. *Disarmed and Dangerous: The Radical Lives and Times of Daniel and Philip Berrigan*. New York: Basic Books, 1997.

Rubin, Jerry. *Do It! Scenarios of the Revolution*. New York: Simon and Schuster, 1970.

Santoli, Al. *Everything We Had: An Oral History of the Vietnam War by Thirty-Three American Soldiers Who Fought It.* New York: Random House, 1981.

The Environment (Peter Berg)

Carson, Rachel. *Silent Spring.* Boston: Houghton Mifflin, 1962.

Planet Drum. www.planetdrum.org.

San Francisco (Peter Berg, Elsa Marley Skylark, Barry Melton)

Coyote, Peter. *Sleeping Where I Fall: A Chronicle.* Washington, D.C.: Counterpoint, 1998.

Selvin, Joel. *Summer of Love: The Inside Story of LSD, Rock & Roll, Free Love, and High Times in the Wild West.* New York: Dutton, 1994.

Rock and Roll (Barry Melton)

Gillett, Charlie. *The Sound of the City: The Rise of Rock and Roll.* New York: Pantheon, 1970.

Jackson, John A. *Big Beat Heat: Alan Freed and the Early Years of Rock & Roll.* New York: Schirmer Books, 1991.

Makower, Joel. *Woodstock: The Oral History.* New York: Doubleday, 1989.

Palmer, Robert. *Rock & Roll: An Unruly History.* New York: Harmony Books, 1995.

Selvin, Joel. *Summer of Love: The Inside Story of LSD, Rock & Roll, Free Love, and High Times in the Wild West.* New York: Dutton, 1994.

Shelton, Robert. *No Direction Home: The Life and Music of Bob Dylan.* New York: W. Morrow, 1986.

Woliver, Robbie. *Hoot! A Twenty-Five-Year History of the Greenwich Village Music Scene.* New York: St. Martin's Press, 1986.

Gimme Shelter. Film (documentary), dir. David Maysles, Albert Maysles, Charlotte Zwerin, 1970.

Monterey Pop. Film (documentary), dir. D. A. Pennebaker, 1968.

Woodstock. Film (documentary), dir. Michael Wadleigh, 1970.

Country Joe and the Fish. *Electric Music for the Mind and Body.* CD, Vanguard, 1967.

———. *I Feel Like I'm Fixing to Die.* CD, Vanguard, 1967.

Communes (Lee Weiner, Elsa Marley Skylark, Verandah Porche)

Houriet, Robert. *Getting Back Together.* New York: Coward, McCann & Geoghegan, 1971.

Mungo, Ray. *Famous Long Ago: My Life and Hard Times with Liberation News Service.* Boston: Beacon Press, 1970.

The Counterculture (Peter Berg, Elsa Marley Skylark, Verandah Porche)

Hoffman, Abbie. *Soon to be a Major Motion Picture.* New York: Putnam, 1980.

Jezer, Marty. *Abbie Hoffman: American Rebel.* New Brunswick, N.J.: Rutgers University Press, 1992.

Lee, Martin A., and Bruce Shlain. *Acid Dreams: The Complete Social History of LSD, the CIA, the Sixties, and Beyond.* New York: Grove Weidenfeld, 1985.

Rubin, Jerry. *Do It! Scenarios of the Revolution.* New York: Simon and Schuster, 1970.

Women's Liberation
(Elsa Marley Skylark, Marilyn Salzman Webb, Verandah Porche)

Boston Health Collective. *Our Bodies, Ourselves.* New York: Simon and Schuster, 1973.

Brownmiller, Susan. *Against Our Will: Men, Women and Rape.* New York: Simon and Schuster, 1975.

——. *In Our Time: Memoir of a Revolution.* New York: Dial Press, 1999.

Friedan, Betty. *The Feminine Mystique.* New York: Norton, 1963.

Gay Liberation (Frank Kameny)

Duberman, Martin. *Stonewall.* New York: Dutton, 1993.

Marcus, Eric. *Making History: The Struggle for Gay and Lesbian Equal Rights, 1945–1990, an Oral History.* New York: HarperCollins, 1992.

Sports (David Meggyesy)

Lipsyte, Robert. *Sportsworld: An American Dreamland.* New York: Quadrangle, 1975.

Meggyesy, Dave. *Out of Their League.* Berkeley, Calif: Ramparts Press, 1970.

Kent State (Doris Krause, Barry Levine)

Davies, Peter. *The Truth About Kent State: A Challenge to the American Conscience.* New York: Farrar, Straus, Giroux, 1973.

Michener, James A. *Kent State: What Happened and Why.* New York: Random House, 1971.

Stone, I. F. *The Killings at Kent State: How Murder Went Unpunished.* New York: Vintage, 1970.

Viorst, Milton. *Fire in the Streets: America in the 1960s.* New York: Simon and Schuster, 1979.

Index

Evers, Medgar, 16, 21–22, 36, 40, 44, 50

Fahey, John, 201
Famous Long Ago (Mungo), 226
Farrakkhan, Louis, 44
Fatigue Press, 132
FBI, 18, 64, 71, 74, 88, 95, 102, 103, 113–115, 179, 189–190, 197–198, 218, 244, 257, 259–260, 264
Fonda, Jane, 133
Fordham University, 106
Foreman, Jim, 31, 33
Freedom Rides, 6, 10, 14–19, 31, 40, 55, 100, 198
    to Mississippi, 16
    See also LaFayette, Bernard
Froines, John, 82, 92
Fuller, Jesse, 199

Gaines, Bill, 68
Garcia, Jerry, 201
Garvey, Ed, 222
Gazette, The, 189
Gelb, Jeff, 252
Gelston, George M., 53, 58–59
Georgetown University, 185, 186
Gifford, Frank, 221
Ginsberg, Allen, 137, 141
Goddard College, 180
Goldberg, Art, 77
Good Death, The: The New American Search to Reshape the End of Life (Webb), 180
Grateful Dead, 158, 201, 203
Greatest Generation, The (Brokaw), 1
Grossman, Stefan, 201
GROW (Grass Roots Organizing Work) project, 46
Guardian, The, 175, 218
Gunning, John Francis, 202

Guthrie, Arlo, 87
Guthrie, Woodie, 197, 229

Hamer, Fannie Lou, 40, 45, 50
Hampton, Fred, 88, 95
Harmony settlement, 225
Harrington, Michael, 215
Harrisburg Seven, 101
Harvard University, 185
Hastings College of Law, 207
Hay, Henry, 184
Hayden, Casey, 172
Hayden, Tom, 86, 92–94, 110
Hendrix, Jimi, 204
Highlander Folk School, 30
Hirsh, Gary "Chicken," 202
Hoffman, Abbie, 74, 75–78, 82, 88, 91–92, 96
Hoffman, Julius, 82, 94
Hoover, J. Edgar, 64, 101, 114, 189–190
Hopkins, Lightning, 201
Horton, Myles, 30
HUAC (House Un-American Activities Committee), 197–198, 202
Huntingdon College, 29, 49

"I Have a Dream," 61
    See also King, Martin Luther Jr.
"I-Feel-Like-I'm-Fixin'-To-Die Rag," 194–195, 202, 204
    and Rock and Roll Hall of Fame, 202
    See also Country Joe and the Fish; McDonald, Joe: Melton, Barry

Jackson, Jesse, 213
Jacobs, Linda. See Porche, Verandah
Jefferson Airplane, 201, 203
Johnson, Lyndon B., 42, 73, 118
Jones, Brian, 204
Joplin, Janis, 155, 204–206